Cambridge

Cities of the Imagination

Cities of the Imagination

Cambridge

A cultural and literary history

Martin Garrett

Signal

Signal Books
Oxford

First published in 2004 by
Signal Books Limited
36 Minster Road
Oxford
OX4 1LY
www.signalbooks.co.uk

A catalogue record for this book is available from the British Library

ISBN 1-902669-78-9 Cloth
ISBN 1-902669-79-7 Paper

Drawings by Wendy Skinner Smith

Cover Design: Baseline Arts
Typesetting: Devdan Sen
Cover Images: Alan McArthur; Baseline Arts; Charles Darwin by permission of the
Syndics of Cambridge University Library; Britain on View

Printed in Canada by Webcom

Contents

CHAPTER FOUR
CAMBRIDGE DONS

CHAPTER FIVE
CAMBRIDGE CHURCHES AND RELIGION

CHAPTER SIX
CAMBRIDGE WOMEN

CHAPTER SEVEN
CAMBRIDGE POETS

CHAPTER EIGHT
CAMBRIDGE SCIENCE

CHAPTER NINE
CAMBRIDGE DRAMA, MUSIC AND ART

Foreword

It was love that brought me to live in Cambridge; John Townsend loves the city, and I love him. I came with some misgivings, aware that it might not be entirely comfortable to live on the outside of a magic circle of any kind. The misgivings were mistaken. Although there is occasional friction over controversial research projects, and occasional mugging of students, the border between town and gown here is not defended; it is porous in both directions. Many university occasions, lectures, concerts, theatricals, are open to all, and retired academics seem to take no time at all to transfer their teaching to the University of the Third Age, so that an excellent on-going education is freely available. For an Oxford girl like myself there is a constant *Through the Looking Glass* feel to Cambridge, a same-but-different experience of just about everything about it, which keeps me continually engaged and surprised.

As well as the spectacular beauties of academic Cambridge, lovingly explored and explained in this book, the city contains a little East Anglian market town, bursting at the seams nowadays; hugely successful research-based industries, and the persisting remnants of the pasture and farming of a low-lying and watery landscape. The Cam is a mere thirteen miles from its official source to the confluence with the Ouse, but a force to be reckoned with all the same. Its propensity to flood has threaded through Cambridge from the pubs in Grantchester to the Ditton Plough, a broad green ribbon of flood plain— Grantchester Meadows, The Lammas Land, the Backs, Jesus Green, Midsummer Common, Stourbridge Common, and then farmland on either bank to Baitsbite Lock, and beyond. One can walk in pastures green, with real cows in summer, from demotic Cambridge in the south, right through the heart of academic Cambridge, and out towards the demotic Cambridge of the fen edges on the north and east of the city, where roads through Chesterton peter out alongside the river, in an eclectic mix of panel-beating establishments, office furniture suppliers, caravan sites and grazing horses.

This band of green space makes Cambridge more diffuse than

Oxford. The hub of the place is probably the market, still lively and definitely demotic. There is no Dome to claim centre spot on the skyline, like the Radcliffe camera, and no Cathedral—the bishopric is Ely, ten miles to the north up the A10. Cambridge, having no bishop, was not technically a city until George VI in almost the only independent act of his reign declared it to be one in 1952. Like Oxford, Cambridge does have one absolutely crucial tree; in Oxford it is the plane tree at the curve of the High Street; in Cambridge it is the spectacular chestnut tree between the road and the eastern end of King's College Chapel. Come when it is in flower to see the ultimate competition between art and nature.

In almost every way Cambridge is a level sort of place to live. The Hills Road is named for the Gog Magog hills, towards which it makes with Roman directness; those hills reach an elevation of some 230 feet above sea-level. A faint persisting Puritanism lingers in which swank appears out of place. Neither what you earn nor what you own will greatly impress people here, but the ambient intelligence is high. The second university here had the self-respect and fidelity to its origins to keep the word *polytechnic* in its name. There are a few houses good enough to be mentioned in Pevsner, and some three or four street names with a bit of cachet, but most Cambridge housing is pleasant, solid Victorian terraces and semis, built of a blessedly soft grey to beige brick—nothing like the rampant red excesses of North Oxford, though the cities share the rather dreary eastwards expansion of between-the-wars suburbia. Until very recently for a town of the size and prosperity of Cambridge there was an extraordinary dearth of good places to eat, pubs apart, though that is changing fast. For good or ill there is also a dearth of really posh shops—you would be hard put to it to spend a fortune on a frock here, and rather hard put to it to find a really posh frock at all. Likewise, if antiques are your liking, you will not find many places to browse for them within the city. Bookshops are another matter; the place is infested with them, of every conceivable kind.

It is infested also with bicycle shops, and with cyclists riding through red at traffic-lights, riding without lights while wearing dark clothing, and often riding fast and unheeding in pedestrian areas, or the wrong way down one-way streets. Motorists should beware—

indeed, visitors coming by car should use the excellent park-and-ride provision.

With the use of a car, or by bus, there are pleasant local excursions in every direction from the city; the land may be flat but it is full of exceptionally pretty villages, speaking eloquently of the trading and farming prosperity of the past. I particularly like Hemingford Grey, with the oldest continuously inhabited house in England, the Manor House, which belonged to the late Lucy Boston, and has a literature all of its own; Hilton with its flood-posts at every ditch, and an ancient turf-cut maze; Commercial End, just one street, which once had a navigable lode and access across the North Sea to Holland and the markets of the world; Earith where one can contemplate the wonders of the Dutch drainage engineer Vermuyden's twin dykes, one tidal and brackish, one fresh flowing steadily seawards. Those who love birds can find, not far away, exotic ones in cages at Linton zoo and wild ones at the RSPB's hide at Welney.

There are good places for memorials, if those are your liking; there is a particularly interesting one on the death of a child in the church at Hemingford Grey, with such a vernacular and modern turn of phrase it must have been taken down from dictation by the mason; there is a wildly metaphysical one to a blacksmith "my bellows now have lost their wind..." in the churchyard at Houghton; and my favourite of all—a touching lament to a little girl who was the daughter of "An English Dame" and a freed African Slave, on the wall beside the porch at St. Andrew's Chesterton. Everyone will have their own favourite local outings.

The city itself can offer urban swans, both black and white, and the ducks which enliven the Cam. It is a good place for gardens; as well as the scholarly delights of the Botanic Garden, college gardens are accessible for hours of the day.

When one lives among glories one tends to ignore them until a visitor arrives to be shown around. After hundreds of times taking someone punting—surely the best water-born journey this side of Venice—or into King's College Chapel or Trinity Great Court I am still as amazed as they are every time. On reflection I think what is so inspiring is not the absolute splendour of the architecture, but the endangered, fading and beautiful ideal of which it is the shell. What shaped these buildings was the idea of learning as the occupation of a community; as withdrawn from the outside world and self-sufficient; as the vocation of a life-time. That is why each college needed its own dining-hall, library, chapel and living quarters with the beautiful results in brick and stone which surround us here. It was monasticism which carried the learning of antiquity to us through the dark ages, and the colleges have preserved some of the quality of monasticism even though they no longer preclude matrimony, and are sisterhoods as well as brotherhoods. They do still inspire life-long loyalties, and a certain amount of gentlemanly tribal sniping between them is still to be heard.

In spite of one or two television dons, and spectacularly successful scientific inventors, the pursuit of learning still involves worldly sacrifice. The beauty of the present city is a product of the values of the past, and continued devotion to those values in the present, Appreciation of it is deepened for locals and visitors alike by understanding such as this book offers. There are two kinds of guide-book—the sort you take in your hand and the sort you take to heart. This is the latter kind.

Jill Paton Walsh

Preface

Writing a book about the place where you live has evident advantages, although at first it can make walking or cycling through town into a kaleidoscopic and rather unreal experience. Later, when you have covered a respectable number of sites, there is still a temptation to think that any fine door-knocker you come upon, any interesting pattern of swirled leaves, must have a special Cambridge importance. More reasonably, it is tempting to treat the reader, when you return from the latest notebook-brandishing foray, to a detailed account of, say, your feelings on a thundery day amid the silent brick walks and wooded gardens of Robinson College. There is a sense of frustration not to have conveyed the exact shape of Jesus Green, its changing, if inexplicit, significance in your life if, like me, you cross it almost every day.

Fortunately the format of a literary and cultural history enables one to shape, challenge or replace one's personal impressions; to cull what is apposite, informative or outrageous from the work of an extraordinary variety of writers. Cambridge can be experienced with the assistance of poets from Chaucer to Plath; university memorialists and wits; actors and directors; novelists "literary", historical, comic and detective; authors of guidebooks antique and modern; architectural historians rational or apoplectic; biographers; scientists; Quakers and Catholics. To return to the personal, however: I have lived in Cambridge since 1994. Before that for nineteen years, as undergraduate, graduate student, and occasional tutor, I was in—oh word of half-serious horror to the Cambridge soul—Oxford. Possibly this makes me more distanced from the material than someone who has always been here. On the other hand, my sense of complete involvement with Oxford, of which I retained at first a distractingly powerful mental image, gave way, soon and naturally, to an equal fascination with and immersion in Cambridge. In both cities I now feel by turns insider and outsider. I have been involved in the life of both universities, but have also spent some time observing them from the edge.

I should like to thank John Benger, John Edmondson, Jennifer Fellows, James Ferguson, Helen Gilbart (Artist in Residence at the Sedgwick Museum 2002-3), Eric Marland (of Eric Marland Lettering Arts), Paul Nixon, and Roy and Doreen Sherwood, for their many helpful suggestions. I am particularly grateful to Robert Inglesfield, who told me much about Cambridge, listened patiently to my accounts of work in progress, and read and commented on several chapters. And as usual I thank Helen, Philip and Edmund for their ideas, practical help, and support.

Anyone writing about Cambridge and literature owes a great deal to Graham Chainey's comprehensive and readable *A Literary History of Cambridge* (1985; revised edition 1995). Alan H. Nelson's *Records of Early English Drama* volume for Cambridge (1989) was equally indispensable.

Martin Garrett
Cambridge

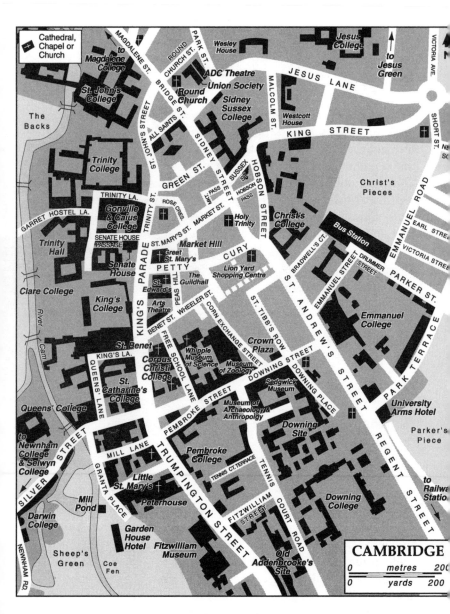

CAMBRIDGE

| 0 | metres | 200 |
| 0 | yards | 200 |

INTRODUCTION

"The atmosphere of these venerable halls standing in such peaceful and dignified seclusion seemed to me likely to induce a state of languor and reverie, excluding both the rude shocks and the joyous revelations of the rough world without." This was Augustus John's verdict on the Cambridge of 1909 in his autobiography *Chiaroscuro* (1952). The secluded inmates of the colleges might have replied—with caution, perhaps, since John engaged in pub-brawls as well as portrait painting during his visit—that they were participating in the "rude shocks and the joyous revelations" of intellectual endeavour. But both views are tenable: Cambridge has been a centre for punting, for daydreaming on the Backs, as well as for scientific discovery, philosophy and literary criticism. Traditionally words like "austere" and "ascetic" are used to describe the city of predominantly pale stone, searching enquiry and penetrating textual analysis; yet it has also produced many of the country's best and most innovative comedians.

Like other places, Cambridge does not always fit its stereotype. Even the weather, which is supposed to be piercingly cold and windy to go with the asceticism or provoke the austerity, seems to have changed. This may be because of global warming and the increasing size of the city, but no doubt it was always, to some extent, part of the myth. Flat places can, of course, be very windy, as at the beginning of Penelope Fitzgerald's Cambridge novel *The Gate of Angels* (1990), where "cyclists coming into the town in the late afternoon looked more like sailors in peril." The situation is rarely so extreme that cows fall down confused, their horns "festooned with willow boughs"; but as they wallow on their backs, still munching, Fitzgerald's cows give the reader pause, once more, about stereotypes: "a scene of disorder, tree-tops on the earth, legs in the air, in a university city devoted to logic and reason."

On the calm days when no cow turns turtle, people in Cambridge may cycle or walk on the Backs, to Grantchester, or on various other surviving greens and spaces like Christ's Pieces or the somewhat wilder

Coe Fen. There are also a few more hilly—or at least less flat—areas near the city. To the south-east are the low, green Gog Magog Hills, often known locally as "the Gogs", on one of which was an Iron Age fort, Wandlebury Ring. (Although some earthworks remain the site has been considerably altered since the seventeenth century.) Near Wandlebury is the conservation area at Magog Down, where 163 acres of formerly farmed land have been re-planted with native chalk grassland plants and trees. And towards Newmarket is the Devil's Dyke, an Anglo-Saxon defensive structure, seven and a half miles long—defending whom from whom is debated. As Bill Bryson observes in *Notes from a Small Island* (1995), it has "a kind of menacing, palpably ancient air, but also a feeling of monumental folly." It has ceased—since armies would simply have gone round it—"to have any use at all except to show people in the fen country what it felt like to be 60 feet high."

There is countryside to be seen, although much of it consists of cornfields rather than chalk meadows, and it is seen more often from roads than from Anglo-Saxon ridges. The amount of traffic today is another factor cutting Cambridge off from an earlier stereotype, from Augustus John's secluded halls or the place which still had for C. S. Lewis in 1954, arriving from Oxford, the atmosphere of a farming town. A year before Lewis came, Olive Cook's guide to Cambridgeshire painted a now almost unimaginable picture of King's Parade in the long vacation: "August afternoons when scarcely a soul has been abroad to disturb the sleepy silence of the intense heat," when one or two cars are parked outside the Senate House, college buildings are deserted and "a woman in a pale dress and big straw hat" walks past languidly. Traffic and tourism, obviously, have increased immensely since 1953, and Cambridge has become much more prosperous—and expensive—than ever before. A major factor in this growth has been the so-called "Cambridge Phenomenon", the emergence of the city as a centre for high-tech companies over the last twenty years. The area now has about 1,350 such firms, employing some 32,000 people. The population is rising rapidly. According to one calculation, the area will need 100,000 new houses by 2020; plans for where to build them are, inevitably, controversial.

Earlier redevelopment had already brutally changed parts of the city. A number of inns and other historic buildings were destroyed when the Lion Yard shopping-centre was built in the 1970s. As *The Cambridge Review* (21 September 1975) saw it, "a picturesque townscape" with "narrow, winding alleys" had been replaced by "a lumbering, crudely trendy composition of standard architectural units". In 1984 the Grafton Centre was built over much of the area of houses and small shops known, from its approximate shape, as the Kite. (The Kite Community Action Group fought long and hard to resist the change.) The centre was greatly expanded in the mid-1990s. But Cambridge can still be the idyllic city of some earlier accounts, its halls still often "peaceful and dignified". Even in the high tourist season it can be surprisingly quiet on the small bridges across the Cam at evening—if not quite as quiet as it must have been in Cook's day. A row of poplars on the way to Grantchester seems to be in the middle of the country, perhaps in rural France. Sun plays on the ivy or Virginia creeper in a college court.

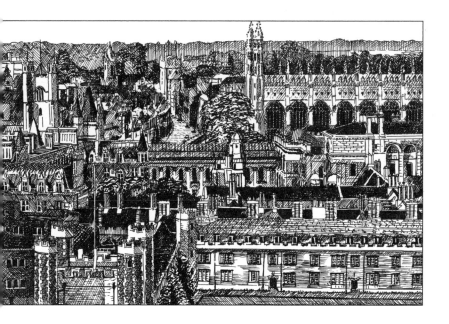

University and Town

Inevitably one comes back to college courts. In this book much space is devoted to the university and colleges. Perhaps this sounds like a reluctance to face John's "rough world without", but in fact it reflects the dominance of the university in the affairs of the town for much of its history. The town was there first: a settlement on the higher ground of what is now Mount Pleasant and Castle Hill began in the Iron Age or earlier and formed the basis of a small or medium-sized Roman fort and town. (There were also suburban developments, some where Arbury Road is now, not far from the no-longer visible pre-Roman fort of Arbury Camp.) In the late Roman period the town of Camboritum declined, for reasons so far undiscovered, to the point of near or total extinction. Anglo-Saxon settlers eventually took over the site, retaining the defensive function of the hill, but shifted the trading focus of the town down to the River Cam and, across it, to the marketplace and what would remain the town-centre. (For the later history of the hill see pp.37-8) Relatively few traces of this early period remain above ground, but the Museum of Archaeology and Anthropology displays a fairly good range of excavated objects. A more spectacular find, made when new sewers were laid in Chesterton Lane a few years ago, dates from a much later period: 1,800 coins—silver pennies and a few gold nobles and half-nobles—gathered together almost certainly around the time of the Black Death, in the late 1340s. The hoard has been acquired by the Fitzwilliam Museum.

When scholars came to the town of Grantebrycge from Oxford and Paris and gradually coalesced into a university in the thirteenth century, they provided trade and employment opportunities for the townspeople. There was also, however, friction between town and gown; the university and colleges (the first of which, Peterhouse, was founded in 1284) were granted an increasing degree of jurisdiction over the affairs of the town, especially after violent attempts to reverse this trend in 1381. The growing university came inevitably, besides, to dominate its small town. Real change came only with the rapid expansion of the town after the coming of the railways in the 1840s. New districts appeared, old were transformed; Eglantyne Jebb, in *Cambridge: a Brief Study in Social Questions* (1906), noted that Mill Road, which was a peaceful country road in 1830—maps show it passing between fields to Mill Road Nursery and Polecat Farm—was now a busy thoroughfare with side streets full of the "giddy monotony" of terraced houses. Building work was in hand, Jebb realized, which would make "the town east of the railway line... by itself equal the extent of the mediaeval city". New Chesterton had united with Old Chesterton. "Side by side with the beautiful mediaeval city, so dear to the hearts of successive generations of Englishmen [and, no doubt, women like Jebb], another town has grown up, one with a population four times as great and covering a much larger area." Between 1800 and 1900 the population had increased from 9,275 to 38,375; the census of 2001 records a population of nearly 109,000.

Amid all this change the civic authorities at last regained their power. But the university remained an unavoidably important local presence. It was still, above all, a provider of employment (direct or indirect). Teachers and students needed lodging, feeding, clothing and transporting. Institutions like Cambridge University Press, where printing commenced in 1584, needed workers. (Among the best known publications of the Press are bibles, including the Geneva Bible of 1591, the New English Bible in the 1960s, G. E. Moore's *Principia Ethica* (1903), and the various Cambridge Histories and New Cambridge Histories. From the 1830s it was based in the grand, towered Pitt Building in Trumpington Street; most of its operations have now transferred to a site close to the railway station.)

While not reliant on the university as much as their predecessors, Victorian and later businesses in Cambridge continued to benefit from its patronage; and in striving to do justice to the town one continually finds unexpected connections with the university. At the individual level, Charles Sayle, son of Robert Sayle (whose drapers' shop grew into the well-known Cambridge department store) worked at the University Library and was known in university literary circles in the days of Rupert Brooke and Ronald Firbank. David Marshall (1873-1942) worked in the kitchens at Trinity from the age of fourteen, revamped the university Pitt Club in Jesus Lane (now a branch of Pizza Express) and in 1909 started a company that hired out chauffeur-driven cars to wealthy undergraduates; his son, Sir Arthur Marshall, was more "respectably" connected with the university as a graduate of Jesus College and the Department of Engineering (1925) who went on to develop Marshall Aerospace on the foundation of the motor company. Marshall's garage in Jesus Lane, converted from a former inn and stables, remained active until a few years ago. Some friends expected Arthur the respectable Cambridge student to be embarrassed by the proximity of his college to his father's business premises, but he was made of more sensible stuff.

On a larger scale, there are many links between academic and commercial science. The Science Park, off Milton Road, was established by Trinity College in the 1980s. Just opposite, St John's College has developed St John's Innovation Park for the benefit of early stage knowledge-based businesses. The university also, of course, obtains and generates income from tourism and conference visitors. There must be many inhabitants of the modern city who have never set foot in a college, but the university remains essential to the role and image of Cambridge in a wider world—even, at times, in the "rough world without".

Oxford and Cambridge

William Thackeray coined the term "Oxbridge". Rarely have two places—collegiate university towns, for centuries the only ones in England—been so closely associated. The results range from mutual respect to mutual hostility. One place often likes to define itself by contrast with the other, and to move between the two can be disconcerting or, as the Oxonian Robert Graves found in Cambridge in 1923, "all Looking-Glassy": "everything was so much the same and yet so disturbingly different." There were punts, for instance, but (still a point of some amazement for travellers in either direction) they were propelled from the wrong end.

Clearly there are differences between the two towns. "To move from Oxford to Cambridge is," Noel Annan observes, "like moving from a gallery displaying paintings by Veronese and Rubens to one in which are hung the austere simplicities of Piero della Francesca." With its river and green spaces the centre of Cambridge often seems more peaceful; there are equally fine green spaces in Oxford but visitors are more likely to have to ask how to get to them. "Cambridge is certainly a cosy, sympathetic spot after the grim grandeurs of Oxford," Lytton Strachey told Dora Carrington on visiting his Alma Mater in 1918.

Cambridge has traditionally liked to think of Oxford as flippant, dilettante, and obsessed with politics and power while Oxford has labelled Cambridge earnest, coldly philosophical or scientific. The differences were more marked before the age of rapid travel and communication. And while Cambridge was long a small, university-dominated place, Oxford was always an important city in the middle of the country, more closely connected with London.

It was, interestingly, as communications improved, as Cambridge expanded and the two became rather more "Oxbridge", that many of the terms that distinguish the one from the other emerged or were solidified: the spellings Magdalene and Magdalen, the accurate placing of the apostrophe for Queens', Cambridge, and Queen's, Oxford (though to confuse matters, Cambridge has Queen's Road). Cambridge had, more clearly and consistently from the nineteenth century than before, combination rooms for Oxford common rooms, courts for quads, bedders and gyps for scouts, supervisions for tutorials. Such niceties have helped maintain a healthy sense of difference in the face of increased similarity.

CHAPTER ONE

Greens and Waters

The Backs

Once there were active docks at the back of the colleges on the river. When the river became less navigable the scene became more picturesque. Henry James described it in "English Vignettes" (1879):

> *Six or eight of the colleges stand in a row, turning their backs to the river; and hereupon ensues the loveliest confusion of Gothic windows and ancient trees, of grassy banks and mossy balustrades, of sun-chequered avenues and groves, of lawns and gardens and terraces, of single-arched bridges spanning the little stream, which is small and shallow and looks as if it had been turned on for ornamental purposes. The thin-flowing Cam appears to exist simply as an occasion for these brave little bridges—the beautiful covered gallery of John's or the slightly collapsing arch of Clare.*

The flowers on the Backs are equally appealing: the flood of purple crocuses near the back gate of Trinity in mid- or late February, or some weeks later the massed anemones and daffodils in the controlled wilderness at the edge of St John's. The most conspicuous example of fauna was, before the foot and mouth outbreak of 2001, the cows of King's. Their disappearance (temporary, it is hoped) makes it difficult not to think of the absent or present cow on which Rickie tries philosophically to focus at the beginning of E. M. Forster's *The Longest Journey* (1907); in his second year at King's Forster lived in Bodley's building, by the river.

Midsummer Common and Jesus Green

The common takes its name from the fair which, from the reign of Henry III onwards, began on Midsummer Day. There are still visiting funfairs, circuses, November fireworks displays for crowds of up to 35,000, and Strawberry Fair (a large event in June attracting many people from outside Cambridge; not always popular with local residents).

One of the most imaginative, and imaginatively marketed, fairs was the Cambridge Coronation Festival of 28 June 1838. In Queen Victoria's honour a specially formed committee for "the rustic sports" on Midsummer Green (or Common) was pleased to announce fixtures including a blindfold Wheelbarrow Race, Biscuit Bolting ("twelve boys to eat a pennyworth of biscuits each"—first prize a Victoria waistcoat), Royal Pig Races, Dipping for Eels, and a Grinning Match "or, which is the ugliest phiz!!" This, now more often called a "gurning" match,

will be contested by men of all ages, and all complexions—all description of physiognomy—and every degree of ugliness and beauty—whether short or tall, little or big, lean or fat, young or old, green or grey, and must be performed according to the usual customs on these occasions, exhibiting, in Grimaldian [as in the great clown Joseph Grimaldi] excellence and bold relief, the various contortions of the 'Human face divine', by peeping through a Pegasian Cravat—or, as the vulgar would profanely designate it—a Horse's Collar! The party who shall be declared the winner will be rewarded with a brand new pair of velveteen trousers, and a new wipe. The other competitors will be rewarded with a gallon of Sam Moore's regular, right-sort, head-strong, out-and-out, strong-bodied, ram-jam, come-it-strong, lift-me-up, knock-me-down, how d'ye-like-it, ge-nu-ine Midsummer-Green Stingo! and a new hat each.

When there are no fairs the common looks fairly countrified for the middle of a city. It is now again, after an absence following the foot and mouth crisis of 2001, grazed by a small herd of cows. Across Victoria Avenue sports including football and volleyball are played on Jesus Green. Quite frequent flooding permits less orthodox games like water-bicycling—not necessarily intentional—and even kayaking between the plane trees of the avenue. Jesus Green also hosts a beer festival in May and a comedy festival in August. The open-air swimming pool was built in 1923.

Parker's Piece

Victoria's coronation was also marked on Parker's Piece (named after Edward Parker, the Trinity college cook who once leased the land), this time by a great charity meal. The senior university official Joseph Romilly, who carved at one of the tables, noted some of the statistics in his diary:

> Round the Promenade were tables in a circle for the Sunday scholars (about 3000). Radiating from these were 60 tables for the poor: about 12,000 of these sat down. And round the extremity of these tables was an outer promenade where the servants etc. walked with gratuitous tickets from the subscribers. The subscription amounted to £1758: the pounds of meat were 8120, the plum puddings 1650, the barrels of beer 99.

Everything "went off admirably" except that the orchestra "was not effective enough, and the singing 'God Save the Queen' was very feeble from being sung in parts." The "Immense Fire Portrait of Her Majesty the Queen" to be seen over Parker's Piece the previous week must have been more impressive; it was part of a grand fireworks display that also included, according to the official programme, "Batteries of Jewelled-Headed Cobras" and a "Salvo of Golden Saucissons".

On more ordinary days areas of Parker's Piece are used for games including football. Here, indeed, some of the earliest games of Association Football in something like its modern form were played. The Cambridge Rules, drawn up in 1848 and redrafted in 1856, were a principal source for the Association rules adopted in 1863. (One of the main rival codes was based on the game played at, and so named after, Rugby.) The beginnings of Cambridge United Football Club are supposed, more simply, to have been a match beneath a street-lamp in Stanley Street in 1912. The club, originally called Abbey United because it was based in the Abbey area around Newmarket Road, disbanded in 1914 but re-formed after the First World War. The Abbey Stadium opened in 1932 and the name Cambridge United was adopted in 1951. At one time Cambridge Town (later City) was its great rival; the rivalry sometimes erupted into violence, especially in the 1960s. One of the most successful United managers (1974-8) was Ron Atkinson.

There are also reminders of cricket. Hobbs' Pavilion, now a restaurant, is named after Sir Jack Hobbs (1882-1963), who first played for Cambridgeshire in 1904 and scored 197 centuries in first-class cricket. Not far away, beyond the baroque sweep of the glassy new swimming pool, is Fenner's, the university cricket-ground, which opened in 1846. (Frank Fenner owned the land.) England cricketers who played here as undergraduates include David Sheppard, Ted Dexter, Mike Brearley and Mike Atherton. Also near Parker's Piece is Mill Road, where there are oriental and continental mini-markets and delicatessens, take-aways, cafés, bookshops, a hardware store and many other small shops of the sort no longer found in the centre of the city; for some people this is now "the real Cambridge".

The Cam

Jawaharlal Nehru, who was as yet more interested, according to his memoirs, in riding, tennis and gambling than politics, described his time at Trinity College in 1907-10 as "Three quiet years with little of disturbance in them, moving slowly on, like the sluggish Cam." The river is "sluggish" or "slow-winding" (Thomas Gray) as persistently as the Tiber was yellow; its banks are muddy or sedgy or worse; "that big sewer at the back of the college" Leslie Stephen has a friend call it in *Sketches from Cambridge* (1865). Matters improved when a steam pumping station was opened in 1895 at Cheddars Lane; it functioned until 1968 and now houses the Museum of Technology, showing and demonstrating a wide range of pumping engines, gas engines, boilers, early radios and printing equipment.

Partly because of its happy associations for people who have spent much time walking by it or floating on it, the river is also Phineas Fletcher's "lovely Cam". For much of its course it flows through meadows, past Midsummer and Stourbridge Commons, colleges, and boathouses. (There are some eighteen of these. Several survive from the late nineteenth century, among them Pembroke's highly decorated specimen; later boathouses include David Roberts' of 1958-9 for Corpus Christi and Sidney Sussex, steel-framed and with external spiral staircases.) Beyond Bait's Bite lock is a quieter stretch where kingfishers are sometimes seen. From there the path leads on eventually to Clayhithe, where the Cam Conservators built their grand Dutch-gabled house in 1842.

Rowing

The first inter-collegiate bumping races or "Bumps" on the Cam occurred in 1827. The competitions took this form—bumping the boat in front instead of simply racing it—because of the narrowness of the river. (The faster Oxford and Cambridge Boat Race took place first on the Thames at Henley in 1829, subsequently in London from 1856.) The early boats, moreover, were much broader than the increasingly streamlined craft of the 1840s onwards, broad enough to carry substantial picnics and the equipment necessary for their consumption. The Lady Margaret Boat Club, of St John's College, was presented with "2 kettles, 9 cups and saucers, 9 teaspoons, 9 plates, 4 dishes, 4 basins, 1 pepper box, 1 salt box, 1 mustard pot, 2 graters, 9 eggholders, 9 eggspoons."

In the late nineteenth and early twentieth century large crowds, from the town as well as the university, turned out to watch the Bumps. Some came for the fun of the fair. The day climaxed, for those who hired boats or brought their own, in chaotic unofficial races back to Jesus Green. Some meditated more deeply on the muscular and "manly" efforts they had cheered. "It was a noble sport," decides Charles Kingsley's Alton Locke:

> a sight such as could only be seen in England—some hundred of young men who might, if they had chosen, have been lounging effeminately about the streets, subjecting themselves voluntarily to that intense exertion, for the mere pleasure of toil.

Just such "grim, earnest, stubborn energy", Locke maintains in spite of his anti-establishment instincts, won Waterloo and built Birmingham and Manchester. Certainly such energy makes for "very good fellows", Leslie Stephen, once a keen oarsman himself, agrees in *Sketches from Cambridge* (1865); "excellent raw material for country parsons", he goes on, "or for any other profession where much thinking power is not required."

The "manly", or at least traditionally male aspect of the Bumps is observable in victorious teams' habit of burning boats (old ones, rather than the highly expensive craft in which they sat earlier in the day) and vigorous, hard-drinking Bump suppers. But women's crews—no more "lounging effeminately" than Kingsley's machos—have been in action on the river since the 1890s. In 1962 a crew from the Cambridge University Women's Boat Club was at last permitted to enter the Bumps, although the captain of Selwyn had opined that "women rowing... is a ghastly sight, an anatomical impossibility (if you are rowing properly that is) and physiologically dangerous." He was prepared, nevertheless, to let them enter; it was not the function of the University Boat Club "to stop them making complete fools of themselves." About seventy women's crews (to a hundred men's) now take part in the May Bumps. Men and women have raced in separate divisions since 1974.

The Dean in Tom Sharpe's *Porterhouse Blue* (1974) would not be a man to countenance such newfangled notions as women in the Bumps. Watching the races inspires him with memories of "the unquestioning innocence of his own rowing days" before the First World War, "and the fitness of things then... an acceptance of life without... the dangerous speculations which had gained momentum since. A guiltless time, that, a golden age of assurance... when there was honey still for tea and a servant still to bring it too." That assurance included, at least for the Dean's old enemy, the Senior Tutor, an unambiguous belief in the virtues of competition. On one occasion the Dean preached, in Porterhouse chapel, on the text "Many that are first shall be last". The Tutor, who was coaching the college boat, was so incensed that he stormed out of the service and began training the eight so hard that they peaked too soon and were bumped three times in the May races.

Punting

On quieter days punts dot the river, between Jesus Green and Grantchester, with a degree of gondola elegance. On busier days, near the colleges and boatyards at least, it looks more like the sort of painted sea-battle where you cannot see the water for close-packed wood. Henry James is only one of the more distinguished people whose head—unfortunately very bald by this time—has been struck by a friend's poorly managed pole. He recovered, Geoffrey Keynes remembered, to spend the rest of the trip "lying comfortably on the cushions and gazing up though prominent half-closed eyes at Brooke's handsome figure in white shirt and white flannel trousers." Rupert Brooke, the golden-haired poet, had taken over the poling from the dangerously less adept Charles Sayle. Some have even wielded a pole or paddle in anger, or at least mock-anger, as in the Rag punt-battles between King's and Clare, which flourished until safety concerns put a stop to them in 1963.

In earlier times at least one more serious clash involved river craft and their crew. On a summer evening in 1781 two St John's undergraduate canoeists were near Magdalene Bridge when a bargeman (these were the days of busy river-trade) grappled one of the canoes with his boat-hook. The occupant of the other canoe leapt at once onto the barge, brandishing his oar, and knocked the bargeman into the Cam. The remaining crew of the barge did the same for the rash youth. The undergraduates returned with reinforcements from St John's but the fiercely pole-wielding bargemen soon forced them to seek sanctuary in Magdalene. The bargemen were set to besiege the college when, in the nick of time, the President of St John's appeared on the scene with Samuel Weston, the private tutor of the ducked undergraduate Charles Yorke. Weston, clearly a man with some diplomatic skills, "by mixing alternately with the people on the outside and on the inside of the gate, persuaded one party to retire to their houses, and got the other into college by a quarter after ten."

Back in their rooms, however, the bruised Johnians began to contemplate revenge. The word was that a miller by the name of Anderson had shouted encouragement to the bargemen from the bridge. (According to some witnesses, however, he had actually come to Yorke's assistance.) Perhaps Anderson would be easier to deal with than the barges. Again, in the morning, Weston had to step in as mediator, going between groups of young men he did not know but "to whom I thought it my duty to represent the probable consequence of a second riot... namely that lives must inevitably be lost on both sides." At first reason seemed to prevail, but by evening some of the students were back at Magdalene Bridge looking for trouble. Their elders, led again by the indefatigable Weston, "followed and mixed with them, and, drawing them off in small parties, once more lodged them all in college before ten." Weston feared another flare-up, but in the morning, clearly somewhat to their own surprise, he and the

President succeeded in negotiating "a general and cordial reconciliation".

More peaceful river experiences are possible, for instance the summer idyll presented in Vladimir Nabokov's autobiography *Speak Memory* (1951). (Nabokov came to Trinity as a student in 1919 after his family fled the Russian Revolution.)

> *I remember the dreamy flow of punts and canoes on the Cam, the Hawaiian whine of phonographs slowly passing through sunshine and shade and a girl's hand gently twirling this way and that the handle of her peacock-bright parasol as she reclined on the cushions of the punt which I dreamily navigated. The pink-coned chestnuts were in full fan; they made overlapping masses along the banks, they crowded the sky out of the river, and their special pattern of flowers and leaves produced a kind of en escalier effect, the angular figuration of some splendid green and old-rose tapestry.*

He would watch the "delicate union" between a falling petal and its reflection, "with the magic precision of a poet's word meeting halfway his, or a reader's, recollection." The scene survived in memory, even if in the next paragraph Nabokov confesses that a visit to Cambridge nearly seventeen years later on "a raw February day" did not have the same lyrical effect.

Hobson's Conduit

Sanitation in medieval Cambridge, as in many medieval places, left much to be desired. One of the main water supplies was the King's Ditch, dug mainly as a defence for the town in the tenth century and renewed and extended by Henry III in the thirteenth. (The ditch ran from the river at what is now Mill Lane to the river at what is now Quayside.) It was frequently clogged with rubbish and sewage. The problem more generally is illustrated by the ambitious anti-pollution statute agreed by the parliament held at Cambridge in 1388: waters and other places full of "dung and filth of garbage and entrails, as well of beasts killed as of other corruptions" were infecting the air so that "intolerable diseases do daily happen." The polluters were to remove the debris by the following Michaelmas, or pay the then enormous fine of £20 to the Crown.

In spite of such well-intentioned measures the ditches continued, on the whole, to fester. Eventually in 1574 the vice-chancellor of the university, Andrew Perne, proposed building a conduit to bring purer water into the town, but it was not until 1610 that his scheme was carried out, financed partly by the well-known university carrier, Thomas Hobson (1544-1631). One reason he was well known was his policy on hiring out horses to "the scholars", as described in *Cantabrigia Depicta* (1776): "he made it an unalterable rule, it seems, that every horse should have an equal share of rest and fatigue, and therefore would never let one out of his turn; from whence came the saying, 'Hobson's Choice': this or none." He was also famous for the energy and persistence with which he continued to drive his eight-horse team to London and back, delivering goods and people. Only inactivity, it appeared, could kill him, as is suggested by the title of Milton's two poems "On the University Carrier, who sickened in the time of his vacancy, being forbid to go to London, by reason of the plague". In a much later poem, John Holloway's *Civitatula*, he is saluted as "forthright as a hammer".

The first stretch of Hobson's Conduit runs from Vicar's Brook, near Long Road, to what is now the corner of Lensfield and Trumpington Roads. Here since 1856 has stood the hexagonal fountainhead that from 1614 had been in the marketplace, to which one branch of the conduit flowed. The other, still operational branch inconveniences the very schoolmasterly schoolmaster Herbert Pembroke in Forster's *The Longest Journey* (1907): in his undergraduate days, he complains, there was no "swaggering three abreast along the pavement and charging inoffensive visitors into a gutter." The gutter in which Herbert's sock is soaked is one of the two runnels still to be seen on either side of Trumpington Street. Unwary cyclists, as well as pedestrian schoolmasters, have sometimes fallen foul of them, but they are a (picturesque) improvement on the stream running down the middle of the road which, in 1788, they replaced.

The Fens

It was right and reasonable, said Charles Kingsley in his "Prose Idyll" on the fens published in 1873, to transform, through drainage, "a waste and howling wilderness" into "a garden of the Lord". "And yet the fancy may linger, without blame, over the shining meres, the golden reed-beds, the countless water-fowl, the strange and gaudy insects, the wild nature, the mystery, the majesty... which haunted the deep fens for many a hundred years."

The draining of the fens (north of Cambridge) was by no means complete even in Kingsley's day. It was a long and difficult process. There had been some progress in Roman times, probably brought to an end by flooding in the third century. The next concerted effort began in 1630, when Francis, 4th Earl of Bedford, and thirteen other "Adventurers" invested capital in exchange for the ownership of land successfully drained. The most important of those who "adventured" their resources was the man most involved in the work: Sir Cornelius Vermuyden, a Dutch engineer knighted in 1629 following his successful drainage work in Yorkshire. Vermuyden's measures included digging two straight "cuts", the Old Bedford River in the 1630s and the New Bedford River or Hundred Foot Drain in 1654. For some time the flow of water on the fenland rivers—among them the Ouse and its tributary the Cam—seemed to have been efficiently regulated. But extensive flooding later in the century suggested otherwise. Vermuyden and his contemporaries did not know that peat, once drained, shrinks by about an inch a year and so lowers the level of the fields.

In the eighteenth century the struggle was continued with the aid of further engineering work and wind pumps, one of which has been restored to working order at Adventurers' Fen, part of the National Trust Wicken Fen estate seventeen miles north of Cambridge. After 1818 more powerful and efficient steam beam engines began to replace the wind pumps. The Old Engine at Stretham, which operated between 1831 and 1941, could lift some thirty tons of water at a single revolution. Such machines, and the even more powerful diesel pumps that in turn replaced them, were one of the chief factors enabling wide-scale land-reclamation. But although cornfields have often replaced fenland, the landscape remains distinctive with its raised roads, long straight drains, and huge views with, for many miles of southern fenland, Ely Cathedral on the skyline. And Kingsley's "shining meres", "golden reed-beds" and wildlife (200 species of birds, nineteen of dragonflies, many a mollusc) are still to be encountered at Wicken Fen.

Once Cambridge itself had seemed close—too close—to the watery expanse: John Evelyn, in September 1654, pronounced "the whole town situated in a low dirty unpleasant place, the streets ill paved, the air thick, as infested by the fens"; Tennyson's friend Hallam could still describe it to his sister as a "college-studded marsh". But as the drainage system improved, the area became more popular with Cambridge people apart from the traditional hunters and anglers. There was still quite enough water for the growth, in some of the hard winters of the nineteenth century, of the sport of fen skating. According to the enthusiastic and informative *Handbook of Fen Skating* (1882) by Neville and Albert Goodman, expert skaters could cover a mile in three minutes; most people could comfortably manage ten miles per hour. In Cambridge they used flooded land on Stourbridge Common or Lingay Fen, near Grantchester. More ambitiously, as Tom (visiting the winter of 1895 from the future) and Hatty do in Philippa Pearce's novel *Tom's Midnight Garden* (1958), they might skate along the frozen river to Ely or beyond.

The Goodmans are at pains to distinguish their sport from figure skating: theirs is "the *going* as opposed to the *showing* style of skating". In *Tom's Midnight Garden* a "town-urchin" vigorously proves the point:

> *In one place an orange had been set centrally upon the ice, and four top-hatted, dignified gentlemen were describing a harmony of figures to it—from it—round it. Suddenly a town-urchin, on rusty Fen runners, partly strapped, partly tied with string to his boots, dashed in, snatched up the orange and dashed away again with his teeth already in it. The swaying, shifting crowd of skaters closed up behind him, and the figure-skating gentlemen stopped skating, and were extremely annoyed.*

Fen runners are the curved skates especially suited to the "going" style. A pair wrapped in paper and concealed beneath the floorboards has a vital role to play in bridging the gap between Hatty's time and Tom's— as well as the practical advantage of turning what ought to be one pair of runners into two.

Skaters and others, as they issued into the fens from Cambridge, encountered and commented on the inhabitants. Kingsley liked to see them as honourable figures, toughened by their struggle with the elements and by a good dose of Scandinavian blood, people like the stalwart Hereward the Wake, Saxon hero and subject of one of his novels. Hereward long held out against the Normans on what, because of the surrounding fens, became known as the "Isle" of Ely. ("Ely" itself almost certainly refers to the plentiful eels which were an important element in the less romantic sphere of fenland trade and diet.) The Goodmans, too, find that, "although there is perhaps not much refinement" (Kingsley probably would have applauded), "there is plenty of good solid English cheer" in the fens. But the people they met were more evidently human than Kingsley's noble natives of the distant past.

One of the peculiarities of the Fen folk is that having so much water round about them, and having experienced the difficulty of defending themselves against it, they are very chary of admitting it into their systems, at least in an unadulterated state. If the tourist asks at any of the little inns on the banks for water, milk, lemonade, tea, or coffee, the hostess will probably gaze upon him with unfeigned astonishment, if not with ill-concealed contempt, and reply 'we don't keep such as them.'

Another local trait was (Neville Goodman perhaps uses the past tense in hope rather than assurance) a certain "rough humour". One form this took was digging holes in the ice for skaters to fall into.

Magdalene College

"The 'Maudlin Men' were, at one time, so famous for Tea-drinking, that the Cam, which licks the very walls of the college, is said to have been absolutely rendered unnavigable with Tea-leaves." Thus, in 1827, J. M. F. Wright of Trinity caricatured the Evangelical and teetotal fervour of a number of fellows and undergraduates at Magdalene. (Their first boat was later called the Tea Kettle.) True, he allowed, things had changed recently—enough to justify his phonetic spelling of the name of the college—for "the modern men of Maudlin... fully attest, by their copious libations, the immense strides they have made in civilization." (In 1954, however, C. S. Lewis, having moved to the college after many years at Magdalen, Oxford, lamented to Joy Davidman that "they only get *one* glass of port after dinner, to Magdalen's three!")

The first residents of the two houses by the Great (now Magdalene) Bridge that grew into the college were, if not tea-drinkers, at least religious. Crowland Abbey obtained the land in 1428 in order to build a hostel for some of the few Benedictine monks studying in Cambridge. By about 1480 this was known as Buckingham College, patronage provided by the family of Henry Stafford, Duke of Buckingham, the original of Richard's overreaching henchman in Shakespeare's *Richard III*. The college consisted at first only of the north and south ranges of the first court. The chapel, on the north side, has been frequently altered; on a visit in 1904 A. C. Benson, later Master, was disappointed to find "a feeble modern Gothic building". It was much improved by the removal of some very dark nineteenth-century glass in the 1960s. The hall, which may date from 1519, seemed to Benson to have been painted so as to look "smeared with stale mustard"; he transformed it not only by re-painting the walls but by designing and installing new glass and a new ceiling. But the greatest change in the appearance of the court came in the 1950s when the eighteenth-century stucco was removed to reveal warm red brick.

Buckingham College closed in 1539 following the dissolution of the monasteries. But in 1542 the Lord Chancellor, Thomas, Lord Audley of Walden, established a new foundation, Magdalene College, in the former court of the monks. Possibly the name was intended not only to honour the saint but, in the rather heavy Tudor manner, as a play on the founder's name: "M-Audley-n". Four years earlier Audley had also acquired the Benedictine abbey at Walden in Essex, which he turned into a country house, Audley End. His grandson Thomas Howard, Earl of Suffolk, expanded this into a great Jacobean palace (later much altered; still one of the most notable stately homes within easy reach of Cambridge). Appointment of the Master of Magdalene remained the responsibility of Audley's descendants of the Howard and Braybrooke families, but in its first century or so the college enjoyed nothing like the magnificence of Audley End. The first court was eventually completed later in the sixteenth century. The entrance gate of about 1585, described by Pevsner as "handsome... and unusually restrained for its date", suits the quiet atmosphere of the brick court as a whole.

Expansion into a second court came mainly during the seventeenth century. Its most remarkable feature, the Pepys Building, was possibly begun as early as the 1580s but is mainly a late seventeenth-century creation, with decoration still being added to the façade after 1700. A colonnade, inscriptions and busts proclaim classical dignity, although everything is on a small enough scale to harmonize easily with the more modest surroundings. Since 1724, apart from a period in the mid-nineteenth century, this building has housed Samuel Pepys' library: three thousand volumes collected by the diarist and his nephew and heir John Jackson, and kept, as stipulated by Pepys, in its twelve original oak cases. The prize possession is Pepys' own diary: six brown calf-bound volumes containing 1,250,000 words and covering his public and very private life between 1 January 1660 and 31 May 1669. Pepys wrote in shorthand, using the system devised by Thomas Shelton. Shelton's work went through more than twenty editions between 1626 and 1710; had he come across it, life might have been easier for John Smith of St John's College, who deciphered the diary with difficulty between 1819 and 1822.

Pepys and Benson: Two Magdalene Diarists

Pepys had studied at Magdalene in 1651-4. The diary includes brief reminiscences of this time and accounts of later visits. He does not mention, as the college records do, that he was officially reproved, on 21 October 1653, for having been "scandalously overseen in drink the night before". He remained fond of beer and wine; in Cambridge he often stayed at the Rose Tavern (the name is preserved in Rose Crescent, off Trinity Street) and there in February 1660 took the opportunity to drink many healths to the soon-to-be-restored King Charles II. And in May 1668 at Magdalene he went "into the buttery as a stranger and there drank my bellyful of their beer," which pleased him—perhaps partly out of loyalty or nostalgia—"as the best I ever drank." (The college brewhouse had been built in 1629. The building survives, in adapted form, between the Pepys Building and the river.) He also mentions, with characteristic frankness, that as a student he was well acquainted with a certain Elizabeth Aynsworth, a procuress who later, having been banished from the town of Cambridge, transferred her activities to the Reindeer Inn in Bishop's Stortford.

More refined relations between the sexes presumably figured in *Love a Cheat*, the romance Pepys wrote at Cambridge and came upon when sorting out his papers ten years later. He "liked it well and wondered a little" at his own achievement, but destroyed it nonetheless. On the whole, however, Pepys the future senior naval administrator, skilled amateur musician and indefatigable diarist (he stopped in 1669 only in fear of damaging his eyes) was a diligent student. The Puritanism of those in positions of power in 1650s Cambridge—and England—made it rather easier to be reprimanded for being "overseen" than in some periods. Seven years after the incident, in a different political and religious climate, he enjoyed "a very handsome supper" with some of the fellows in the very room of his disgrace and "could find that there was nothing at all left of the old preciseness [Puritanism] in their discourse, especially on Saturday nights." But his fondest, most personal recorded memory of Magdalene was not of hard study or high living; while drinking his nostalgic "bellyful" of college beer, he talked about old times with "the butler's man, who was son to Goody Mulliner over against the college that we used to buy stewed prunes of."

Above "Bibliographia Pepysiana 1724" on the library façade is inscribed Samuel Pepys' motto in later life, "Mens cujusque is est quisque", a quotation from Cicero meaning approximately "One's mind is what one is"—in other words, a person's true worth inheres in what he or she truly is, not in external appearances. This motto was, in the opinion of I. A. Richards, "the prime utterance point of... the most inexhaustibly enheartening facade in Cambridge". Richards (1893-1979), an undergraduate and then a fellow at Magdalene, was, more than any other teacher and writer, responsible for a revolution in the twentieth-century understanding and criticism of poetry, the form regarded by many of his followers as "the prime utterance point" of language. In the late 1920s in Cambridge (subsequently he moved to China and to Harvard) Richards carried out the experiment that resulted in his *Practical Criticism* (1929): he gave students copies of poems without date or author's name. Their reports or "protocols", often preferring trite and straightforward poems to richer, more challenging examples, were then analysed; this method enabled Richards to demonstrate the prevalence of readers' "stock responses", based on untested assumptions about what poems "ought" to be like.

As a corrective, he recommended training in close reading: close attention to words and their range of possible meanings, to ambiguity and irony. Richards' pupil at Magdalene, the poet and critic William Empson (1906-84), produced for one of his supervisions the "central 30,000 words or so" of perhaps the most inventively detailed example of close reading, *Seven Types of Ambiguity* (1930).

When Richards came up to Magdalene in 1911 A. C. Benson immediately took an interest in him. Benson had come to the college as a fellow in 1904 and was President (or Vice-Master) from 1912 and Master from 1915 until his death ten years later. During the twenty-one years of his involvement with the college he transformed it from a small, poor, failing institution into a respected and confident one. This process was greatly assisted by Benson's personal wealth—the result mainly of writing a string of popular novels, essays and reminiscences. He himself thought little of the books that flowed so easily from his pen; he was aware that his work was slight, pleasing, unchallenging. In 1908 Max Beerbohm drew "Mr Arthur Christopher Benson vowing eternal fidelity to the Obvious" in the shape of a dull, stout but laurel-crowned lady on whom he is advancing with determined stride and definite moustache. He was aware, too, as were some of his friends, of the great contrast between the blandness of his books and the sharper observation and humour of his conversation. Fortunately, he was also an even more extensive diarist than Pepys, and it is in the diaries that this sharper element survives. He observes keenly his fellow denizens of academe: the white-bearded Master of Trinity, Dr Henry Montagu Butler, "like the Almighty in Blake's designs for Job"; Doctors of Divinity as rooks at the Senate House; Richards, briefly a "silly boy" having proclaimed, over dinner, his youthful faith in anarchism, but on further talk the following day "a sincere lover of liberty", "an interesting creature", and soon someone Benson admired.

Benson also observed himself, reflecting quizzically, for instance, on his own position as a college dignitary. Recurring depression made him focus more acutely on the oddness of identity. As he cycled along Huntingdon Road one June afternoon in 1917, "the ludicrous thought was lurking in my mind that no one who passed a stout, rather bronzed, ill-dressed man on a bike going very slowly, had the smallest idea that they saw a martyr at the stake." In the attempt, sometimes successful, to escape the martyrdom of depression he would often cycle far out of Cambridge. Occasionally he pedalled across the great flat to Ely. Once, after a hot day, he went south with his younger friend Percy Lubbock, through the night to the villages of Barton, Haslingfield and Harston and on at dawn to Grantchester, "where the mill with lighted windows was rumbling, and the water ran oily-smooth into the inky pool among the trees."

When his depression lifted, Benson was an energetic achiever. He was responsible, among much else, for the expansion of the college to include land on the other side of Magdalene Street, although it was after his death that most of the building and conversion of the "delicate court of cottages" of John Holloway's *Civitatula* (houses, some medieval, were incorporated) took place. Mallory Court, named after the ex-Magdalene mountaineer George Mallory who died on Everest in 1924, was built in 1925-6. The first building of Benson Court (1930-2) is by Sir Edwin Lutyens. David Roberts and associates worked further in these two courts in the 1950s and added Buckingham Court in 1969-70. It was originally gifts and loans from Benson that made such projects possible; he had already contributed several thousand pounds to the college before, in 1915, an American admirer of his books, Mme de Nottbeck, persuaded him to accept £40,000, most of which went to Magdalene.

The atmosphere of the college is sometimes described as "domestic". It is the peaceful place of warm brick, studious monks, the quiet garden by the glinting river. This atmosphere is perhaps enhanced by the contrast with the modern cafés, bars, flats and punt proprietors across the Cam in the 1990s Quayside development. In Benson's day and for much of the twentieth century, however, the contrast was grimmer. The punts were there for hire, and before them the working river boats, but for Benson the dominant feature was "the Electricity Supply Works, that noisy, smoky, bare-walled place, so barbarously planted down opposite the Magdalene Garden, and disfiguring so unpleasantly the old waterway into Cambridge from the north." In earlier times the noise emanated from docks and coal-barges on the river and from the five nearby inns, of which only the sixteenth-century Pickerel, opposite the college, remains active. The Cross Keys, a little further along the street, may have been a brothel; this is a possible explanation for the phallically well-endowed grotesques still decorating the wooden frame of the building. A few doors further along, on the corner of Northampton Street, the White Horse, which closed down in 1934, has housed the Folk Museum since 1936. Here surviving traces of the inn include the carefully preserved bar with its pots, measures and casks, and what is supposed, on the first floor, to be a "wig-powdering closet" of about 1700. The museum packs in a remarkable assortment of cooking utensils, lace bobbins, thatching tools, toys, old signs from local pubs, early vacuum cleaners, hats, an eighteenth-century portable "parlour sink", mantraps, mousetraps and a Demon Beetle Trap of 1955.

Inside the college, too, life could be far from quiet, if we can believe even part of the complaint sent by William Bulkeley, the college President, to Lord Burghley, Chancellor of the university, in 1578. The new Master, Degory Nicholls, had said, for reasons best known to himself, that he "would root out all Welshmen in the college" (which had lands and connections in Wales) and had accordingly lost no opportunity "either to take away some thing from such Welshmen as were in the college or to hinder them of some benefit that might befall them." The butler and the Greek lecturer had lost their jobs only because they were Welsh. (The lecturer was soon reinstated but not the butler.) Later Nicholls also sacked Bulkeley, who was also, of course, Welsh. "Item", the aggrieved letter continues, Nicholls is less interested in "the perfecting of the scholars" in his care than in "the feeding of his kine [cattle] which commonly lie in the court and often are milked before the hall door, his wife standing by." Mistress Nicholls was herself a particular bone of contention. The fact that she may well have been virtually the only woman in college—fellows were not allowed to marry—may have attracted some of the animus against her. As far as her critics were concerned, she made the atmosphere at Magdalene all too domestic: "Item: his wife is so chiding that often she is heard all over the college to the disturbance of the students so that it were to be wished she had another dwelling house." The Master's only defence, when questioned by Burghley, was that he had the right to act as he had acted. But eventually, whether alienated by the complaints or chidden by his wife, Nicholls retired in 1582 to his living in Cornwall and resigned the Mastership soon afterwards.

Clare College

Clare, says the 1790 edition of *A Concise and Accurate Description of the University, Town and County of Cambridge,*

> *is pleasantly situate on the eastern bank of the river, over which it has an elegant stone bridge, leading to a fine vista, beyond which is a beautiful lawn, surrounded by lofty elms, and cornfields extending as far as the eye can reach to Coton and Madingley; a more pleasing prospect cannot be conceived in a level country. This delightful spot is much resorted to on summer evenings.*

The view is now interrupted by the substantial presence of Clare's own Memorial and Thirkill Courts. But the bridge, erected by Thomas Grumbold in 1639-40, is still elegantly in position and the college and its grounds remain a popular place to linger. The Fellows' Garden, which is often open to the public, was redesigned by Professor Nevill Willmer in 1947 as a series of open-air "rooms" of carefully gradated colours and levels. The rooms are grouped around the central sunken garden with lily-pool, inspired by a similar arrangement that Willmer had seen at Pompeii more than twenty years earlier. His "triumph of landscape gardening", suggests Duncan Robinson in an essay in *Clare Through the Twentieth Century* (2001), pays "equal homage to the serpentine paths and concealed bounds of William Kent's eighteenth-century gardens, and to the combination of formal design and thickly planted flower borders which Gertrude Jekyll introduced into English gardens in the early twentieth century."

The college itself was founded by Richard de Badew in 1326 and re-founded by Lady Elizabeth de Clare, a granddaughter of Edward I, in 1338, but the earlier buildings were replaced by the much admired court built mainly by Thomas and Robert Grumbold between 1638 and 1715. Work was interrupted by the Civil Wars but in 1654 John Evelyn found Clare already "of a new and noble design". When the work was finished, others continued to find it noble or, in the words of one eighteenth-century Cambridge student, "neat beyond description, and though it might not at first strike your fancy as much as Trinity, yet the more you consider, the more you admire it."

The present chapel, of 1763-9, is the work of James Burrough and James Essex. The guide *Ambulator* (1835), varying only slightly the wording of *A Concise and Accurate Description*, describes the interior as "very pleasingly ornamented with stucco-work, and a neat wainscoting. Over the altar, in a beautiful alcove, is a picture of the Salutation, by Cipriani. The ante-chapel is of an octagonal form, and is lighted by an elegant dome." Stained glass commemorates two of the most notable religious leaders in the history of the college, Hugh Latimer (c. 1492-1555), fellow and Protestant martyr (see pp.113-14) and Nicholas Ferrar (1592-1637), who came to Clare at the age of thirteen and was later a fellow. He was the close friend of George Herbert and in 1625 established an Anglican community at Little Gidding in Huntingdonshire (an inspiration for the last section of T. S. Eliot's *Four Quartets*).

Mansfield Forbes, a twentieth-century fellow of Clare, wrote enthusiastically about Ferrar, especially his interest in the colony of Virginia, in the massive, often rambling, often perceptive two-volume history of the college that he edited (1928-30). This was Forbes' only substantial publication but he is remembered as a brilliant and sometimes unconventional teacher and a founder of the new English tripos. ("Tripos", the Cambridge term for a degree examination, originated from the three-legged stool used by the official opponent in oral disputations.) He encouraged in his pupils an open-minded, carefully meditated response to the text, and furthered the early careers of I. A. Richards and F. R. Leavis; Leavis, with unusual generosity, said years later that Forbes, who was "himself a vital force of intelligence, had... the impulse and the power to stir intelligence into active life in others." Known everywhere as "Manny", he figured in innumerable anecdotes and quotations. It is said that once, when he was carrying a huge pile of books, he responded to a woman who offered to help, "Pray do not disturb me, I have the stability of a pregnant kangaroo." Queenie Roth, the future Mrs Leavis, had seen him, when she was a student at Girton, as a different sort of creature, "a mooncalf or an archangel" (as reported in Gwendolen Freeman's Girton memories, *Alma Mater*).

Forbes' other much talked-about venture was his home in Queen's Road, Finella, a Victorian house completely transformed by the architect Raymond McGrath. The once grey brick exterior was painted rose-pink and the woodwork lemon-yellow. Inside there was much imaginative use of glass, jade ornaments, a fountain; Forbes himself, in characteristic style, described some of the features for *Country Life* in March 1930: "Gold mirrors on either side assist the axial gold lunette in westward extension of the glassy corridor, as the transparent entrance door aerially projects it eastward." He showed thousands of visitors round in person. After his early death in 1936 shortage of funds and then the risk of bomb-damage led to some alterations, most obviously a reduction in the amount of glass, but Finella (owned by Caius College and not open to the public) remains relatively intact.

Clare's own most visible art holdings are at Memorial Court (by Sir Giles Gilbert Scott, 1923-34). John Julius Norwich thinks the buildings here "perfectly agreeable in a nice, safe, Georgian way." Henry Moore's "Falling Warrior" (1956-7) reflects the memorial theme. His "Standing Figure" is on the lawn at the front and there is also a Barbara Hepworth: "Two Forms–Divided Circle".

Queens' College

At Queens' the Cam is spanned by the structure often called the Mathematical Bridge because, supposedly, Isaac Newton designed it and it was built without the aid of nails. This is an attractive story, but misleading—the first version of the bridge was put up twenty years after Newton's death and, if nails were not actually used, iron pins were. The present version (1905) is held together with orthodox nuts and bolts. The buildings on the east bank are mainly medieval, Renaissance and Victorian. On the west bank the Fisher Building, curving along Silver Street, was completed in 1936 and the large white Cripps Court in 1980; Cripps expanded in 1989 into Lyon Court with its Fitzpatrick Hall, a theatre with retractable seating which can be adapted for drama, concerts, badminton or social events. At least initially, criticism of these new structures abutting the Backs was much fiercer than Pevsner's verdict on the Fisher Building as too like "a friendly block of flats", "timidly imitative" in style. For Norman Scarfe, in the *Shell Guide to Cambridgeshire* (1983), the newcomer Cripps "bares its backside, bicycle stores, etc., under the very windows of the Fisher rooms"; another cause for complaint, apparently, is that "the students' rooms look comfortable to the point of luxury."

The college queens developed their plural apostrophe in the nineteenth century in honour of the royal patrons Margaret of Anjou, wife of Henry VI (founder of the neighbouring King's) and, in 1475, Edward IV's wife Elizabeth Wydvil or Woodville. The original founder, in 1447, a year before Margaret became involved, was Andrew Dokett, rector of St Botolph's Church. He was the first President or head (called Master in most colleges, while the President is his deputy), and under his aegis Old Court was built, probably by Reginald Ely, who was also master-mason at King's, in 1448-9. It retains much of its original appearance, helped by the fact that here, as at Magdalene, the red brick has been left uncovered. The most visible alteration is the sundial of 1733 (replacing or restoring a seventeenth-century original): "no small ornament to the Court to enliven it", says William Coles in his manuscript account of the college a few years later.

Old Court leads to Cloister Court, originally built between about 1460 and 1495 but dominated by the late-sixteenth century long gallery of the President's Lodge, a timber-framed, two-storey building above the north range of the cloister. The central oriel is supported by wooden pillars. The court, one of the quietest and most secluded in Cambridge, looks like some corner of a great Tudor country house.

An earlier, probably less impressive, lodge existed when Desiderius Erasmus lived in the college between 1511 and 1514. His letters, especially those to an Italian friend in London, Andrea Ammonio, suggest that he was both too busy and too uncomfortable to spend much time pacing the windy cloister. His rooms are said to have been in the turret overlooking Silver Street, now in Pump Court. According to Andrew Paschal, a fellow of Queens' in 1680, the turret commanded "the best prospect about the college, viz. upon the river, into the corn-fields, and country adjoining. So that it might very well consist with the civility of the House to that great man" to let him live there. Erasmus records neither his college hosts' "civility" nor his rapture at the "prospect". His one brief reference to his accommodation is part of a more general lament about the town in November 1513:

I have been living like a snail now for several months, Ammonio; confined and cooped up at home, I brood over my work. There is hardly anyone here, since most people have left for fear of the plague; even when everyone is here, besides, it is a lonely place to me. Expenses are impossibly high, and there is no money to be made.

Cambridge might have been more bearable if the drink had been better. Soon after Erasmus arrived in August 1511, by way of a long, hungry journey in heavy rain, he told Ammonio that "the beer in this place suits me not at all and the wines won't quite do either." Given the poor quality of drinking water at the time, and the fact that he was convalescing from a bout of sweating sickness, this mattered significantly. Erasmus therefore asked his friend to send a small cask of dry Greek wine from London. This came safely and was much appreciated. Having spent some days enjoying even the smell of the wine in the empty cask, he sent it back for a re-fill. This time, however, it returned half full; Ammonio had, said Erasmus, made the mistake of "consigning it unsealed to the hands of men to whom nothing is sealed." Two more casks arrived, one broached, the other not, to add variety to the scholar's remaining time in the town. Drinking local beer when the wine ran out had made him ill—"a dangerous grapple with the stone", he told Archbishop William Warham, perhaps in the hope of being sent some good prelatical wine.

It is possible, however, to exaggerate how miserable Cambridge made Erasmus. His Latin letters to Ammonio and others are exercises in wit as well as personal feeling, and on one occasion he even admits that "this place really suits me fairly well." Certainly he managed to work, giving public Greek lessons, publishing volumes including *De ratione studii* (*On the Method of Study*), and making good progress with his edition of the Greek New Testament, one of his most important contributions to the new learning of the time and, unintentionally, to the Reformation. England was dear to Erasmus above all for the fellow humanist scholars who were his friends, met on his first visit to the country in 1499-1500: Thomas More, John Colet, Thomas Linacre. But they were mainly in London rather than Cambridge, and this contributed to the town's imperfections. Yet he was able to do battle on their behalf against the university's "Thomists and Scotists", the proponents of the old Scholastic theology. This, Colet flattered him, was an unequal fight, "for what lustre do you gain, when you have repulsed a swarm of flies, and stabbed them to death?"

Erasmus became part of the college pantheon. In the Grove, on the west bank of the river, "Erasmus' Walk" was planted in 1685, rather too late for him to walk there. Queens' owns what is supposed to be his chair and at one time also displayed his "huge corkscrew"; "I am afraid," observed Isaac Milner, President in 1788-1820 and a noted Evangelical, "that there was nothing in his principles to keep him from making very assiduous use of it." There is an Erasmus Room. And Sir Basil Spence's Erasmus Building (generally more admired than Cripps Court) was erected in Friars' Court in 1959-60.

But it was to the Middle Ages rather than the Renaissance that the Victorian architects and decorators of Queens' turned for inspiration. The original chapel in Old Court (now a library) was restored by George Frederick Bodley in the 1840s and 1850s. *The Ecclesiologist*, published by the neo-Gothic-promoting Cambridge Camden Society, was especially pleased to see surfaces of "polished alabaster, enlaid with encaustic tiles, and marbles of various colours... while the foliage is most judiciously gilt." Judiciously or not, however, the college subsequently called on Bodley to build an entirely new, larger, and more thoroughly Gothicized chapel, completed in 1891. (A number of memorials and some of the glass were transferred from the old building.) The new chapel in Walnut Tree court—where, as the name suggests, the college once kept an orchard—gives the vigorous impression of a single inspiration: glass, altar-hangings, statues, painted gold-winged angels, stalls, all aspire to the medieval ideal as conceived by Bodley, Ruskin or Morris. Bodley had also worked, to more spectacular effect, on the refurbishment and alteration of the medieval college hall in Old Court. This is now Old Hall, used, since a new dining hall opened in Cripps Court in 1978, for college feasts, concerts, and other functions. Here, mainly in the 1860s and 1870s, with William Morris and others, he provided sumptuous decoration, perhaps most notably in the red and green ceiling with its 885 stars of gilded lead. The stars were, like the fireplace tiles contributed by Morris and company, additions rather than restorations. The tiles showing the months of the year personified in Book of Hours tradition were designed by Burne-Jones (January, February, and probably October), Madox Brown (March, May, November, December), Morris (April, June), and Rossetti (July, August, September).

Darwin College

The university's first college for postgraduate students was set up in 1965 by Caius, St John's and Trinity. Three existing buildings, Newnham Grange, the Hermitage and the Old Granary, were skilfully adapted and extended to form the core of the college. The Hermitage was built in the early 1850s and enlarged in the 1870s, but its name derives from the chapel kept somewhere in the vicinity by the pre-Reformation hermits who maintained, and collected tolls from people crossing, the small bridges later replaced by the Silver Street bridge. Newnham Grange was the home of Charles Darwin's son the mathematician Sir George Darwin and various members of his family between 1885 and the death of his son Sir Charles Galton Darwin, Master of Christ's, in 1962. The atmosphere of much of the college remains that of a friendly small country house and gardens, a place that has expanded and adapted gradually and naturally rather than being purpose-built. Space for any grander scheme is limited by Newnham Road, Silver Street, the Silver Street mill-pond, the Cam and its backwaters. But the riverside location allows for contemplative areas including wooded walks on the two "islands" already colonized—with the aid of wooden bridges—by the Darwins.

Newnham Grange, built in 1793 but not given this well-known name until the Darwins arrived and altered it, has always been a useful observation post. Gwen Raverat, daughter of George and Maud Darwin, who was born in the house in 1885, recalls in her popular *Period Piece* (1952) that "nearly all the life of Cambridge flowed backwards and forwards over the [Silver Street] bridge, and before our house":

> ...*the rush and rattle of the butchers' traps and their furious little ponies... and the yellow milk-carts, like Roman chariots, with their big brass-bound churns of milk and their little dippers hooked on at the side; and the hairy-footed shire-horses, who drew the great corn-wagons in from the country.*

When Raverat was eighteen she saw something on Silver Street bridge that was well calculated to disconcert a respectable Edwardian young lady. One evening she was puzzled and horrified to see "a small gang of rather disreputable undergraduates" in "smashed-in caps and tattered gowns" running towards her across the bridge,

> carrying, flat out, the body of a woman who seemed to be dead. Drowned in the river? That was my first thought... Murdered? Or captured for some nameless purpose? Something horrible and vague and improper? It did not occur to me that she might be drunk. Men got drunk; women didn't.

The frightened, guilty-looking men rushed on into the riverside pub, the Anchor, somewhere she could not follow them, for a "public-house was a mysterious sinister haunt, full of Bad Women." Raverat, known for her wood-engravings long before she wrote *Period Piece*, accompanies her tale with a whimsical illustration; this, and especially the frightened youth at the back, ferrying the girl's hat, catches the same naïve but amused tone as the writing. She writes and illustrates throughout the book almost as if she were the child and young woman of fifty-odd years before, but retaining nearly always some trace of amusement at that distant self and the very different society in which she grew up.

She looks back at that upper middle-class and academic society, its proprieties, costumes, old-fashioned notions, games, eccentricities, hypochondria, and in particular at her very individual family, sometimes with frustration but generally with fondness. There is a danger, she says, that her account of her father and his four brothers may make them sound "too good, too nice, too single-hearted to be true". But then, in a way, "that was what was wrong with them. I always used to feel that they needed protecting and cherishing, for they never seemed to me to have quite grown up." (To some extent they were living in the shadow of their father, Charles Darwin.) They had "a sort of innocent lack of imagination, which was exceptional. They were quite unable to understand the minds of the poor, the wicked, or the religious."

On reaching Newnham Grange after seeing the girl-bearing undergraduates, she contemplated telling her father but feared that, if something "improper" was going on, it would embarrass both of them too much. All the same, she burst into the study, where her parents were sitting in their usual imperturbable manner. George Darwin, with his feet on the fender, was working at his "long neat rows of little figures and symbols". Maud Darwin sat nearby, surrounded by papers of one sort or another. (Again, an illustration sums up the situation.) Their daughter felt like a bomb, charged with horror and emotion, about to go off. But Maud spoke first: "Gwenny dear, just add up the milkman's book, will you, please? I can't make it come right."

CHAPTER TWO

Cambridge Beginnings

This chapter is concerned with a series of beginnings: the Norman castle, Cambridge archaeology, the first colleges, the new humanist college of St John's in the sixteenth century, new colleges and architecture in the twentieth.

The Castle Mound

All that remains of Cambridge Castle is its motte, which provides excellent views of the city and its surroundings, and traces of two of the earthen bulwarks with which the defences were shored up during the Civil War. Construction of the original castle was ordered by William the Conqueror in 1068. It was one of many Norman castles designed to police Anglo-Saxon townspeople, the headquarters of Sheriff Picot, a man with a reputation worse, if anything, than that of the legendary Sheriff of Nottingham: according to the *Liber Eliensis* he was "a hungry

lion, a ravening wolf, a filthy hog". But it was another two centuries before the castle itself looked particularly intimidating. Under Edward I it acquired, between 1283 and 1299, several towers, a gatehouse and a drawbridge connecting the gatehouse with a barbican across the moat (where Castle Street is now). But this formidable fortress saw no serious military activity. By the late sixteenth century it was much decayed. Most of the land was used as pasture, although a prison survived and justice was administered from the Elizabethan Shire Hall, eventually demolished in 1747.

When Oliver Cromwell, as a Cambridge MP, secured the town for the Parliamentarian cause in 1642, the decay was arrested for a time. Bulwarks were made and soldiers of the Eastern Association marshalled, but the fighting happened elsewhere and as early as 1646 the new defences were removed. Stone, as before the Civil War, was diverted to local use. In 1788 *Cantabrigia Depicta* reported that "there are now but few remains, except the Gateway, which serves for the County Gaol." This too was demolished in 1842 to make way for a new Shire Hall, predecessor of the 1930s building still standing. In these halls, in the area once dominated by prison and gallows and ravening Picot, Henry Morris conducted his more positive activities as Chief Education Officer for Cambridgeshire from 1922 to 1954. He pioneered the idea and practice of the Village College—the school as well-equipped centre of a community rather than place for educating children only.

Further down the hill, tradition has it, the less community-minded Dick Turpin was wont to lurk. The great eighteenth-century highwayman is supposed to have hidden from the law at the Three Tuns, a long-demolished inn on the town side of the County Arms. Across the road the Castle Inn, with the steep slope of the mound beyond it, displays the missing castle on its sign.

The Museum of Archaeology and Anthropology
The Cambridge Antiquarian Society was formed in 1840 and donated its growing collection (pots, flints, Bronze Age swords, tiles) to the university in 1883. A purpose-built museum to house both archaeological and anthropological materials was built in 1910-20. Although Archaeology, on the ground floor, displays interesting

artefacts from Africa, the Americas, India, the Mesolithic site at Star Carr near Scarborough and many other places, it also has a strong local showing. There are bronze swords and shorter, thinner "rapiers" from Cambridgeshire sites. From a barrow at Lord's Bridge, Barton, near Cambridge, comes an iron fire-dog with bull's head terminals. It was found, more disturbingly, with an iron chain for binding slaves together; presumably the owner of the fire-dog wanted to be served in the hereafter. From another burial, this time of a Roman child at Arrington, are figurines of a mother-goddess and a ram.

There is an upsurge of local survivals from Anglo-Saxon times: a wealth of cruciform and other brooches, beads, the bronze mounts for a drinking-horn, daggers, a ploughshare, from places including Barrington, St John's College cricket field, and Linton Heath. Then, the brighter colours and fuller shapes a little incongruous after all the fragments, comes a later medieval section with decorated pitchers and jugs, alabaster figures mostly from the village of Milton, a fifteenth-century wooden saint or bishop with large mitre, a processional cross in copper and rather gaudy gilt, and the head of a hilarious or irritating jester, in clunch (fire-clay), from mid-fourteenth-century Wilburton. Less exotic later items include some stout eighteenth-century wine bottles, and the growth of the town is well illustrated with maps of different periods.

Anthropology, upstairs, has more immediate impact. A Haida Indian totem pole from British Columbia reaches the roof. Other eye-catching exhibits include the spiralled wooden sternpost of a Maori war canoe, Balinese gold lacquered masks, and an Inuit bleached walrus-skin parka, decorated with beaks and feathers. But since 1990 the collection has been organized so as to demonstrate just how little anthropology is concerned with the merely eye-catching. Objects are placed clearly in their cultural context—trade, shamanism, hunting, for example—and there are displays on larger themes like religion, ritual and kinship in the Mediterranean.

The way collections are constructed is studied in a section on such groupings as "Baron von Hügel's Fijian Cabinet": Anatole von Hügel, the first curator from 1884 until 1922, had lived in Fiji in 1875-7. Mixing with Fijians and learning their language, he was struck by the European settlers' strange lack of interest in the people as opposed to the flora and fauna; they collected "a few scattered native weapons or implements," he noted in his journal, "but they were kept as 'curios', often for the sake of some sensational history which the owner could attach to them. Every dish was a cannibal dish, every club had been the instrument of some atrocious murder, and every stain on either was caused by blood." The Fijians "might have been so many cabbages for anything their white fellow creatures cared to know of them, their customs or their history." Armed with this sort of awareness, abundant personal funds and the gift of persuasion, the Baron firmly established the museum enterprise. His most important colleague was Alfred Haddon, originally a marine biologist, whose expedition to the Torres Straits in 1898—one of the first serious anthropological expeditions—looked in detail at the role of artefacts in structures of belief and social life. (Von Hügel, comparatively enlightened though he was, tended to arrange his collection as much with an eye to pleasing symmetry as to function.)

Peterhouse: the First College

The first of the colleges was founded in 1280 by Hugh de Balsham, Bishop of Ely, on part of the site later occupied by St John's. The statutes were modelled on those of Merton College, Oxford. In 1284 the bishop moved his few collegians to the present site, where they took over two tenements. The more substantial hall was completed a few years later; apart from providing a space for eating and debating, the hall was important, as in most medieval institutions, as the main place where a fire was kept burning. Its medieval features, submerged in the eighteenth century, were restored and added to by George Gilbert Scott in the 1870s: panelling and timber roofing, William Morris tiles in the fireplace, colourful glass in the new oriel by Morris, Philip Webb and Ford Madox Brown.

Like other early colleges, Peterhouse had no chapel of its own, worshipping next door at its conveniently placed parish church, originally called St Peter's-without-Trumpington-Gate and now known as Little St Mary's. A gallery was built to join college and church. But in the 1620s the Master, Matthew Wren (Sir Christopher's uncle) decided to erect a separate and more modern chapel. The original tenements were finally demolished as part of the restructuring. From

Trumpington Street this unusually prominently placed building contributes to a generally rather stony and forbidding impression. Yet, as Basil Willey suggested in a lecture of 1949, Peterhouse's baroque religious poet Richard Crashaw (1613-49) would still "recognise, in gazing at the west front with its negative volutes, its surviving cherub-faces, its floral decoration and arabesque lozenges and its air of fantastic grace, an expressive architectural emblem of his own mode of religious sensibility."

Inside Wren's chapel decoration and worship were more obviously flamboyant. The college was unequivocally Laudian Anglican in sympathy; Crashaw, who was a fellow between 1635 and 1644, and John Cosin, Wren's successor as Master, were among those deprived of their posts by the Parliamentarian authorities. By then the poet, lamenting the loss of his "beloved patrimony in [the college of] St Peter", that "little contentful kingdom", had fled to Holland. That soon afterwards he converted to Roman Catholicism can have come as no surprise to such fierce Puritans as William Prynne, who in *Canterbury's Doom* (1646)—a work exulting in the execution of Archbishop Laud—recorded, with pious if gleeful incredulity, that

> *in Peterhouse Chapel there was a glorious new altar set up, and mounted on steps, to which the Master, Fellows, Scholars bowed, and were enjoined to bow by Dr Cosens the Master, who set it up; that there were basins, candlesticks, tapers standing on it, and a great crucifix hanging over it... that there was likewise a carved cross at the end of every seat, and on the altar a pot, which they usually called the incense pot.*

William Dowsing, a Puritan with a more practical streak than Prynne, had already visited this den of iniquity in December 1643. It was his job to cleanse the churches and chapels of East Anglia of their popish accretions. Here, he notes in his diary, he and his colleagues "pulled down two mighty great angels with wings, and divers other angels, and the four Evangelists, and Peter, with his keys, over the chapel door—and about a hundred cherubims and angels, and divers superstitious letters in gold."

Gray and Amis at Peterhouse

Nearly a century later, in 1742, Thomas Gray moved into rooms in the newly finished Burrough's Building (named after its architect, the Master of Caius; later came Gisborne Court (1825), Fen Court (1939) and, in the gardens, the eight-storey but discreet William Stone Building (1963-4) by Sir Leslie Martin.) This was the beginning of Gray's second period at Peterhouse. He had left the college without a degree in 1738, but now returned, successfully became a Bachelor of Civil Law (1744), and stayed on, working on classical translation and composition and also, increasingly, on his English poems. Here in the mid-1740s he began his "Elegy Written in a Country Churchyard" (1751). Mid-eighteenth-century Cambridge was not, however, known for its intellectual or artistic interests, and it was no doubt with some real feeling, mixed with conventional irony about his Alma Mater and imitation of Alexander Pope's manner in *The Dunciad*, that Gray addressed his "Hymn to Ignorance" to

> *...ye ever-gloomy bowers,*
> *Ye Gothic fanes and antiquated towers,*
> *Where reedy Camus' slow-winding flood*
> *perpetual draws his humid train of mud.*

In 1756 Gray had some concrete confirmation that Ignorance ruled the town. He suffered from a phobia about fires, probably exacerbated when his old home in London burned down in 1748. Acting sensibly by modern standards, risibly by eighteenth-century ones, in 1756 he had a strong iron bar fitted outside his window so that he could escape, if necessary, by rope ladder. Either because the bar was attached so well, or in remembrance of the poet, it has remained there ever since, clearly visible from the street. It was, as Gray's biographer Maynard Mack says, "an unadvisedly public pronouncement of [his] private phobia to the undergraduate population of the University". Mack gathers the various versions, some of them apocryphal, of what happened next. In one account a group of students including Viscount Percival, from Magdalene, was passing Peterhouse early one morning on the way to hunt. They decided to have "a little sport" first. One of them shouted "fire!" up the stair leading to the sleeping poet's door.

According to a story now widely discredited, but which no-one can resist repeating, the naked Gray opened his window and rapidly descended his ladder into a waiting tub of water and the wild laughter of the pranksters. A more sober and believable version is that he thrust his head out of the window in terror, realized what was going on, but still excited the ridicule of those below.

Whatever exactly happened, Gray took offence. It also seems likely that the prank brought to a head other perceived slights. The alleged presence of the viscount may suggest a class element—Gray was a scrivener's son, even if he had been to Eton. He was not satisfied when the Master dismissed the affair as a typical undergraduate caper and took no action against those involved. Probably within days, he had transferred himself permanently across the road to Pembroke College.

A later and very different figure who left Peterhouse unexpectedly early was Kingsley Amis. He found the college itself, where he was a fellow in 1961-3, "an oasis in Cambridge of good nature and common sense", and found supervisions enjoyable if draining. But the whole town seemed "cold and lonely, a setting more appropriate to an unhappy love affair than to the bustling exchange of ideas that is supposed to go on." From his colleagues he usually got not "original and well-grounded talk about English literature" but "talk about intra-faculty discord and personal quarrels, syllabus changes... the attendance at old Joe Soap's lectures, etc." Amis thought "Cambridge meant too much to Cambridge." He also felt that there was too wide a social gap between dons and undergraduates. From this "a clever person would, I think, have foreseen the student troubles of the later Sixties," he concludes in his *Memoirs* (1991). Amis was, besides, earning more from his books than his job. He left to write full-time. F. R. Leavis had muttered about Peterhouse appointing "a pornographer". Few people, according to Amis, deigned to discuss his work; "A writer in *Delta* did complain that he had not found a novel of mine so much as funny, but Cambridge is the least damaging place in England in which not to be found funny."

Corpus Christi College

Corpus Christi, unlike the other colleges of the university, was founded by townspeople. In 1352 the newly merged guilds of Corpus Christi and St Mary, based in the parish of St Bene't's, planned and provided funds for the institution whose statutes were drawn up in 1356. At first it was a fairly modest enterprise: the small, enclosed Old Court (to the left of New Court, where the main entrance now is) provided ample space for the Master and two fellows. While pursuing their studies in canon law and theology, they repaid the guild by ministering to it as chaplains and through their prayers. St Bene't's Church served as their chapel until about 1500—the college itself was often known as Benet College.

Yet the town association counted for little when, in 1381, a group of disgruntled townspeople turned their attention to the college during a more general attack on the privileges and monopolies of the university. Thomas Fuller, in his *History of the University of Cambridge* (1655) is alliteratively eager to condemn this "rabble rout" which "rolled to Benet College" where, one Saturday night in June, they broke open the gates, "violently fell on the master and fellows," and "took all their charters, evidences, privileges, and plate, to the value of four score pounds."

The triumph of the rioters was predictably short-lived. College and guilds continued to display their wealth and power in the annual Corpus Christi procession (maintained by the college long after the guild had ceased to exist). Fuller explains that the "grand solemnity was held... according to this equipage": first came the alderman of the guild as master of ceremonies, "then the elders thereof... carrying silver shields enamelled in their hands, bestowed on the brotherhood" by its patron the Duke of Lancaster, "then the master of this college, in a silk cope under a canopy, carrying the host in the pyx, or rich box of silver gilt, having two for the purpose" (one, allegedly, made from a griffin's egg). Next came the Vice-Chancellor and other "University-men" and finally the "Mayor of the town and the burgesses thereof". From St Bene't's

> they advanced to the great [Magdalene] bridge, through all parts of the town, and so returned with a good appetite to the place where they began. Then in Corpus Christi College was a dinner provided them, where good stomachs meeting with good cheer and welcome, no wonder if mirth followed of course. Then out comes the cup of John of Goldcorne (once alderman of the guild) made of an horn with the cover and appurtenances of silver and gilt, which he gave the company, and all must drink therein.

The horn, probably from the now largely extinct European aurochs or wild ox, remains a prize possession of the college. Fuller, who as curate of St Bene't's Church in 1630-3 no doubt partook of the horn, is happy with this convivial quaffing, but has some reservations about the Catholic pomp of the procession. Once, he avers, the canopy under which the host or consecrated bread was carried "fell on fire, leaving men to guess, as they stood affected, whether it was done casually, by the carelessness of the torch-bearers, or maliciously, by some covertly casting fire thereon out of some window, or miraculously, to show that God would shortly consume such superstition." As indeed He did, through Henry VIII, when the procession "was finally abrogated" in 1535. (Nevertheless town and gown had the temerity to process together for the six hundred and fiftieth anniversary of the college in 2002.)

Christopher Marlowe and Matthew Parker

The college's best-known graduate, Christopher Marlowe (1564-93), would no doubt have enjoyed the idea of "covertly casting fire" onto the papist canopy; his Faustus and Mephostophilis fling fireworks about the papal court itself, having stolen the Pope's food and drink, and hit him "a box of the ear". Presumably, however, Marlowe personally cast no fire or fireworks during his time at the Catholic seminary in Reims, which apparently he infiltrated on behalf of the government. The university, having listened to "those that are ignorant of the affairs he went about", attempted to deny him his MA in 1587 but the Privy Council intervened on his behalf, explaining that his stay at Reims had been temporary and that "in all his actions he had behaved himself orderly and discreetly whereby he had done Her Majesty good service, and deserved to be rewarded for his faithful dealing."

The statement by the Privy Council is the only solid evidence that Marlowe worked as a spy. Next to nothing is known about his time at Corpus, which he entered in 1580 at the age of sixteen on a scholarship restricted to boys of King's School, Canterbury, who showed prowess in singing. He probably wrote some of his poems and the early *Tragedy of Dido* here, and embarked on the more ambitious *Tamburlaine*. But while studying for his MA he would have been entitled to spend much of his time away from Cambridge—spying, perhaps, or more likely frequenting the London playhouses or the fringes of the court. While he was at Corpus, however, he seems, to judge from the plays, to have read widely and studied hard, wanting perhaps, with Faustus, to "make our schools ring with *sic probo*". On the other hand, his family's record of violence and civil disorder in Canterbury, the daring matter of his plays and poems, and the circumstances of his death all make it difficult to believe that he, any more than Faustus, really had much desire to "live and die in Aristotle's works." (Christopher Isherwood (1904-86) is a later Corpus student who—from a position of somewhat greater social and financial safety than Marlowe—is known to have taken an unambiguously dissident approach to his studies.

Refusing to take the "enormous tacit bribe" offered by Cambridge, according to his autobiographical novel *Lions and Shadows* (1938), he wrote limericks and other verses in answer to the questions in Part One of the History tripos and was persuaded to leave Corpus quietly.)

In 1953 a portrait of a man stated to be, like Marlowe, twenty-one in 1585, was discovered amid rubble that was being removed from the Master's Lodge in New Court. It bears the enigmatic inscription "Quod me nutrit me destruit", "what nourishes me destroys me." Identification with Marlowe has proved irresistible for most people, although the clothing seems too expensively fashionable for a poor scholar. The notion that the finery is a reward for espionage is improbable: spies are not supposed to flaunt their status, and a young Elizabethan shoemaker's son could not have transgressed the sumptuary code quite so flagrantly. Just conceivably, the work was painted after Marlowe's death in 1593, the clothes emblematizing the glory—or at least the theatrical connections—of the departed. The portrait, its expression giving little away (defiantly, perhaps), hangs in the college hall. There is also a plaque in Old Court honouring both Marlowe and John Fletcher (1579-1625), an undergraduate here in the 1590s. Fletcher lived long enough, unlike Marlowe, to enjoy the fruits of a London career. He succeeded Shakespeare as staple dramatist of the King's company and wrote or co-wrote many theatrically viable tragedies, comedies and, more distinctively, tragi-comedies which seek the unMarlovian *frisson* of "the danger, not the death".

The college which Marlowe and Fletcher attended owed much to Matthew Parker, a fellow from 1527, Master in 1544-53, and still keenly interested in Corpus and Cambridge affairs while serving as the first Elizabethan Archbishop of Canterbury in 1559-75. He reorganized records and administration, recovered income and land lost to the college under his Marian successor as Master, and endowed fellowships and scholarships (including Marlowe's). To particular long-term benefit, Parker also gave or bequeathed many books and manuscripts, often volumes dispersed at Henry VIII's dissolution of the monasteries. He was, as his early eighteenth-century biographer John Strype puts it, "a mighty collector of books, to preserve, as much as could be, the ancient monuments of the learned men of our nation from perishing":

> *And the world is for ever beholden to him for two things; viz., for retriev-*
> *ing ancient authors, Saxon and British, as well as Norman, and for*
> *restoring and enlightening a great deal of the ancient history of this noble*
> *island... Indeed he was the chief retriever of that our ancient native*
> *language, the Saxon I mean, and encouraged heartily the study of it.*

Much though Strype likes the word "ancient", Parker's interest was not purely antiquarian. He and his Latin secretary John Josselin trawled early English texts for anti-papal material to be used in doctrinal and nationalistic polemic: defiance of or independence from Rome, married priests, Protestant-sounding attitudes to the eucharist. But in the process Parker and his associates also laid the foundations of modern study of Anglo-Saxon literature and culture. Thanks to Parker, some of the most important manuscripts are preserved in the Parker Library at Corpus, including the "Parker" text of the *Anglo-Saxon Chronicle*. The later medieval texts in the collection include the brightly illuminated Bury Bible of 1121-48 and Chaucer's *Troilus and Criseyde* with frontispiece in which the author, mounted in a wooden pulpit, reads to a noble and sumptuously coloured audience.

The Parker Library (above the Butler Library, for more general college use) is in New Court, William Wilkins' substantial neo-Gothic addition of 1823-7: "a compact and simplified version", notes his biographer R. W. Liscombe, "of the traditional quadrangle, geared to a small [£60,000] budget". (Such compactness leaves little room for accommodation; fortunately, Corpus already owned the land off Grange Road on which Leckhampton, housing graduate students, opened in 1963. The site has space for extensive grounds and a seated figure by Henry Moore.) The chapel, opposite the college entrance, replaced one from the sixteenth century. Wilkins considered the new buildings as his "most complete and satisfactory" to date and was buried in the chapel in 1839.

St John's College

"It is a well-known fact that it is possible to walk all the way from Oxford to Cambridge entirely in the wine-cellars of St John's College, Oxford and St John's College, Cambridge. This has always served to unify the two universities and, indeed, the masters of the two colleges meet annually in the little room where the cellars meet underneath Stansted airport, for a glass of Madeira." So claims David Mitchell's "Up the Cam" column of *Varsity* for 3 November 1995. There is a more plausible, if no less unfounded, tradition that the two colleges between them own land that stretches from one to the other. The stories illustrate the considerable wealth of the institutions in question. In the case of St John's, Cambridge, this originated in the foundation of the college under the will of Lady Margaret Beaufort, the rich and influential mother of King Henry VII.

At the beginning, though, money was a problem. With the help of her confessor Bishop John Fisher, and probably under his inspiration, Lady Margaret had already re-founded Christ's College in 1505. She was keenly interested in the plan to convert the old hospital of St John into a sizeable new college. But her death in 1509 left Fisher with a two-year struggle to secure the funds from rival claimants, clear various legal obstacles, and remove the few remaining nuns from the hospital. Having done that, he set to work in earnest. Parts of the hospital were adapted, and its chapel taken over largely unchanged, but there was sufficient repair and new work for the builders to take delivery of 800,000 bricks from Greenwich. The college opened in 1516, four years before the completion of First Court, to be followed by a second in the late 1590s and a third in the seventeenth century. The 1620s Old Library, on the north side of Third Court, holds an important collection of medieval and later manuscripts, including a text of Sir Philip Sidney's "Old" *Arcadia*; among the printed volumes is an illuminated 1474 edition of Ovid which once belonged to Lorenzo de' Medici. (Edward Cullinan Architects provided an attractive new library, discreetly using the shell of the 1880s Penrose Building and adding a new extension, in 1993.)

In later centuries the college continued its inexorable expansion across the river. The attractive red brick and human dimensions of the early courts contrast with the vast neo-Gothic stone fantasy of the "Bridge of Sighs" and New Court, built by Thomas Rickman and Henry Hutchinson in 1831. The centrepiece of New Court— prominent in views of the Backs—is the octagonal "wedding cake", for Hugh Casson "an elaborate lantern guarded by sentinel pinnacles, rising out of the river mists, half-nursery fortress, half-Walter Scott abbey, throwing all caution to the winds." Next to this court, and crossing Bin Brook, is the Cripps Building (1964-7, by Powell and Moya), faced in Portland stone and divided into several small courts. And finally, as you seem to be wandering in the outlying areas less of an educational institution than of some city-state, beyond the Cripps Building you may come upon the early thirteenth-century house, known, apparently for no good reason, as the School of Pythagoras, which St John's bought only in 1959 from its original owners, Merton College, Oxford. It has now been adapted for plays and other events.

Fisher, who launched this mighty enterprise, did more to change Cambridge University as a whole than most individuals. Especially in his roles as the first Lady Margaret Professor of Divinity from 1502 (this was another of the educational benefactions in which he encouraged Margaret) and as Chancellor of the university from 1504 until his death in 1535, he initiated major changes in the medieval curriculum. The often arid study of biblical commentaries was replaced by concentration on the Bible itself in its original Greek and, sometimes, Hebrew. Knowledge of classical texts and mathematics also assumed a new importance. By 1520 Fisher had done much to impose the pattern of study recommended by the Dutch reformer Erasmus. Probably the best means Fisher found to persuade his university of the virtues of this New Learning was to invite Erasmus himself to Cambridge as one of his successors as Lady Margaret Professor.

St John's was established as a centre of the New Learning. The Yorkshireman Fisher was responsible for another important element of the college. He decided that since the north of England was "more barren of learning and so ruder in manners than the south", he must get as many northerners as possible into St John's and remedy the situation. He succeeded so well that a statute of 1545 restricted northerners to not more than half of the fellowships. (The measure was aimed partly to decrease the influence of traditional Catholics, still strong at this time in Yorkshire and Lancashire.) The presence of the large regional contingent in the college led, in the seventeenth century particularly, to some brawls with the neighbouring, mainly southern Trinity men. The northern connection continued into modern times.

St John's loyally offered its co-founder moral and financial support when he fell from grace for refusing to take Henry VIII's Oath of Supremacy in 1535. Even more daringly, the college publicly mourned Fisher following his execution. Soon, however, with the king's right-hand man Thomas Cromwell installed as the new Chancellor of the university, Fisher's emblem or rebus—a fish with an ear of corn for "Fish-er"—was being erased from the college chapel. (The arches of his chantry-chapel are, however, one of the rare survivals in the Victorian ante-chapel, together with the tomb of Lady Margaret's Comptroller, Hugh Ashton.) His library, intended for St John's, was confiscated by the Crown. And once Fisher had been recognized as a Catholic martyr (even if he was not actually canonized until 1935) it was inevitable that the college would privilege Lady Margaret over him in subsequent founder's-day celebrations.

Fisher himself, besides, had made potent the myth of the foundress. Her heraldry has dominated the front gate of St John's since the beginning: a huge Tudor rose and Beaufort portcullis, smaller roses, vines, forget-me-nots for her motto *Souvent me souvient*, daisies—marguerites for her name—and curving fantastic "yales" (beasts combining elements of antelope, deer, and goat but who, unlike such everyday creatures, can swivel their horns in different directions), gold-spotted, gold-maned, gold-horned. Above this display is a statue of St John the Evangelist, probably a 1660s replacement for an original removed or vandalized in the 1640s. A small, fine eagle in gold—his symbolic creature—is tucked in next to him, and many another sculpted eagle will be found in the college grounds. But the saint himself, portrayed on the gate as the usual angelically blue-robed and golden-haired young man, tends to take second place to Margaret's emphatic emblems and pictures. We meet her portrait and half-length figure in the ante-chapel. At the entrance to the chapel her 1860s statue treads down Ignorance, opposite a now safely mentionable Fisher, who tramples Vice. There is another statue, of 1671, by Edward Burman in First Court. Often, here as elsewhere, her hands are clasped in prayer; Fisher's funeral sermon for her emphasizes her devoutness, fasting, and "sober temperance". She was also, however, a highly experienced political survivor of the dangerous times when her son was an exile and a rebel rather than a monarch, and a skilled administrator.

Another woman, Mary Cavendish, Countess of Shrewsbury, achieves the honour of a statue in the second court, whose building she helped to finance. The statue is again the work of Edward Burman: a Restoration lady, slightly windswept in the fashion of the time. But this is a rare exception. Even the college rowers took the name Lady Margaret Boat Club in 1825.

The financial and educational investment of Margaret and Fisher, undertaken partly as an act of Roman Catholic religious devotion, benefited a new Protestant-leaning generation. Sir John Cheke (1514-57), Greek scholar and mathematician, was a fellow of St John's between 1530 and 1548, and tutor to the young Protestant King Edward VI. His pupils included William Cecil, Lord Burghley (1520-98), Elizabeth I's chief minister, and Roger Ascham (1515-68), who taught at St John's and was university Public Orator before becoming tutor to the then Princess Elizabeth at the end of the 1540s. Ascham, David Starkey concludes in his *Elizabeth* (2000), made her household, "with its central mission to educate its young mistress and its close connections with St John's, Cambridge... genuinely a university extension college." His experiences at St John's and with Elizabeth are the basis of *The Schoolmaster*, a readable study of how best to lead "young wits into a right and plain way of learning", written in the mid-1560s and published in 1570. Scholars also need their relaxation, if preferably, Ascham's contemporaries tended to believe, with some educational element to it. His *Toxophilus* (1545), written at St John's, argues ingeniously—with much learning and some wit—the overwhelming physical, mental, and moral advantages of the sport of archery.

Nashe and Wordsworth at St John's
Bliss was it in that dawn to be at St John's, as Wordsworth might have put it. The college was still trailing clouds of glory, apparently, when Thomas Nashe (1567-1601) was a student in the 1580s. In the preface to *Menaphon* (1589), a romance by his fellow Johnian Robert Greene, he looks back lovingly at

> that most famous and fortunate nurse of all learning, Saint John's in Cambridge, that at that time was an university within itself, shining so

> *far above all other houses, halls and hospitals whatsoever, that no college*
> *in the town was able to compare with the tithe of her students.*

"Grave men of credit" reported that some of the students were up working by candlelight at four in the morning.

No doubt Nashe is partial, but the college, like the university as a whole, was shining less brightly by the time William Wordsworth did arrive in 1787. In *The Prelude* he remembers, tempering dissatisfaction with a degree of humour, the "three gloomy courts" of "the Evangelist St John" ("gloomy" became "Gothic" in the more polite revised version published in 1850). In the first court, on Staircase F

> *Was my abiding-place, a nook obscure;*
> *Right underneath, the college kitchens made*
> *A humming sound, less tuneable than bees,*
> *But hardly less industrious.*

Issuing forth from his cramped quarters (later demolished), he enjoyed the usual undergraduate sauntering, rioting, and "unprofitable talk" and, with his companions,

> *Drifted about along the streets and walks,*
> *Read lazily in lazy books, went forth*
> *To gallop through the country in blind zeal*
> *Of senseless horsemanship, or on the breast*
> *Of Cam sailed boisterously, and let the stars*
> *Come out, perhaps without one quiet thought.*

Such a life gave only superficial satisfaction to one used to wandering the hills in solitary meditation. True, he was sometimes able to go off alone and find solace even in "the fields, the level fields,/With heaven's blue concave reared above my head." True, he is aware that "after-meditation" may have distorted his recollections—*The Prelude* is, besides, a poetic construction, not a record, of events—and feels that perhaps he was as much the problem as Cambridge, that he "was not for that hour,/Nor for that place." Nevertheless, Wordsworth and many others had good grounds for alienation. Contemporary witnesses confirm the poet's picture of most late eighteenth-century dons as exemplars of "blind Authority beating with his staff/The child that might have led him."

The ideal university, Wordsworth says, would, unlike Cambridge and St John's in the 1780s, be:

A habitation sober and demure
For ruminating creatures; a domain
For quiet things to wander in; a haunt
In which the heron might delight to feed
By the shy rivers, and the pelican
Upon the cypress spire in lonely thought
Might sit and sun himself.

This vision of serious freedom (not a literal call for a wildlife park, although St John's almost has room for one still) is difficult to realize, but there was some progress towards it later in the nineteenth century. The college saw its mighty new chapel, completed at great expense by George Gilbert Scott in 1869, nineteen years after Wordsworth's death, as one sign of the new earnestness of endeavour in the mid-Victorian university. Wordsworth himself finds a place among the painted worthies on the amber-gold vaulted ceiling; there is a bay for each century, moving out from Christ at the east end for the first century. Johnians dominate several bays, especially the sixteenth, with Lady Margaret, Fisher, Cheke, and Ascham, and the nineteenth, with Wordsworth, William Wilberforce, and James Wood, Dean of Ely and Master of the college, who earned his place partly by leaving, at his death in 1833, £20,000 which went towards the building of the chapel. West also merits a statue in the ante-chapel, moved from the old chapel, as does Wilberforce.

At its consecration in 1869 the chapel was anything but "a domain/For quiet things to wander in." Nine hundred members and former members of the college attended, many arriving from London by special train, a good number nostalgically filing, early in the morning, into the last service in the old chapel (which obligingly collapsed soon afterwards). A great procession of dignitaries delivered the Bishop of Ely and five other prelates to the new building, and the whole town, reported the woollen draper and diarist Josiah Chater, was "alive... with parsons... Bells ringing all day, and not much business doing." Inside the chapel the parsons were able to marvel at its fine Ancaster stone with, as the enthusiastic chronicler in the college magazine, *The Eagle*, explained, details picked out in Ketton stone, Peterhead red granite, Devonshire, Irish and Serpentine marbles, Purbeck, Sicilian, and black Derbyshire, and an oaken altar with "a single slab of Belgian marble for its top". Not everyone liked Scott's work: "invariable bad proportions and bits of mongrel Gothic", spluttered one Johnian, Edmund Dennison. The dominant tower, substituted for the more graceful one Scott intended, came in for particular criticism. But familiarity—it is a prominent feature of the Cambridge skyline—bred acceptance.

New Institutions: Churchill College, Clare Hall, Robinson and Fitzwilliam Colleges

During a rainy holiday in Sicily, soon after his resignation as Prime Minister in 1955, Sir Winston Churchill discussed with Lord Cherwell and Sir John Colville the founding of a new college. It was, as Roy Jenkins puts it, "intended to provide a British answer to the Massachusetts Institute of Technology." Churchill College was founded on a forty-two acre former farm site in 1958 and opened in 1960, with the nuclear physicist Sir John Cockcroft as the first Master.

The "brutalist" architecture of this new endeavour prompted the following comment in James Lees-Milne's diary for October 1982: "Beastly building, like enormous public lavatory." (He thought Churchill would have hated it.) Some observers are more positive. Pevsner concedes that the building containing the hall is "1960 at its most ruthless," but admires the force of Richard Sheppard's overall conception and the successful combination of strength and intimacy. The chapel, far apart and separately controlled because it was deemed unsuitable for a scientific foundation to be too closely associated with religion, is reached across grounds of park-like extent and has glass by John Piper and Patrick Reyntiens in submarine greens, blues, yellows and purples. Nearby, lighter and generally more popular than the main buildings, is the Møller Centre for Continuing Education by Henning Larsen, built following a large gift from a Danish foundation in 1992.

The grounds of the college display modern sculptures (several of them on loan) including Barbara Hepworth's "Four Square Through" (1966). At the front, in Storey's Way, are Sir Anthony Caro's "Forum" in brown rusted and waxed steel—suggestions, but not too specific, of industrial or scientific processes—and Dhruva Mistry's "Diagram of an Object".

The archives centre (1973) is constructed, outwardly at least, as if ready to resist invasion with Churchillian strength. It holds Sir Winston's papers and many other collections relating to British political life, including papers of Lord Hailsham, Lady Thatcher and Neil Kinnock.

Clare Hall, a graduate college set up by Clare College in 1966, achieved full separation in 1983. Ralph Erskine's plan is, as Nicholas Ray indicates in his book on Cambridge architecture, "founded on a social model of an academic village," with two "pedestrian streets, or walks" running though it; "its deliberately unmonumental quality is in refreshing contrast to the pompous rigidity of much twentieth century building for colleges." Robinson College, next door, was founded in 1977 by the businessman and philanthropist David Robinson. The architects are Andrew Macmillan and Isi Metzstein. It seems to Ray "formally effortful" by comparison with Clare Hall. Tim Rawle (*Cambridge Architecture*) calls it "a vast, brick-clad concrete monolith". The gatehouse, with its ramp and "portcullis-like screens", is "blatantly defensive". But the wooded gardens, as Rawle says, "remain calm and private," watered by Bin Brook. The chapel has stained glass by John Piper.

Fitzwilliam College originates from an organization set up in 1869, near the museum of the same name, for students not attached to a particular college. Somewhat paradoxically, it evolved, by way of institutions called Fitzwilliam Hall and Fitzwilliam House, into a college, established in 1966. In that year it moved to the present site on Huntingdon Road, where an unwelcoming façade conceals a rich garden, some older buildings like the Grove (a house of 1813 onwards), and what Michael Grant in 1969 called the "up-rearing fantasy of the hall"—its "transparent, glass-filled vault, with widely spreading half-pointed arches which soar and undulate in splendid contrast with the two solid floors at the building's base."

The Sidgwick Site

The Arts Faculty buildings between Sidgwick Avenue and West Road have had rather a rough reception. This is particularly true of James Stirling's mid-1960s History Faculty Building, which David Watkin describes as a "neo-Constructivist essay in pseudo-functionalism". The former Cambridge historian David Cannadine, as quoted by Martin Thompson in the alumni magazine *CAM* in 2002, goes further: it is "a monstrosity—dry-as-dust implausibly clad in the leaking raiment of high-as-tech. Part bunker, part factory, part greenhouse, all folly... ugly, strident, unpopular, aggressive, unwelcoming, antihumanist and anti-architecture." Millions of pounds have had to be spent on repairs. But as Thompson points out, this is a place of pilgrimage for many architects: an imaginative conception of "an open book stood on end with a quadrant of industrial glazing hung between the arms to roof a multi-storey library."

Sir Norman Foster's spectacular glass-and-stone Law Faculty (1995) is easier for most people to admire. Here, too, there were teething troubles; a glass screen had to be put in to stop noise travelling from the atrium up into the reading areas. Also worth seeing at the Sidgwick site is Edward Cullinan's Divinity Faculty Building (2000), the most prominent element of which is sometimes known irreverently, from its shape, as "the jam jar".

Interesting modern buildings elsewhere in Cambridge include several of those in the Science Park (off Milton Road); at the West Cambridge site, off Madingley Road, Schlumberger Cambridge Research (1985) with its distinctive central roof—a white, translucent glass-fibre membrane—and the William Gates Building (2001); and John Outram's striking and richly coloured Judge Institute of Management Studies, converted in 1995 from the main Old Addenbrooke's hospital building in Trumpington Street. (The out-patients' department had already become the less architecturally innovative, but useful, Brown's restaurant.)

Imaginary Cambridge

Notable as edifices and institutions though the colleges are, imaginative writers have felt the need to add to their number. There are archetypal (if rather Trinity-like) institutions like Boniface College, Oxbridge in

Thackeray's *Pendennis*, with its resident poet Sprott. Tom Sharpe's Porterhouse sounds like Peterhouse, is supposed to owe part of its inspiration to Corpus, but is not particularly like either. Penelope Fitzgerald's St Angelicus, in *The Gate of Angels* (1990) has the quirkiness of a college in one sort of guided tour: it is remarkably small, a "toy fortress" with no accommodation for students and a legacy of jokes about the difficulty of finding it; in theory it does not exist, because it was founded by a Pope who was subsequently dethroned.

Often the locations are fairly exact without corresponding closely to real colleges: St Angelicus, or "Angels", is not far from Christ's Pieces and its cellar extends under Butt Green. Detective work on Jill Paton Walsh's sleuth novels *The Wyndham Case* (1993) and *A Piece of Justice* (1995) shows that St Agatha's, where Imogen Quy is the perceptive college nurse, runs roughly from the Castle Mound to Chesterton Lane. St Bartholomew's in Michelle Spring's *Nights in White Satin* (1999) is, a little more loosely, in the vicinity of the police station and New Square and has a view of Midsummer Common. Elizabeth George's St Stephen's in *For the Sake of Elena* (1992) slips in between Trinity College and Trinity Hall. One advantage of the fantasy college is that authors can say what might be libellous or unfair if directed at an identifiable institution: Spring's St Bartholomew's, for instance, has "a reputation as one of the randier colleges around", and various crime writers' murderous or duplicitous dons are best kept fictional. Spring's investigator Laura Principal was at Newnham, but her acumen makes that a compliment even if she did have "a small and shabby room".

Architects and planners have also created Cambridge fantasies: Hawksmoor's plans of 1712 for a town centre of imposing classical symmetries; Wren's alternative, circular library for Trinity; the university MP William Bankes' more extreme scheme of 1824 to replace Caius College with a building "of the exact dimensions and proportions of the Parthenon at Athens (the sculpture omitted)" and to install the Fitzwilliam Museum there. Another sort of fantasy, vigorously advanced in the sixteenth century and later, often in a desperate attempt to deny Oxford's claim to greater antiquity, had the university founded by the Spanish prince or duke Cantaber in the fourth century BC or, failing that, at least by Sigebert, King of the East Angles, in about AD630. Finally, of course, innumerable Cambridges are constructed by memory, inspired by three years' residence, by a day-trip starting from the porters' lodge at Selwyn, or by a misremembered conversation which did not take place in the Baron of Beef in Bridge Street.

CHAPTER THREE

Cambridge Students

Cambridge students have engaged in a remarkable variety of extra-curricular activities: rioting; going to the races at Newmarket (established in the seventeenth century); playing and betting on billiards in Chesterton, then a small riverside village outside university jurisdiction; climbing out of Magdalene at 3 AM, with Charles Kingsley, to ride nine miles in heavy rain for the sake of a few minutes' successful trout-fishing at Duxford; incurring the charge of "dishonestly handling a policeman's helmet"; acting; debating; taking part in political demonstrations; conducting mock funerals for those who have been sent down; propelling friends through the streets in beds to raise money for good causes in Rag week.

Sports and Hoaxes

In the early nineteenth century "our University bucks"—those with money and some panache—disported themselves, according to the satirical guide *Gradus ad Cantabrigiam* (1803), by strutting about the town not in the prescribed gowns and caps but in "forbidden boots, with hat, and stick, and eke a dog!" Later in the century university and college sports acquired a respectability denied to dubious boots and non-regulation dogs. By the mid-twentieth century there were, in addition to rowing, rugby, cricket and football, such activities—listed by Mark Weatherall in his analysis of student life as covered in the weekly *Varsity*—as "lacrosse, sailing, water polo, badminton, fencing, real tennis, Eton fives, Australian rules football... gliding, cycling, rallying, hare and hounds... pelota, petanque, modern pentathlon" and "ultimate frisbee".

A competitive sport less likely to meet with senior approval (there have been unsuccessful attempts to ban it) is the King Street Run, in which undergraduates proceed along the street in question as fast as is compatible with swallowing a pint of beer in each of its pubs. The King Street Run gives its name to one of the pubs; its sign shows wild capped and gowned students trampling a fellow drinker as they rush up the street with their pints. (King Street now has not only pubs but several cafés, notably the excellent family-run Italian café-restaurant Clowns.) Charles Stuart Calverley (1831-84), although he claimed in "Beer" that "The heart which Grief hath canker'd/Hath one unfailing remedy—the Tankard," was too enterprizing simply to drink in, or race between, hostelries; as an undergraduate at Christ's he is said to have removed the sign from the Green Man in Trumpington. He fled with it back to college, pursued by the inn-keeper and his confederates, and explained to the Dean, playing on Matthew 12:38-9, "Sir, an evil and adulterous generation seeketh after a sign, and there shall no sign be given it." This exploit may be apocryphal, but Calverley had been known for both his wit and his athletic feats at Balliol College, Oxford, before migrating to Christ's—he had been sent down from Balliol after one feat of adventurous climbing too many. At Cambridge his energies were diverted more often into his verse, humorous, parodic or classical. His "Ode to Tobacco" valiantly denies rumours that devotees of the "sweet" weed "All grow by slow degrees/Brainless as chimpanzees." The poem concludes by saluting Bacon Brothers the tobacconists; it can still be read on a plaque at the Market end of Rose Crescent where their shop once stood.

Conceivably tobacco helped the cogitations of the perpetrators of the "Zanzibar Hoax". According to Adrian Stephen (son of Sir Leslie Stephen, brother of Virginia Woolf), one evening in 1905 he and another Trinity undergraduate, Horace Cole, "set ourselves to think out some plan of amusement." His idea was that they should disguise themselves as German officers, march some troops across the French border in Alsace-Lorraine, and cause an amusing international incident. But they decided to take up Cole's idea, positively sane by comparison, of impersonating the Sultan of Zanzibar, who was in England at the time, and paying a state visit to Cambridge. Since the Sultan's photograph had appeared in the newspapers, Cole and Stephen soon realized that it would be safer to impersonate his "imaginary uncle" and—two friends joined the plot—followers. With surprising prudence they also decided that they would be less likely to be sent down if they hoaxed the mayor rather than the university authorities. In London a theatrical costumier made them up and provided them with exotic turbans and robes. An Oxford undergraduate in more everyday clothes, but unlikely to be recognized in Cambridge, joined them as "interpreter". A telegram announced their imminent arrival to the mayor. (It was signed "Lucas" because, one of the group claimed, "high colonial officials always bore that name.") Verve, luck, steady nerves and civic credulity won the day; the town clerk received the distinguished emissaries at the station. Speaking to each other and their interpreter much nonsense punctuated by a few words of Swahili, the group went on to meet the mayor at the Guildhall, paid a "royal visit to a charity bazaar" where Cole as the uncle made "enormous purchases", and were shown round the colleges. Finally the town clerk escorted them back to the station. Not wanting to end up back in London, they made off through the crowd on the platform, jumped into hansom cabs and had themselves driven out into the country, near the house of some friends. Here they changed, washed and dined before making their way back to college.

Cole, originally against his confederates' wishes, took the story of their escapade to the *Daily Mail.* On reading of his discomfiture the mayor asked the Vice-Chancellor to send the offenders down. The Vice-Chancellor, however, suavely "advised the Mayor for the sake of his reputation to think it over" and no further action was taken. But there was greater controversy when, several years later, Cole, Stephen, his turbaned and bearded sister Virginia and others, this time as the Emperor of Abyssinia and his entourage, were formally received on HMS *Dreadnought.* For in the eyes of some, Stephen pointed out, the mayor had been "only a Cambridge tradesman" (he kept a chemist's shop), whereas naval officers, as one critic said, were "different"—they were "men of honour".

Instead of, or often in addition to, such manifold activities, many undergraduates have studied hard. Those who needed to obtain a church benefice needed to work for a degree. There have always, besides, been people who are passionate for learning, although not necessarily the learning their courses have to offer. For instance, the studies of John Sterling of Trinity, said Thomas Carlyle (with characteristically Carlylean grandeur or grandiloquence), "were of the most discursive, wide-flowing character, not steadily advancing along beaten roads towards college honours, but pulsing out with impetuous irregularity," following now one track, now another, "towards whatever spiritual Delphi might promise to unfold the mystery of this world." In *May Week Was in June* (1990) Clive James describes, in less exalted tones, his habit of reading anything not written in the early nineteenth century as a way of avoiding working at a (soon abandoned) PhD thesis on P. B. Shelley.

Nevertheless, committed work became the norm rather than the exception once, in modern times, the main criterion for admission became academic merit rather than social position, wealth, or family or school tradition, and once courses began to address student needs and interests more fully. In the 1980s in particular the resolve to work hard was also stiffened by the threat of graduate unemployment. Even before this, in 1976, study was sufficiently popular for a "work-in" to be staged at the University Library in protest against reduced opening hours. Professor Trefusis, in Stephen Fry's novel *The Liar* (1991), laments just how staid undergraduates had allegedly become by 1979: "They're are all getting firsts and married these days, if you'll forgive the syllepsis... Decency, discipline and dullness. There's no lightness of touch any more, no irresponsibility... There's no lack of respect today, that's what I miss."

The end of undergraduate life can come as a shock—a relief or an ejection from paradise. Most people carry forward some knowledge, useful skills, friendships, and powerful memories. There may be a natural progression into a career or postgraduate study, or there may be a sense of pointlessness when the three (or in some subjects four or more) years of intense activity reach their full stop. The comedian Peter Cook, interviewed on BBC television in 1979, remembered that "Cambridge seemed to be the hub of the world. We didn't think that much of the outside world. When I left, I was fully equipped to stay at Cambridge forever." For a while at least, people coming back to visit may agree with Tennyson's friend Arthur Hallam: "I don't think I could reside again at Cambridge with any pleasure. I should feel like a melancholy Pterodactyl winging his lonely flight among the fowls and flying fishes of the post-acdamic world."

Early Days

Bertrand Russell first came to Cambridge, to be examined for an entrance scholarship in mathematics, in December 1889. He stayed in Trinity New Court but, he says in his autobiography, "was too shy to enquire the way to the lavatory, so that I walked every morning to the station [about a mile and a half] before the examination began." He also noticed the Backs through the gate of New Court, "but did not venture to go into them, feeling that they might be private." Once he returned to take up residence as an undergraduate Russell began to develop more confidence. He also found himself, on moonlit nights, careering around the countryside "in a state of temporary lunacy", unaware at the time that "the reason, of course, was sexual desire." Where Cambridge did provide him with fulfilment, he felt, was in friendships, intellectual discussion, and the habit of intellectual honesty. During the First World War, when he was ejected from his lectureship at Trinity (and imprisoned) for his pacifism, he was sad to find that "even at Cambridge, intellectual honesty had its limitations."

People are always full of advice for new students, whether they are shy Russells or more confident characters. Dickens' eldest son Charles Junior, in *A Dictionary of the University of Cambridge* (1884) tells freshmen what precautions they must take if they want to hide their "verdancy". He fails to supply a map showing college lavatories, but does know how you should and should not dress: you must not alight at the station with "high-hat on head, or hat-box in hand; chimney-pots and their cases must on all accounts be left at home." The "ordinary round felt" hat is safe, apparently. Boaters are out because the colour of the straw and the ribbon will depend on which college club you subsequently join; "Scotch bonnets, wide-awakes, and other soft things may be donned later according to taste, but the diffident ones had better begin with billycocks." Choice of headgear is, fortunately, less of a problem for the modern Cambridge undergraduate; it was hair and clothing which, for a time in the 1960s and 1970s, became more of a talking-point. Basil Willey, writing in 1968, four years after his retirement as King Edward VII Professor of English Literature, was baffled by the appearance of male students "with their dirty unsightly jeans, beards and hair-mops, and often with their arms around equally dirty and unsightly but often shorter-haired girls." They seemed to him "almost a different race of beings" from those he had taught.

Dickens has other prescriptions, which must contain at least a degree of exaggeration but suggest something of the way Cambridge students of the time saw themselves. Sugar-tongs must be left behind:

> for lump-sugar, in Cambridge, is generally passed round and taken with the clean finger and thumb. The hands have little other social use, for there is total abstinence from handshaking, except on the first and last occasion of seeing an acquaintance in any term. When two men meet in the street or road who have nothing to say, they do not stop and say it, nor even mutter in passing, 'Do?' but the tiniest nod or the least perceptible motion of the near eyelid suffices. The fresh springy youth, who comes up with some boyish bubbling gush and sentiment, need not let himself be frozen by the seeming coldness and formality of the social atmosphere; and must never imagine himself 'cut', but rather believe, till he meets with proof absolute, that his seeming haughty senior is really short-sighted, or that his own sight is not clear enough to distinguish the courtly motion of the eyelid.

By 1922, when Cecil Beaton came up to St John's, fashions had changed in this as in other respects. His diary records that even people he "used to hate and turn my back on [at Harrow] now come up and shake hands. The most weird types have spoken to me... I suppose *I'll* have to become friendly with the world too!" A fellow Harrovian, however, suggested to him that "people are more friendly here out of insincerity"; unlike Harrow, Cambridge was so full of people that "one can afford to be amicable without worrying about having to see them again and again." Relationships remained accordingly superficial; Beaton felt, summarizing his remaining years at Cambridge, that he remained "deeply insecure" and "took refuge behind a façade of formality." But, as befitted his future career in high-class photography, fashion and theatre design, the façade was a stylish one. On settling into his rooms at 47 Bridge Street, he luxuriated in the sense of his own independence and originality. "I must buy lots of things for this sitting-room: emerald green curtains, green cushions [he was already cushioned by a generous allowance from his father] and green china. I must also get some of those tall, twisted wooden candlesticks." If this sounds decorous enough, Beaton's tastes in dress were clearly more extraordinary. In his diary he wonders, perhaps disingenuously, why people stare at him. He is not, as far as he can see, "fantastically dressed or odd looking". But since, as he comments in a later footnote, he "was possibly wearing fur gauntlet gloves, a cloth of gold tie, scarlet jersey and flowing 'Oxford bags', perhaps it is reasonable to suppose that I was noticeable." His friend Steven Runciman, the future historian of the Crusades, who "wore heavy rings, carried a parakeet on his fingers, and had his hair cut in an Italianate fringe," was no less noticeable.

Rooms

Discovering where you are to be quartered is one of the first delights or disappointments of arriving at university. Will the room be as large—there may be a "set" with separate bedroom—or as poky, with such a wonderful view or terrible smell as the one you had when you came for interview? Accommodation ranges, as Frank Stubbings says in his *Cambridge Glossary* (1995) "from a late medieval attic with exposed timbers to an architect-designed bed-sitting-cell". Today in some respects it will certainly be more comfortable than college accommodation used to be; as Stubbings says, "the world of the hip-bath survived until the First World War, that of the chamber-pot until the Second." The *Corpus Christi College Association Letter* for 1966 notes that "Improvements are being made in the provision of lavatory and washing facilities on various staircases: the college takes the view that some abatement of the rigours of life is not a sign of decadence." Very nearly all student rooms now have their own decadent wash-basins. (Far fewer students live "out" than used to be the case; colleges have now extended on site or developed their own off-site accommodation, replacing the earlier private but university-licensed lodging-houses.)

Aesthetic comfort is another consideration in evaluating a room. Christopher Isherwood, at Corpus in the 1920s, had problems not only with a smoky coal-fire but with the "bright unfriendly brown" of his sitting-room walls. The "eight hard, leather, brown chairs" made you feel "surrounded by stiff, invisible presences. Altogether, the place was like an old-fashioned dentist's waiting-room." But, as Isherwood found in his friend "Chalmers'" rooms on the same staircase, the occupant could have as much effect as the décor. Chalmers (the novelist Edward Upward) had many books, three Dürer engravings and "a big inverted lamp-shade, like a half-pumpkin", which "filled the room with warm red light." His possessions were few, but scattered, and his untidiness gave a homely, inhabited feel. Isherwood, try as he might, had a "proper position" even for his matchbox.

Riots and Unrest

In 1810 five disorderly Trinity undergraduates were brought before Isaac Milner, the formidable President of Queens', who was Vice-Chancellor at the time. He took the opportunity to inveigh against such student practices as

> *breaking of lamps and windows, shouting and roaring, blowing of horns, galloping up and down the streets on horseback or in carriages, fighting and mobbing in the town and neighbouring villages; in the daytime breaking down fences and riding over cornfields, then eating, drinking and becoming intoxicated at taverns or ale-houses and, lastly, in the night frequenting houses of ill-fame, resisting the lawful authorities and often putting the peaceable inhabitants of the town into great alarm.*

Milner was famously illiberal, but the problem was clearly a real one. In his day such breaches of the peace were caused mainly by those with the money and the privileges not to worry too much about consequences. Noblemen were exempt from examinations until 1822; they and the other socially distinguished Fellow Commoners were treated generally with some deference. The wilder excesses were on the whole too risky and too expensive for the Pensioners—the bulk of undergraduates—and the poorer Sizars, who received some financial aid in return, traditionally, for performing various menial tasks. Affronting "the inhabitants of the town" also drew on the wider tradition of Town and Gown conflict, which was usually at its most violent each 5 November. Nonetheless, students also, whether they take it for granted or feel guilty about it, have traditionally relied on townspeople to attend to their personal needs. "The bedder was a woman who made your bed," explains Clive James. Perhaps she might, instead, have been working for society or seeking spiritual fulfilment, but as it was she "was earning a pittance by squaring up our crapulous sheets and blankets."

Conscience, rather than simple belligerence, inspired the student-led protest and scuffles outside the film *Our Fighting Navy* at the Tivoli cinema in November 1933. Several days later the Armistice Day anti-war march proceeded, amid a hail of pro-war eggs and tomatoes, to the War Memorial near the railway station. (Fighting on the anti-war side were the communist spies-to-be Burgess and Maclean.) There was a huge "Hands Off Cuba" rally on Parker's Piece in 1962 and protesters against the Vietnam War managed to hang a banner between the pinnacles of King's College Chapel. Internal issues, including the content and structure of courses, prompted a number of demonstrations and sit-ins beginning in the late 1960s. But foreign affairs prompted the famous and controversial events at the Garden House Hotel in February 1970. At the height of the Greek dictatorship of the "Colonels", the hotel participated in a Greek Week. Some 400 demonstrators arrived to picket one of the events. There were set-tos with police, some damage occurred inside the hotel, and nine students were later convicted for unlawful assembly and riot. The present Garden House Hotel is the result of rebuilding after a fire in 1972.

Study and Examinations

What undergraduates are supposed to study has changed many times over the centuries. Medieval students took degrees in liberal arts (mainly logic, rhetoric, philosophy and mathematics), theology, canon or civil law or, more rarely, medicine. In the late fifteenth and early sixteenth century "humane letters"—classical and biblical texts—and mathematics became increasingly important. Other subjects continued to evolve, with some changes confirmed, and others effected, by Thomas Cromwell's injunctions of 1535: there was to be an emphasis on the Bible "according to the true sense thereof and not after the manner of" such medieval commentators as Duns Scotus. In the arts subjects Scotus and his ilk and their "frivolous questions and obscure glosses" were to be replaced by Aristotle and, among others, the contemporary Lutheran Philip Melanchthon; the study of canon law was abolished.

Development seems to have been arrested amid the distractions of religious conflict over the following century and more. Conservatism or sheer inertia also played its part: Francis Bacon, who had come up to Trinity as a twelve-year-old undergraduate in 1573, found, he says in *The Advancement of Learning*, that the dons possessed "abundance of leisure and small variety of reading, their wits being shut up in the cells of a few authors, chiefly Aristotle, their Dictator." In 1649 John Hall of St John's, petitioning parliament for university reform, demanded in vain to know where was "Chimistry", which has

> *snatched the keys of nature from the other sects of philosophy by her multiplied experiences?... Where any manual demonstrations of mathematical theorems or instruments?... Where an examination of all the old tenets?... Where a survey of antiquities and learned descants upon them? Where a ready and generous teaching of the tongues?*

A fair number of students did in fact engage in the sort of studies Hall specified, but outside the curriculum. Some individual college fellows and private tutors provided teaching in such subjects. Elisabeth Leedham-Green points out that John Ray, author of an early catalogue of flora in the environs of Cambridge, was probably teaching botany in the university in the 1650s and that Giovanni Francesco Vigani of Verona lectured in pharmaceutical chemistry from 1683. Language teaching was widely available, and both the university and private benefactors continued to endow chairs: there were, for instance, professors of modern history and of geology from the 1720s. But only some of the professors actually gave lectures; Janet Browne in her biography of Darwin cites the aptly named William Lax, professor of astronomy and geometry from 1795 to 1837, who "never, as far as is known, delivered a single lecture." Most of those who did lecture were unlikely to attract much interest as long as their subjects failed to feature in students' examinations.

What did feature was a little classics, philosophy and divinity and, increasingly, much mathematics, especially geometry. This emphasis resulted partly from the prestige of such Cambridge mathematicians as the Lucasian professors Isaac Barrow and, above all, Isaac Newton, although the average student worked, of course, at a much more rudimentary level. Up to 1850 any serious student (anyone taking an honours degree rather than the more basic "pass" degree) needed to be mathematically well versed. The pass degree, too, had its fair share of the subject: in the early 1830s it required knowledge of Euclid, arithmetic and algebra together with some Latin and Greek, Paley's *Evidences of Christianity* and *Principles of Moral and Political Philosophy*, and Locke's *An Essay Concerning Human Understanding*. But only partial, superficial and, especially in Paley's case, unquestioning knowledge of the material was required. According to George Pryme, a Trinity undergraduate of 1799 who later became professor of political economy, "Two books of Euclid's geometry, simple and quadratic equations, and the early parts of Paley's *Moral Philosophy* were deemed amply sufficient." A classical tripos was instituted in 1822 but until 1850 could be taken only following success in the mathematical tripos.

From the mid-nineteenth century, however, there was a rapid increase in the diversity of available triposes. Moral Sciences (philosophy) and Natural Sciences triposes were established in 1850, Law in 1858, Theology and Semitic Languages in the 1870s, Medieval and Modern Languages in 1886, Mechanical Sciences (engineering) in 1894. Many others followed in the twentieth century, including Economics (1905), English (1919), Geography (1920), Music (1948), Computer Science (1972) and Management Studies (1987).

Examinations have always been a tonic to some students and poisonous to others. In Margaret Drabble's *The Peppered Moth* (2000) Bessie Bawtry, inspired by Drabble's unhappy mother, does not enjoy Part One of her tripos. This is not helped by the fact that until recently she has been blissfully unaware that the lectures she attended have delivered no mere "background information, which she could take or leave as she chose," but the subjects on which she will be examined in "English B":

> *Three hours of [the first paper] and a warm day; the sun shone outside, and indoors, pens scratched on paper. Three hours of questions on La Tène firedogs, the Beaker people, bronze shields and the Mildenhall burials: to be followed by other papers on other hot days on the Vikings, on Teutonic brooches, on socketed axes, on the Plymstock and Arreton Down*

hoards, on trade routes and runes and ruins. Was it for this that Miss Heald [at school] had encouraged Bessie Bawtry to read J. Alfred Prufrock and Edith Sitwell? What had all this to do with English Literature? What was she doing here?

Bessie survives Part One, finding amid the brooches and burials some more congenially literary questions on Fate and *Beowulf*. Part Two, although she does less well than would once have been expected, is at least concerned with literature, as would her Part One have been if she had come to Cambridge a few years later. (The other material became the preserve of the new Archaeology and Anthropology tripos in 1928; Anglo-Saxon became a separate tripos in 1958 and part of Anglo-Saxon, Norse and Celtic in 1971.) But "for the rest of her life those teasing terrible objects and subjects would rise up before her to torment her in her dreams—the Jellinge stone, the Oseberg Viking Ship... They were scorched and scarred into her. They would be incinerated with her upon her funeral pyre."

Peter Cook took a more relaxed approach to his final Modern Languages examinations. Harry Thompson's 1997 biography reports that one day Cook brought in, as he had discovered that he was entitled to do, a carton of fruit-juice. This annoyed the invigilating don, "himself sweating in full rig". "Peter kept up a running battle with this gentleman. The following day he openly swigged copious draughts from a bottle of brandy, informing the fuming official that he didn't want his answers to lack spirit."

Proctors and Bulldogs

Two schoolboys snigger as a man encounters a youth outside Macmillan and Bowes bookshop in Trinity Street, now the Cambridge University Press bookshop. The man, bearded, begowned, begoggled, grandly doffs his academic cap with one hand but points sternly with the other at the cigarette which the nervous youth is trying to hide behind his back. In this *Punch* cartoon of 1909 the undergraduate has committed the offence of smoking while wearing academic dress. The grim enforcer is a proctor, one of the two university officials co-opted to police student conduct—not only to check the gowns but to "walk the round, and see that there is no chambering and wantonness, no rioting and drunkenness" (*Gradus ad Cantabrigiam: or, a Dictionary of Terms… which are used at the University of Cambridge*, 1803). In their pursuit of these misdemeanours the proctors also, for centuries, had the power to apprehend townspeople, especially women suspected of an intention to lead young gentlemen astray.

Since proctors themselves were not always nimble enough to catch malefactors, they were, as Francis Burnand puts it in his reminiscences of 1880, "accompanied by two men generally 'good on their pins' and not bad with their fists, who were styled 'bull dogs'" or constables. Later the bulldogs tended to "walk the round" while the proctors came out in person only if a real emergency threatened. At the end of his first term in 1957 Peter Cook was stopped by them because he was wearing what they decided was an improperly shabby, battered gown (it was second-hand and had cost him 17s 6d., a third of the price for a new one). They told him that he must report to the proctor and asked his name, but, as Thompson's biography records, he was rescued by his gift for improvisation: "Peter started to flap the remains of his gown slowly up and down, while the trio [the bulldogs and his friend Robin Voelcker] looked on in astonishment. Then he informed them that he was *The Vampire*, and flapped off into the dark, leaving Voelcker to explain as best he could."

Clubs

"Political clubs, clubs literary, hunting and boating clubs, clubs for encouraging agriculture by devouring beef-steaks, clubs to perpetuate the dress of the seventeenth century, archery clubs, private debating clubs, and clubs for 'natation' as the French call it, have all in their turns, some for a season, others perpetually, flourished in the University," declares one of the contributors to Rev. J. J. Smith's *Cambridge Portfolio* (1840). Student dining clubs have indulged in such names as the Lucullans and the True Blue. (The Family, in the early years of the twentieth century, catered to the palates of more senior members of the university.) Charles Darwin and his friends founded the Glutton Club with the declared aim of consuming creatures "which were before unknown to human palate"; they tried hawk and bittern before their "appetite for strange flesh" was cured by an unpleasant experience with an old brown owl.

The Pavement Club, true to its aim of lending "verisimilitude to the rapidly disappearing illusion that University life is a Life of Leisure," sat on the pavement in the early 1920s. The many debating clubs were, at least in theory, more serious about life: the Fifty, the Chitchat, the Magpie and Stump (convened under its eponymous stuffed magpie on a tree-stump). At King's in the late 1880s E. F. Benson was, he recalls in *Our Family Affairs 1867-1896* (1920), elected to the Decemviri Debating Society, "though I do not think I ever expressed any wish to belong to it." He did not go to the meetings, and since the society's rules decreed that after a certain period absentees should be expelled, he found that the private business preceding the next debate was to be "the matter of my own expulsion". Usually he was terrified of making speeches and contributed only "a rich silence" to discussions. But "unjustifiable indignation for this time put terror to flight, and," he claims, "I was allowed to open another debate in the place of that already arranged for, and to make a speech to show reason why I should not be expelled. My motion was triumphantly carried, and I never went to a meeting of the Decemviri again."

Much the least ephemeral of such groups was the Cambridge Conversazione Society, called by its members simply the Society, but known more often as the Apostles. (There were usually about twelve of them. The name stuck, however, probably because of their exclusivity—members were chosen as carefully and as secretly as possible.) The group, founded in 1820 and dominated for much of its history by Trinity and then by King's, met every Saturday to discuss a brief paper by one of the members. There was no alcohol but much smoking of pipes and eating of anchovy sandwiches or "whales". Former members were often present as honorary members and, in greater numbers, at the annual dinner.

In the period when Arthur Hallam (elected 1829) was a leader of the Society and F. D. Maurice (elected 1823) increasingly an influence on it, a clear "apostolic" spirit became definable. It was, as it later struck the 1850s Apostle Henry Sidgwick, "the spirit of the pursuit of truth with absolute devotion and unreserve by a group of intimate friends, who were frank with each other, and indulged in any amount of humorous sarcasm and playful banter" while respecting and trying to learn from each other "and see what he sees." "Absolute candour was the only duty that the tradition of the society enforced," and "there were no propositions so well established that an Apostle had not the right to question, if he did so sincerely and not from mere love of paradox." Sidgwick stresses again, perhaps to the reader's relief, that solemnity of manner was not required, although some may find fairly solemn his pronouncement that it was "a point of the apostolic mind to understand how much suggestion and instruction may be derived from what is in form a jest." (The Heretics, a society at its height in the 1920s, was conspicuously more irreverent.) But outside meetings at least, the apostolic tone was not always earnest. Robert Tennant wrote to Alfred Tennyson, who had briefly been a member of the Society in 1829-30, and whose early work it continued to champion, about a dinner attended by his fellow Apostles:

> *most of them stayed till past two: John Heath volunteered a song, Kemble got into a passion about nothing but quickly jumped out again, Blakesley was afraid the Proctors might come in, and Thompson [later Regius Professor of Greek and Master of Trinity] poured huge quantities of salt upon Douglas Heath's head, because he talked nonsense.*

Behaviour like this and, more seriously, the free and wide-ranging character of the debates, were a reaction against the old-fashioned, limited and mechanical approach to learning that prevailed in the university. Even after this attitude changed in the middle and later part of the century, the Apostles often espoused liberal causes or were at least happy to debate them seriously. When Bertrand Russell was one of their number from 1892 (joined by G. E. Moore, soon to become their guiding light, in 1894) "there were to be no taboos, no limitations, nothing considered shocking, no barriers to absolute freedom of speculation." (Even in the 1830s "fornication" had been discussed, to the distaste of a few.)

Russell believed, however, that the principle of detachment was jettisoned by the Apostles of ten years later, led by Maynard Keynes and Lytton Strachey and others subsequently dubbed "Bloomsbury". This generation (which also included E. M. Forster and Leonard Woolf) "aimed... at a life of retirement among fine shades and nice [i.e. delicate, refined] feelings, and conceived of the good as consisting in the passionate mutual admirations of a clique of the élite. This doctrine, quite unfairly, they fathered on G. E. Moore, whose disciples they professed to be." Ignoring Moore's emphasis on morals and other aspects of his philosophy, they "degraded" his ethics "into advocacy of a stuffy girls-school sentimentalising". So much for the finer feelings of early Bloomsbury. (The prevalence of homosexuality in Strachey's group was another aspect Russell did not much like, yet it had been almost equally common when he was an Apostle.) Strachey, Russell claims, never left this world. Keynes did, but when he concerned himself with politics and economics he left his soul behind. He went about believing that "true salvation was elsewhere, among the faithful at Cambridge." Like Russell, evidently, he cared passionately about the Apostles.

Some feel that students might be better occupied than in apostolic debate; Herbert Pembroke, in the Apostle E. M. Forster's *The Longest Journey*, gathers that Rickie's Cambridge friends "discuss what one knows and what one never will know and what one had much better not know... [It] is because they have not got enough to do." But the society, now less secret and admitting female members, goes on meeting.

The Cambridge Spies

In the 1930s many Apostles were Marxists, although how directly their agenda influenced the papers presented has continued to be a matter of dispute. The secrecy of the Society has made it difficult to get at the truth and has encouraged some people to draw parallels between its culture and that of espionage. The future communist spies Anthony Blunt and Guy Burgess were, after all, Apostles.

Blunt was older than the other spies. He came up to Trinity College in 1926 and went on to become a fellow, for a time teaching both Modern Languages and the History of Art, the subject through which he climbed to the establishment height of Surveyor of the Queen's Pictures and Director of the Courtauld Institute before his public exposure in 1979. His aristocratic hauteur and connections helped him conceal his KGB involvement until 1964, when he confessed to the authorities in exchange for immunity from prosecution; he was practised, also, like many of his friends, at concealing his homosexuality. He was, Alan Bennett suggests in the introduction to *Single Spies* (his paired plays on Blunt and Burgess), the sort of don "in whom shyness, self-assurance and deep conviction combine to give an uncongenial impression."

When under investigation, and after Burgess' defection in 1951, Blunt claimed that he had been recruited by Burgess (a graduate of Trinity, like the others apart from Donald Maclean, who was at Trinity Hall). The generally accepted sequence is that Kim Philby, a recent history and economics graduate, was approached by the KGB controller Arnold Deutsch in 1934; soon afterwards Philby put Donald Maclean, who had just gained a first-class degree in Modern Languages, in touch with Deutsch's superior; early in 1935 Burgess was recruited through Maclean and Philby; Burgess in turn, in 1937, contacted Blunt and John Cairncross, another brilliant linguist. Cairncross may have been the "Fifth Man", but Roland Perry in *The Fifth Man* (1994) presents the evidence for yet another Trinity undergraduate and Apostle, Victor Rothschild, later 3rd Baron, possibly recruited as a spy through Philby in 1934. It is conceivable that Blunt was involved at a much earlier stage.

Burgess was much the most noticeable of the group. He was, as Christopher Andrew says in an essay included in *Cambridge Contributions* (1998),

> one of the most flamboyant figures in Cambridge: a brilliant, gregarious conversationalist equally at home in the teetotal intellectual discussions of the Apostles, the socially exclusive and heavy-drinking Pitt Club, and the irreverent satirical revues of the Footlights. He made no secret either of his Communist sympathies or of his enjoyment of the then illegal pleasures of homosexual 'rough trade' with young working-class men.

Usefully for the party cause, "No existing stereotype of a spy remotely resembled Burgess." Donald Maclean projected a more conventional image, but seemed similarly unlikely to be a spy. When the undergraduate Maclean told Robert Cecil, who knew him later at the embassy in Washington and wrote his biography, about his political persuasions, "this elegant young man in his leather armchair was not my idea of a Communist. It was an error into which many people, wiser than I, would fall before Maclean's nefarious career came to an end."

This sense of improbability was one of the factors that enabled such people to infiltrate the British establishment with such apparent ease. Maclean even genially admitted, when asked about his communism at his interview for the Foreign Office in 1935, that at Cambridge he "did have such views—and I haven't entirely shaken them off," prompting, Maclean recalled, nods and smiles; "I think they must have liked my honesty." Had he not been the bright, ex-Cambridge son of a former Liberal cabinet minister he might have been viewed with more suspicion. His colleagues were similarly plausible and well placed. "My analysis of situations, the précis I had to submit at the Foreign Office, were always Marxist. Openly so. Impeccably so," says Alan Bennett's Burgess in *An Englishman Abroad.* "Nobody minded. 'It's only Guy. Dear old Guy. Quite safe.'... And in all the important things I did conform. 'How can he be a spy? He goes to my tailor.'"

"The average Englishman, you see," Burgess goes on, "is not interested in ideas. You can say what you like about political theory and no one will listen." The spies can indeed be seen as people who sought to put ideas into practice, who followed through their convictions to a degree unheard of in "the average Englishman". But they emerged from the much broader group of people, many of them from the same privileged background, who were deeply disturbed by the social inequalities of 1930s Britain and the dire effects of unemployment. By the end of the decade the Cambridge University Socialist Society, run by communists, had nearly a thousand members. (Philby was Treasurer for a time.) Students were bussed from Cambridge to Royston to lend their support to hunger marchers en route for London. Burgess organized a successful strike by underpaid servants at Trinity College.

The political balance had shifted significantly since the General Strike of 1926, when sizeable contingents of Cambridge undergraduates went off to other parts of the country to drive trams, trains or buses or help keep the docks running. Taken further, such social awareness prompted many students to uncritical admiration for the Soviet Union, which projected itself as the home of equality and social justice. Russia seemed also much more likely to fight the fascists than did the appeasing western governments of the time. In 1934 one of Maclean's more frivolously inclined fellow-students at Trinity Hall imagined, in a college magazine, how after the revolution "the colleges have been re-named and re-appropriated. Magdalene is a clinic, King's a delousing station... The tomb of Donald Maclenin in red bakelite in Market Square is used by thousands."

Not everyone was so easily persuaded by men like Blunt and Burgess. Some rejected communism on intellectual grounds. The poet Louis MacNeice (1907-63), who had been a close friend of Blunt at Marlborough College, distrusted all systems. In his unfinished autobiography *The Strings are False* (published posthumously in 1965) he describes visiting Blunt in Cambridge in 1936. With difficulty, manhandling a large stone cyclamen that he was hoping to sell for a sculptor he knew, MacNeice reached Blunt's "coquettishly chaste room with white panelling and Annunciation lilies" in Nevile's Court at Trinity. But he soon found that the friend of Blunt to whom he was hoping to sell the sculpture had just had a baby "and Anthony had now gone Marxist [and] was no longer so eager to push the sale of a work that was primarily abstract or decorative." The plan having failed, MacNeice decided to let Cambridge entertain him, as it had on his last visit three years earlier. "Cambridge was still full of Peter Pans," he noticed, "but all the Peter Pans were now talking Marx." He abused his friend's (about to be former friend's) hospitality in what could be interpreted as both an artistic and a political statement: "The next morning while Anthony was teaching I found a gin-bottle in his room and drank myself blind before lunch; it seemed an exquisite outrage to the room and also to Dialectical Materialism."

Mathematicians

The new Centre for Mathematical Sciences was opened in 2000 by the Chancellor of the University, Prince Philip, who insisted that, at an estimated £56 million, it was much cheaper than the Millennium Dome "and it's going to be a great deal more useful." (The circular Betty and Gordon Moore Library, on the same site, was completed in 2001.) The buildings are sunken but filled with light from glass lanterns above.

Most of the students who frequent the much-praised centre are, no doubt, equally enthusiastic about their subject. In the mid-nineteenth century, when many Cambridge students still found themselves compelled to study it, such keenness was exceptional. "Oh for words to express my abomination of that science. It is starvation, confinement, torture, annihilation of the mind," cried Thomas Macaulay when he was an undergraduate at Trinity in 1818. But between two and four in the afternoon, according to Leslie Stephen's *Sketches from Cambridge* (1865), certain "shabby looking youths in ill-brushed, ill-cut garments" could be observed taking their daily constitutional, "conversing affably on abstruse problems, or stopping to draw strange figures on the ground with the points of their walking-sticks." These were the "reading men" who took their studies seriously, the "embryo Senior Wranglers". (Wranglers, ranked individually from Senior downwards, were those who achieved a first class in the tripos. The word originates from the oral disputation or "wrangling" originally involved in examinations.)

Their habits are supposed to be mainly nocturnal. Their favourite repast is a cup of tea with muffins, and a couple of friends on a Sunday evening. Their conviviality is typified by the very ancient story of the wrangler who, on taking his degree, locked twelve men into a room with one bottle of wine, saying that they should not go till they had finished it. In fact, they inherit the character which our ancestors applied to alchemists—a tribe of semi-insane enthusiasts, venturing occasionally like owls into broad daylight, but ordinarily plunged in the depths of philosophical abstraction.

That, Stephen—himself a mathematician among other things—"may say at once... is, for the most part, a gratuitous libel." And whether this is true or not, one thing to be said for the subject is that it is "so singularly repulsive to the general public that its practitioners seldom"—unlike classical votaries—"intrude it into general conversation." A mathematician "conceals his knowledge as a dentist conceals his instruments of torture."

The University Library

Frederica Potter falls in love, as far as someone "doomed to be intelligent, a watcher, judicious" can, at the University Library. It begins, in the 1950s Cambridge of A. S. Byatt's *Still Life* (1985), as she looks out from the basement tea-room: "a pleasant place, smelling of warm baking," but replaced in the 1990s, to the grief of its habitués, by a less characterful first-floor room. Up until now, like many undergraduates today, she has rarely visited the library. (Colleges and departments have their own, usually well-appointed libraries.) But she comes back to take out Dr Raphael Faber's books and to work in the same reading room, "sitting circumspectly two tables away, with a clear view of the smooth black back of his head." Less circumspectly, she later inspects his notes when he leaves the room: Mallarmé, Rilke, Greek, Hebrew, the human sign of small drawings of various shapes of vase, jar, bottle and urn; above the drawings, "framed in neat square black the words Concrete Universal." Coming up behind her he seems offended at first—"Reading and writing are private matters, Miss Potter. Or so I have always taken them to be"—but the difficult journey towards a degree of intimacy continues.

The "UL", with its books and lovers and "narcotically comfortable" chairs—in one of which Adam Morris in Frederick Raphael's *The Glittering Prizes* (1976) struggles not to sleep over his Sophocles—has occupied its present "greenfield" site near the Backs since 1934. Its earliest home was several chests in the tower of Great St Mary's Church. Then, in the early fifteenth century, it moved to the north range of the University Schools. By the late nineteenth century the library filled the whole Schools Court and the Cockerell Building. There were 122 volumes by 1440 and at least 600 by 1530. A decline during the Reformation was reversed in the 1570s, and photographs of the old library from early last century show rooms in which books are invitingly but desperately crammed into every available space.

After stiff debate (some traditionalists disliked the idea of moving the library even half a mile from the colleges) a decision was taken to build on some former playing fields acquired from Clare and King's in 1922. During the First World War there had been a military hospital here. The architect chosen for the new building was Giles Gilbert Scott. It was intended to complement his Memorial Court for Clare College, next to the site, completed in 1924. Several influential people disliked parts of Scott's original design for the library, most important among them John D. Rockefeller, Jr., whose Rockefeller Foundation provided half the £500,000 it cost to put up the building. A. F. Scholfield, the Librarian, explained to Scott that his design was too "self-effacing, austere, and with no taste of richness". He obliged by substituting reddish brick for grey and by adding the tower, one of the main landmarks on the flat Cambridge skyline. Clive James, in *May Week Was In June*, registers "the vaguely pre-Columbian threat of its appearance".

Over a period of eight weeks in 1934, 1,500,000 books, in 23,725 boxes, were moved to the new library on horse-drawn carts. Unusually for a major research library, many books are available on open access to readers not only in the various reading rooms, but on six floors' worth of what would elsewhere be a staff-only stack. The number of books, manuscripts, periodicals, tapes, microfilms, and compact discs has greatly increased (there are now about 7 million books and 135,000 manuscripts) since the move, mainly because the University Library is, as one of the six copyright or deposit libraries, entitled to receive a free copy of everything published in the United Kingdom and the Republic of Ireland. It also, of course, acquires thousands of items produced abroad. Two miles of new shelf-space needs to be found each year. Recent additions to the main library building include the Aoi Pavilion, for the Chinese, Korean and Japanese collection.

Among the library's rarer possessions are some of the earliest known Chinese texts, on "oracle bones", which, when heated, produced cracks which were interpreted as oracular responses to the question asked; the Winchcombe Psalter, an eleventh-century illustrated text in Latin and Old English; many of the papers of Newton and Darwin; the Aston collection of early Japanese books; and the books, manuscripts, posters, tapes and videos of the East German novelist Stefan Heym (1913-2001), who gave all his material to Cambridge having felt "disappointment" at the new united Germany. The Genizah Collection consists of thousands of fragments, mostly in Hebrew and Arabic and dating from the eleventh century onwards, of documents kept in the *genizah* or storage place of the Ben Ezra synagogue in Cairo. They include a range of biblical, rabbinical, and secular material. They were acquired for the library in 1897, after patient negotiation with the Chief Rabbi in Cairo, by Solomon Schechter, who taught Talmudic literature at Cambridge. A photograph taken probably the following year shows Schechter patiently working in a room of the old University Library crammed with what look at first sight like heaps and boxes of rags. The sorting and recording of the manuscripts was completed only in 1982 after delays occasioned by Schechter moving to New York in 1902 and a general lack of interest and funding until the 1960s. (Schechter arranged to borrow some of the Genizah fragments. Most were returned in the 1930s but the library did not succeed in retrieving others until 1969.) Much work continues, including the production of digitized images of the fragments. Stefan C. Reif, responsible for the collection from 1973, regards it as "matching, if not indeed eclipsing", the Dead Sea Scrolls. Reif's introduction to the Genizah is included in the useful and well-illustrated *Cambridge University Library: the Great Collections*, edited by Peter Fox.

The contents of the library have not always been well cared for. William Pugh, fellow of Trinity College, was employed between 1790 and 1799 to catalogue the University Library. He was eventually removed from his position because the catalogue was proceeding too slowly. According to Henry Gunning's *Reminiscences* (1854), "whenever he came to a work with which he was unacquainted, he was not content with looking at the title page, but applied himself to reading its contents." Pugh, who was already known for his eccentricity, took his dismissal badly. Early in the morning he would throw his dirty linen into the Cam. On at least one night, says another source quoted in D.A. Winstanley's *Unreformed Cambridge* (1935) he went out smashing lamps with a stick, shouting "You are Robespierre!" to one, "You are Danton!" to another. Yet eventually he recovered, won general respect, and was, says Winstanley, "considered to display remarkably good judgement as an examiner."

The Union

The Union Debating Society, founded originally in 1815, used to meet in what Richard Monckton Milnes (Lord Houghton) remembered as a "low, ill-ventilated, ill-lit gallery at the back of the Red Lion" in Petty Cury, "cavernous, tavernous—something between a commercial-room and a district branch-meeting-house". The society left the Red Lion for other temporary homes in about 1830 and moved to its present site by the Round Church in 1866. The building, in red brick with stone dressing, is Alfred Waterhouse's first work in Cambridge. Pevsner finds it "coarse, but not without character". The debating chamber (refurbished in the mid-twentieth century) is a relatively plain, serviceable room with benches facing each other as in the House of Commons. To Milnes, speaking at the inauguration, the contrast with the tavernous room was palpable and the occasion called for some oratory: "How can I compare [the Red Lion] with this superb building, these commodious and decorated apartments, these perhaps over-luxurious applications of domestic architecture, which you will have to enjoy?"

Many future politicians, prelates and journalists have tested their powers of debate at the Union. Either at the time or in red-faced retrospect, speakers' youthful enthusiasms, politicking and blunders have proved an obvious target for satire. Thackeray, having "spouted at the [old] Union" soon after he came up to Trinity in 1829, was serio-comically aware of his own deficiencies as a public speaker. He had, he told his mother,

> *rendered myself a public character... I do not know what evil star reigns today or what malignant daemon could prompt me to such an act of folly—but, however, I got up, and blustered and blundered, and retracted, and stuttered upon the character of Napoleon... In endeavouring to extract myself from my dilemma, I went deeper and deeper still, till at last with one desperate sentence... I rushed out of the quagmire into which I had so foolishly plunged myself and sat down like Lucifer never to rise again with open mouth in that august assembly.*

The eponymous hero of Thackeray's *Pendennis*, student of St Boniface College, Oxbridge, puts in a more confident performance when, having become a fierce young republican in his second year, he vows in debate that "Louis the Sixteenth was served right. And as for Charles the First... he would chop off that monarch's head with his own right hand were he then in the room at the Union Debating Club, and had Cromwell no other executioner for the traitor." Arthur Pendennis, however, performs no better than his creator in dealing with less extreme responsibilities: spending on horses, cards, clothes, dinners for friends, he runs up considerable debts. Some of Thackeray's own debts were incurred on vacation trips to Paris, one with his mother's knowledge, the other surreptitious. But his greatest improvidence was to play and lose at the game of *écarte*; with the assistance of professional card-sharps who had established themselves opposite Trinity, he ran up a further £1,500 worth of debts. He left Cambridge soon afterwards.

To return, unlike Thackeray, to the Union: Clive James was unimpressed by the "foolish interruptions", points of order, and old jokes about Antipodeans walking around on their heads, at this madhouse with a libretto written by Tristan Tzara and choreography devised by Hieronymus Bosch. Another non-Briton, Arianna Stassinopoulos (journalist, author of *The Female Woman*) feared, at the time of her first debate in 1969, that her accent would prevent her from being understood. But listening to the "sparring politicians" soon convinced her "of the immense value in British public life of total incomprehensibility". Nevertheless, she goes on to remember in her essay in *My Cambridge*, it was worth sitting through "all the acres of slogans, far-fetched platitudes, idiotic puns and sub-Wildean witticisms" for the moments of real eloquence, for "the whole magic of people's minds moved by words". Stassinopoulos managed to move enough minds to be elected as President of the Union in 1971. (Ann Mallalieu, four years earlier, had been the first woman President.)

The Senate House

The Senate House, built in white Portland stone by James Gibbs and James Burrough between 1722 and 1730, was saluted by *Cantabrigia Depicta* (1776) as "a finished Piece within and without, and allowed by all that view it, to be one of the most elegant rooms in the kingdom." The architects intended this "room" to be part of a three-sided court of dignified university buildings, but were frustrated by lack of finance and by political opposition. As it is, however, the Senate House coheres well with its neighbours: the equally white and stately Portland façade of the Old Schools range (1754-8), and the Cockerell Building of 1837-42, now adapted as Caius College library.

The Senate House serves important practical and symbolic functions in the university: students' examination results are posted outside, graduation happens here, and honorary degrees are also conferred with much traditional ceremony. The significance and centrality of the place has also made it the scene of protests. In June 1975, for instance, a widely supported action group demanding university nursery facilities seized control of the building for some hours.

The Senate consists of all those possessed of the Cambridge Master of Arts degree, for which holders of the Bachelor's degree are automatically entitled to apply seven years after matriculation. In practice, decisions have been taken, since 1926, by the smaller and more relevant "Regent House", in other words the teaching and administrative staff of the university.

Here, too, students have listened to lectures by the great, the good, the entertaining and the inaudible. In 1959 C. P. Snow came to deliver his controversial *The Two Cultures and the Scientific Revolution*. And in 1860 there were large audiences for Charles Kingsley. Kingsley (1819-79), well known as novelist, social reformer and "muscular Christian", had been appointed Regius Professor of History with "apparently no more reason", claimed his enemy the historian Edward Freeman, "than why he should be... set to command the Channel Fleet." According to the *Reminiscences* of the Irish novelist, journalist and politician Justin McCarthy, who heard him lecturing in London, he cut an unimpressive figure:

> *Rather tall, very angular, surprisingly awkward, with thin, staggering legs, a hatchet face adorned with scraggy grey whiskers, a faculty for falling into the most ungainly attitudes and making the most hideous contortions of visage and frame; with a rough provincial accent and an uncouth way of speaking which would be set down for caricature on the boards of a theatre.*

Nevertheless Kingsley lectured to packed audiences at the Senate House. Most students responded eagerly to his enthusiasm, to "the robust and energetic plain-speaking" acknowledged by McCarthy, "the bluff and blunt earnestness and... transparent sincerity". The manner of most lecturers of more academic backgrounds was distinctly less exciting. Indeed, the audience sometimes broke into loud cheers, amid Kingsley's stuttering protests. It was his passionately maintained belief that history is made not by social and economic forces but by heroic individuals much like the protagonists of his historical novels: Amyas Leigh the Devon seaman fighting the Armada, Hereward the Wake taking on the Normans.

Popular though it was with the young, this viewpoint failed to impress more critical listeners who were sympathetic to the progressive views of Charles Darwin or of Henry Buckle, author of a *History of Civilization in England* (1857-61). Kingsley himself, who according to McCarthy explained, "with characteristic bluntness", that "he really knew nothing in particular about the subjects whereon he had undertaken to instruct the University and the world," came gradually to feel that he had no real grasp of history, and eventually resigned with some relief in 1869.

Edward, Prince of Wales, was one young man happy enough to accept Kingsley's history if it did not interfere too much with such activities as going to the races and seeing the actress Nellie Clifden.

Queen Victoria and Prince Albert judged the professor, somewhat to his own trepidation, the right man to teach their distressingly un-earnest son during his time at Cambridge. Teacher and pupil, of whose more scandalous habits Kingsley remained unaware, seem to have got on well. There were enjoyable dinner-parties at the prince's temporary residence near the town, the sixteenth- and eighteenth-century Madingley Hall, now the home of the university's Department of Continuing Education. But the royal education came to an abrupt end when, in November 1861, Prince Albert died of typhoid less than two weeks after coming to Cambridge to confront his son about Nellie Clifden. The queen—endorsing, in her grief and anger, Kingsley's faith in individual causality—blamed Edward for his death.

There have been some irreverent moments at the Senate House. When Charles Darwin came to receive an honorary doctorate in November 1877 some enterprising undergraduates decided to make sure that everyone knew the nature of the illustrious visitor's views. Adrian Desmond and James Moore take up the tale in their *Darwin* (1991); the students

> strung a cord over the chamber and sent a monkey-marionette dangling above the waiting crowd. A Proctor climbed up and snatched it to antiphonal cheers and groans. Then a real "missing link" appeared, a fat ring garnished with gaudy ribbons, which remained suspended in mid-air throughout the ceremony.

And in 1959, the year Snow lectured inside the building, students contrived to park an Austin 7 van on the roof.

CHAPTER FOUR

Cambridge Dons

Together, though never in unison, they had steered Porterhouse away from the academic temptations to which all other Cambridge colleges had succumbed and had preserved that integrity of ignorance which gave Porterhouse men the confidence to cope with life's complexities which men with more educated sensibilities so obviously lacked. Unlike the Dean, whose lack of scholarship was natural and unforced, the Senior Tutor had once possessed a mind, and it had only been by the most rigorous discipline that he had suppressed his academic leanings in the interests of the college spirit.

In real life dons as dedicated to the "integrity of ignorance" as Tom Sharpe's in *Porterhouse Blue* have become increasingly rare since the university reforms of the mid-nineteenth century. In the eighteenth and early nineteenth century few college fellows were obliged to do any teaching. (Involvement in teaching, administration or research became compulsory only in 1926.) Some of the most effective teaching was undertaken by private tutors (some of whom were also fellows). Once in place, dons in the colleges might stay on indefinitely to pursue their studies or their pastimes or to vegetate, retiring each evening, as the satirical dictionary of university terms *Gradus* (1803) has it, to "take their bottle, or two, of wine after dinner, crack nuts, and conundrums etc" in the Combination Room. A little more intellectual effort than this was expected by 1848, when D'Arcy Wentworth Thompson came to Pembroke College, but he was probably exaggerating only slightly when he maintained that the fellows of the place he called "St Ignavia's" were still for the most part "of the cobra kind. They had swallowed their intellectual goat in early life, and were passing through the years of inactivity requisite for digestion."

Those who moved on, leaving their college to moulder away in Thompson's "beautiful and ivy-clad decay", usually did so when they married (incompatible with a fellowship until 1882) or obtained a lucrative church living or promotion. Administration was mainly in the hands of the college masters, the Vice-Chancellor annually elected from their number, and a few other university officials also elected or appointed by this group.

Dons' diligence, then, has varied in different generations. But in each generation there have been memorable dons, thought of with affection or mirth, taken as examples or deterrents. One undergraduate at St John's was seized with uncontrollable laughter in October 1922 when "the chorus of senile and beavered elders lined up in front of their carved chairs" for grace before dinner; they struck him as a caricature of old age. Yet the freshman Cecil Beaton, looking at the same group, was perceptive or naïve enough to see only "embodiments of profound wisdom and scholarship, with their bald heads, parchment skin and wisps of white beard." One, the young connoisseur felt, "might have been painted by Tintoretto: he had a straight nose and deep, hollow eyes with huge pouches under them." This living Tintoretto may have been wise or he may just have looked it; the much younger Samuel Morland (later Sir Samuel), who taught Samuel Pepys at Magdalene, was more unambiguously memorable: he was renowned, Pepys' biographer Richard Ollard points out, "as a mathematician and as a diplomatist, as a latinist and as an inventor, as a cryptographer and as a double agent." He invented the speaking-trumpet and deserves "a place in the pedigree both of the computer and of the steam-engine".

More intimidating, perhaps, was the mathematician G. H. Hardy, who believed that "the only way to assess someone's knowledge... was to examine him." When dining at Christ's in 1931 he was told that a young fellow, C. P. Snow, knew something about cricket. He interrogated him forthwith: "Did I play? What sort of a performer was I?" Who would he have chosen as the captain for the 1930 Test Match? What would have been his strategy "if the selectors had decided that Snow was the man to save England?" Hardy thus ascertained that Snow would make a suitable companion for matches at Fenner's the following season. The young tended to be put more at ease by the classicist J. T. Sheppard, Provost of King's, "his face," according to Eric Hobsbawm hearing him lecture in

1937, " a cross between Buddha and Mr Pickwick in its all-embracing benignity". Another classicist, Benjamin Kennedy, was Regius Professor of Greek from 1867 until his death at eighty-five in 1889 and was known for his Latin Primer (first published in 1866 but much revised and improved by his daughters, Marion and Julia, for the new edition of 1888, although they receive no mention there.) Kennedy was remembered in less reverent light by M. R. James for his conduct as an examiner for university scholarships, when "he would enter the Senate House with a face like an apoplectic macaw and a give a very prolix notice," duplicating the written instructions about such matters as where candidates should write their names. From the 1920s onwards F. R. Leavis stimulated, outraged or dominated his pupils, many of whom, as teachers, carried his message and methods into the country's schools and newer universities. Such influence might be exerted in supervisions or on less formal occasions, as in the case of Sopwith of Trinity in Virginia Woolf's *Jacob's Room* (1922), who every evening

went on talking. Talking, talking, talking—as if everything could be talked—the soul itself slipped through the lips in thin silver disks which dissolve in young men's minds like silver, like moonlight. Oh, far away they'd remember it, and deep in dulness gaze back on it, and come to refresh themselves again... Sopwith went on talking; twining stiff fibres of awkward speech—things young men blurted out—plaiting them round his own smooth garland.

Another fictional don, Raphael Faber in the 1950s Cambridge of A. S. Byatt's *Still Life*, engages in more precise, more careful and analytical talk with the few who, like Frederica Potter, penetrate his rooms and attempt to penetrate his reserve. His main influence on undergraduates is presumably through his lectures. Frederica, not usually a lecture-goer, hears him speak on Names and Nouns in the poetry of Mallarmé:

His physical beauty was quite as startling as [she] had remembered it, a beauty that could have supported a series of theatrical gestures or impas-sioned recitals, neither of which he indulged in. He paced, evenly and regularly, from side to side of the dais as he talked, his eye fixed, not on his audience but on empty air, arguing passionately and quietly with himself, as though he was the only man in the room. This should have been dangerous but was not; his hearers were rapt.

A don whom Faber would sedulously have avoided, and who sounds distinctly more fictional than him, was Oscar Browning (1837-1923) of King's. He was a champion of academic reform and especially of the study of modern history, in which he held a lectureship from 1880, but was better known as the large, voluble, tricycling, self-absorbed "O. B." M. R. James, his colleague at King's, points out that "*the* O. B." was a later appellation. He irritated James and his fellow old Etonian undergraduates by harping on the injustice of his dismissal as an Eton housemaster in 1875 after allegations of too great intimacy with his pupils. A more venial fault was that he was not a good listener. In a representative scene in James' memoirs O. B. invites him to sit next to him in hall and tell him what he did during the vacation. As James does so "O.B. sits drumming with his fingers on the table and gazing before him with a lack-lustre eye." Soon "he breaks in, 'Oh, did you really? How very interesting' (pronounced 'veynsing'). 'Well, I - I - I -,' and for the rest of the meal there is a monologue." He was often, James concedes, kind to others and had some "big ideas", but the meal-time monologue was symptomatic of the man: "If once he could have pushed past the figure (of O. B.) which bulked so large before him, he might have been a great man." E. F. Benson, at least as perceptive about Browning and a little more generous, sums him up in *Our Family Affairs 1897-1896* (1920). When he entertained in his rooms,

however mixed and incongruous was the gathering, [he] never lost his own hospitable identity in the crowd; waving bottles of curious hock he would spur on the pianist to fresh deeds of violence, make some contribution to the discussion on Determinism, and promise to speak at the next debate at the Union, as he wandered from room to room, bald and stout and short yet imperial with his huge Neronian head, and his endless capacity for adolescent enjoyment... Everyone laughed at him, many disapproved of him, but for years he serenely remained the most outstanding and prominent personality in Cambridge. Had he had a little more wisdom to leaven the dough of his colossal cleverness, a little more prin-

cipled belief to give ballast to his friskiness, he would have been as essentially great as he was superficially grotesque.

James found O. B. particularly maddening at college business meetings: "Oh, the prolixity, the quarrelsomeness, the relentless plying of the grindstone for his own particular axe!" Another fellow of King's, J. E. Nixon, made the meetings even more impossible. According to James, he "behaved like an insane Jack-in-the-Box, and carried the passion for debate so far that on one occasion (perhaps more than one), after speaking for a motion that stood in his name and reducing the company to silent apathy, he claimed the right of reply. It was granted. He replied exhaustively to his own proposal" and even voted against it. To make matters worse, "his oratory was a little difficult to follow," since he was, it was said, capable of pronouncing "laboratory" in one syllable, "official sources" as "fish sauce" and "high opinion" as "hairpin". "How veynsing," O. B. might have replied before launching into his own monologue.

Supervisions

In modern times one of the principal means of teaching undergraduates has been the individual or small-group encounter called, in Cambridge, the "supervision". Today students are often required to hand in a weekly essay in advance of their supervision, but sometimes, as more often in the mid-twentieth century, they read it aloud. Debate, enlightened comment, or near-silence—oracular or embarrassing—may follow. Christopher Isherwood remembers reading his first essay to "the dreaded Mr. Gorse" in *Lions and Shadows* (1938):

The subject of the essay was: "Better England Free than England Sober". I had finished it with some pride: it exactly suited my idea of Mr. Gorse's requirements—snappy, epigrammatic, a bit daring in its language, sprinkled with witticisms borrowed unacknowledged from Mr. Holmes. Only now, for some reason, all my effects seemed to have gone wrong: the verbal fireworks were damp; the epigrams weren't epigrams but platitudes, pompous, painfully naive, inept and priggish. It was positive misery to have to utter them. I writhed with embarrassment, coughed, made spoonerisms.

In the last paragraph Gorse began drumming his fingers on the mantelpiece:

"Yes, yes..." he kept muttering: "Yes, yes..." as though his impatience were increasing with every word. "Well," he told me, when, at last, I had finished: "I'll say this for you—it's not the work of an entirely uneducated fool." He paused. I grinned hopelessly; regarding him like a poodle which is going to be kicked. "Look here, Isherwood," he appealed to me abruptly, "don't you yourself agree that it's all tripe?"

The methods and manner of Edward Welbourne, Master of Emmanuel between 1951 and 1964, had little in common with those of Gorse. Welbourne was an omnivorous reader and a great talker, a "cheerful, prejudiced, limited but uncommonly generous and illuminating old devil", according to his pupil Ronald Gray. Gray "heard tales" of Welbourne supervisions where "the final words might be shouted from the platform of a bus he had just boarded" and himself recalls vast sessions in which "it was normally sufficient to read just the first sentence" of an essay

to let loose the stream of paradox which flowed on undisturbed, except when he paused to munch moodily at a Marie biscuit. "Ah, well," he would say, before flinging himself into some bewildering non-sequitur, which somehow, through devious routes, brought him back to the main track. It was always brilliant, but frequently baffling... Looking at some notes which I attempted to take after one supervision (ostensibly on the Counter-Reformation), I find that we covered inter alia the childhood of Ribbentrop, the real story behind the building of the American railways, why London footmen were usually Irish, the origin of the Lyons Corner Houses, Luther's consumption of liver sausage and the religious significance of porridge. Somehow it all got back to the Council of Trent.

Downing College; F. R. Leavis

It took more than half a century to found Downing College. Sir George Downing, who made the original bequest, died in 1749, but as a result of complicated legal disputes the college was founded only in

1800. Building did not commence until 1807, after the plans of several rival architects had been considered. William Wilkins, a fellow of Caius who had travelled in Greece and Turkey and published *Magna Graecia*, eventually won the contract.

Wilkins' plan was ambitious and unlike that for any other college. Generous spaces replace enclosed courts in the first educational "campus". From the great Propylaeum leading, like that on the Acropolis in Athens, to the main edifices beyond, it would have been a Hellenist's dream. As Cinzia Maria Sicca explains in her study of the building of the college, *Committed to Classicism* (1987), Wilkins planned

> *thick plantations along the outer edges of the estate and huge, plain expanses of lawn at the centre, with hardly any trees at all; the college would thus have been isolated from the town, screened off from it. Once inside the belt of trees, however, the visitor would have been faced with the distant view of classical temples, unexpectedly rising from the ground, almost as if he had been transported to some remote plain in Greece, or to the Valley of the Temples in Sicily. The vision would have been imposing and moving, in a way that is entirely lost to us today.*

To realize even parts of this vision Wilkins had to struggle continually for funding. Not only was the new college not rich, but its Master and fellows often differed from the architect and each other over what should be built how and when. There were particular problems with William Frere, who became Master in 1812 and whose architectural priorities were so different from those of Wilkins that he built a piggery and a cattle-shed and used his lawn to graze his wife's flock of sheep.

By 1820, when the money ran out, Wilkins had succeeded in completing the east and west ranges. Partly because of the unfinished appearance, partly because of their different brand of neoclassicism—more Roman than Greek—a new generation of architects were distinctly unimpressed by the college. "Quadrangle too wide," noted Charles Robert Cockerell in his diary in 1822; "buildings too sunk, like a string of sausages." Charles Barry said that Downing put him off the Greeks he had once been happy to follow: "a Greek portico, exalted on a rock of Attica, was a very different thing from even its exact copy in the streets of London or the gardens of Cambridge." The Greek style was "comparatively cold and insipid... for modern purposes" and was "not sufficiently plastic". Mercifully, Wilkins had been dead for eight years by the time, in 1847, James Elmes expatiated on such coldness in the *Civil Engineer and Architect's Journal*: "Should the Emperor of Russia, in imitation of the Empress Catherine, erect another ice palace at St Petersburgh, no man could have executed the freezing task so well as the cold and chaste architect of Downing College." Essentially a scholar, lacking the true artist's "invention, and freedom from pedantry", his "was the very mummy of the art—as cold, as lifeless, and as much bound up by the bands of precedent."

The college, however, kept faith with Wilkins' ideal. Edward Middleton Barry was at last commissioned to continue and supplement the original plans in 1873. Later additions harmonize with Wilkins' work without copying it too closely: Alex T. Scott's early 1950s chapel, Bill Howell's modern but classically forceful Senior Combination Room, the unashamedly Doric portico of the early 1990s Maitland Robinson Library. Downing retains its generous spaces but no longer, as in the 1820s, seems like a string of sausages, a few buildings marooned in a sea of grass. Some people will agree with Hugh Casson that "the buildings stand to attention round the hollowed square, porticos and pediments denoting rank and importance. The eye looks for a flagpole, the ear strains for a bugle call." But the gravelled walks are better for contemplative strolling than for marching, the porticoes and pediments at least as much the echo of Wilkins' desire for classical purity—of the idealism appropriate to an academic foundation—as markers of rank and importance. Downing remains bracingly different in effect from all other Oxbridge colleges.

The best-known don to stride this hollowed square was F. R. Leavis (1895-1978). Indeed, he became so well-known that even Helen Fielding's Bridget Jones, a character singularly unlikely to have read his work, maintains (in the film version) that she has just been speaking to him on the phone. ("What, the F.R. Leavis ... who died in 1978?") Leavis would undoubtedly have disapproved of Helen Fielding, Bridget Jones, and the way in which I have introduced him. It is difficult to give an account that fairly balances Leavis' important position in

English literary criticism with the wealth of tales and sketches of twentieth-century Cambridge in which he fills such a curious, often such a comic role. His very seriousness, indeed, often informs the comedy. "He even had a serious way of being bald," as Clive James says, and "looked as if walking briskly had been something he had practised in a wind tunnel."

Leavis, initially under the influence of I. A. Richards, who later, like most of his colleagues, fell into disfavour, believed that civilization was under threat from the deadening, dehumanizing effects of mass culture. To learn critical discrimination is one way to combat this situation, and it relies on rigorous close reading, not vague literary history. It is the emphasis on close reading which is Leavis' (and Richards') most helpful legacy. Less acceptable in the long term was the concentration on practical criticism at the expense, often, of detailed understanding of the context of a work. Related to this, and more damaging, was Leavis' prescriptiveness and proscriptiveness, his promulgation of a canon and exclusion from it of many a book which before and since his time has interested, challenged and enthused readers: Milton was out, for instance, as was, for many years, Dickens apart from *Hard Times*. Inevitably, personal taste came into such decisions. And some kinds of literature respond better to Leavisite analysis than others: the concrete world of Keats was more to his taste than the evanescent mists, clouds, veils and waters of Shelley; inevitably he tended to prefer George Eliot's subtlety to Dickens' surrealism. The poet and critic Donald Davie, once a disciple, remembered the practical advantages of the canon for someone who needed to start earning a living from literature: every issue of *Scrutiny*, the magazine dominated by Leavis and his even more fiercely authoritative wife, Queenie, "made me a present of perhaps a dozen authors or books or whole periods and genres of literature which I not only need not, but should not read." Thus one could be spared much literature "and at the same time earn moral credit by the exemption."

Leavis felt strongly that he himself was the victim of exclusion. Although he had many disciples, his message was slow to gain acceptance. The Cambridge establishment was as yet unimpressed by the new English tripos, let alone Leavis' new take on how it should be taught. Clearly there was also some bias against his non-establishment background. Leavis' father's piano shop was the long, narrow building opposite Downing; at present it is a branch of Pizza Hut. Leavis was born above the earlier shop at 68 Mill Road. The father, Harry, was intelligent, well read, and politically radical. Both on those counts and as a tradesman he was distinctly not part of the public school and Anglican world from which most Cambridge dons of the day still emanated. Nevertheless Leavis studied at the Perse School and, after service in the First World War as a stretcher-bearer, at Emmanuel, where he initially read History before changing to English for Part Two. In a time when there were few academic posts to be had—but also because of bias against his uncompromising, original manner and ideas—he failed to gain full-time or permanent teaching posts for some years. A probationary lectureship at Emmanuel from 1927 was followed by appointment as Director of Studies in English at Downing in 1932 and a fellowship there in 1936. Further promotion was frequently blocked by his opponents, or made difficult by the number of enemies he continued to make.

Fuelled partly by their sense of injustice, the Leavises spent most of their careers at war not only with bad literature and sloppy reading, but with anyone who disagreed with them, including many former disciples. In Leavis' later years he attacked his opponents so savagely that, as Clive James observes, "he had no harsh words left over" for Stalin. Partly for this reason, and because of their dogged refusal, for all but brief periods, to leave ungrateful Cambridge, they became high-profile figures. In spite of the emphasis on allegedly objective, impersonal criticism, F. R. Leavis in particular was known as the upright, open-necked moralist on a bicycle, seriously bald, the "magnificent, acid, malevolently humorous little man who looks exactly like a bandy-legged leprechaun" whom Sylvia Plath heard lecture in 1955. For their aggressive exclusivity the Leavises became, F. L. Lucas felt, "tight-lipped Calvins of Art, teaching the young to love literature by first loathing nine-tenths of it." Their influence was great, and their vigorous pronouncements continue to stimulate debate.

St Catharine's College

St Catharine's, whose Main Court was built in reddish brick between 1675 and 1757, is a far cry from the bright neoclassical spaces of Downing. The court replaced the buildings put up after the foundation of the college in 1473. It had been a "mean structure" according to John Evelyn in 1654. The later structure is less mean: Main Court, closed off from Trumpington Street only by elegant iron railings added in 1779, is unassuming, sober rather than austere, presenting, for Hugh Casson, a "mild, modest and rosy face". This is not, it is true, quite the way it struck the restless, troubled undergraduate Malcolm Lowry in 1930, when, writing to his American mentor Conrad Aiken, he compared St Catharine's to a barracks and its dining-hall to a mortuary.

Lowry was taught, initially, by Tom Henn (1901-74), a don as different from Leavis as is St Catharine's from Downing. Henn, a Yeats scholar (himself originally from Sligo), approached literature in a more romantic, impressionistic, at times more mystical spirit than the analytical Leavis. (A. S. Byatt contrasts their lecturing style: "Dr Henn weeping with his head on the lectern over the fate of Lear, Dr Leavis, with two fastidious fingers depositing a copy of *Early Victorian Novelists* [by Lord David Cecil] in the waste paper basket and exhorting his audience to do likewise.") Henn's qualities seem to have been lost on Lowry, and the feeling was mutual. Henn many years later recalled him as "withdrawn, slow-spoken, and rather idle". Lowry soon stopped coming to his supervisions, rarely appeared at the weekly gatherings Henn hosted in college, and did not share his enthusiasm for rowing. Henn was equally unenthusiastic about his pupil's writing. But on the whole Lowry had little time to worry about what he thought of his teachers or they of him: he drank hard, socialized at times, sang his poems while accompanying himself on the ukulele (which he also played in the 1932 Footlights show *Laughing at Love*), told seaman's tales, listened to jazz records, and worked on his novel *Ultramarine*. In 1933 he was allowed to submit a 5,000-word section of the novel as part of his tripos. On the strength of it he was judged to have done just enough to obtain a third-class degree. "He would," said Henn, like many another long-suffering teacher or don, "have done much better if he had worked." Cambridge resurfaces, ambivalently, in Lowry's later work. In *Under the Volcano* (1947), from the distance of Mexico and through an alcoholic haze, emerges a place whose

fountains in moonlight and closed courts and cloisters, whose enduring beauty in its virtuous remote self-assurance, seemed part, less of the loud mosaic of one's stupid life there, though maintained perhaps by the count-less deceitful memories of such lives, than the strange dreams of some old monk, eight hundred years dead, whose forbidding house, reared upon piles and stakes driven into the marshy ground, had once shone like a beacon out of the mysterious silence, and solitude of the fens. A dream jeal-ously guarded: Keep off the Grass. And yet whose unearthly beauty compelled one to say: God forgive me.

Peter Hall, an undergraduate at St Catharine's from 1950, has fonder memories of Tom Henn than had Lowry twenty years earlier:

His rooms were filled with pipe-smoke. I remember him dressed in baggy tweeds in an environment that was more like a country gentleman's study than a Cambridge don's. Fly-fishing rods and double-barrelled guns nestled alongside the letters of Maud Gonne and the journals of Lady Gregory.

Hall wisely failed to mention to Henn that he was a keen attender at Leavis' lectures. But although Leavis had a much greater influence on him, he remembers at least one example of Henn's distinctive teaching method: when elucidating an image in a poem by Yeats, "'Have you ever,' he intoned, 'made love—to a girl—in a cave?' Since we had never made love to anybody, in a cave or anywhere else, we shifted in our seats uncomfortably. Men outnumbered women in Cambridge at the time by eight to one."

Henn, a friend of the don and director "Dadie" Rylands of King's, seems usually to have got on well with the actors among his pupils. Sir Ian McKellen came up in 1958, five years after Sir Peter Hall went down. At McKellen's interview Henn asked him to read some poetry and he leapt onto a chair to recite Henry V's "Once more unto the breach..." How far this panache helped him to win an "exhibition" to the college—a form of scholarship—is unrecorded.

McKellen acted at school, at Cambridge and thereafter. An earlier man of the theatre, James Shirley (1596-1666), came to St Catharine's, it seems, with every intention of pursuing a career in the church. He had studied first at St John's College, Oxford but left, it is alleged, because the Master, William Laud, told him that a large mole on his face would prohibit him from entering holy orders. In spite of Laud, and equipped with a Cambridge degree, Shirley was ordained and became a schoolmaster for several years. This career is supposed to have ended when he converted to Catholicism in 1624. He then became, between 1625 and the closing of the theatres in 1642, one of the best-known London playwrights: author of tragedies of bloody revenge in Italy and comedies of fashionable society in the nascent West End. He served as a royalist in the Civil War before returning to school teaching, drawing more directly now on his Cambridge education. Tradition reports that he died after fleeing his house during the Great Fire of London. He is commemorated in the name of the college literary society, the Shirley Society.

Trinity Hall

Trinity Hall was founded in 1350 by William Bateman, Bishop of Norwich. The full name was "the College of Scholars of the Holy Trinity of Norwich". His stated aims for the college included the promotion of civil and canon law and the benefiting of the commonwealth, "especially of our church and diocese of Norwich". An unstated aim was probably to train priests—and priests well qualified in law—to replace some of the many who had died in Bateman's diocese during the Black Death. The legal emphasis remained strong, and was perpetuated by the London connections of many college fellows; between the late sixteenth and early nineteenth century Trinity Hall effectively controlled Doctors' Commons (the familiar name for the College of Doctors and Advocates of the Court of Arches). The chapel includes memorials to such senior legal figures as John Cowell, Master of Trinity Hall and Regius Professor of Law, who died in 1611. In 1932 G. M. Trevelyan could still talk about "The famous legal and boating college, Trinity Hall". Naturally enough, the interests of the modern college have broadened.

The front court was built in the fourteenth century but thoroughly classicized in the eighteenth, most conspicuously when the walls were faced, in the early 1740s, with six-inch-thick ashlar. Pevsner finds the court "comfortable and a little phlegmatic, an excellent visual representation of what the University then was." It is perhaps a little more exciting than that: harmonious, compact, all of a piece. (The east range, however, was rebuilt after a fire in 1852.) The Screens passage, beneath the white and gold painted cupola, leads to Library Court. The Old Library, a long two-storey building in red brick with stepped gables (c.1590-1600), looks much earlier than the first court. The small oak door at original first-floor level, and with no stair, seems to invite readers absorbed in their studies to fall, gowns billowing, into what is now a capacious and well-stocked flower bed; in fact, until about the mid-eighteenth century the door opened on to a walkway on top of a wall which led to the Master's Lodge. In 1998 the new part-timbered Jerwood Library opened next to, and with wonderful views of, the river.

The Fellows' Garden was what particularly impressed Henry James in the 1870s:

If I were called upon... to mention the prettiest corner of the world, I should draw out a thoughtful sigh and point the way to the garden of Trinity Hall... The little garden at Trinity Hall is narrow and crooked; it leans upon the river, from which a low parapet, all muffled in ivy, divides it; it has an ancient wall adorned with a thousand matted creep-

ers on one side, and on the other a group of extraordinary horse-chestnuts.
The trees are of prodigious size; they occupy half the garden, and are
remarkable for the fact that their giant limbs strike down into the earth,
take root again and emulate, as they rise, the majesty of the parent stem.

There are still horse-chestnuts. Here it would be pleasant to linger as what Robert Runcie, Dean of Trinity Hall between 1956 and 1960, described as "an acceptable college codger".

Avoiding the temptation to become such a codger (someone who did a great deal of teaching but failed to write the "big book" which would win promotion), Runcie soon moved on to become Principal of Cuddesdon Theological College, near Oxford, the next stage on the route to appointment as Archbishop of Canterbury in 1980. (His elevation was celebrated in stained glass by John Heywood in the antechapel at Trinity Hall.)

Leslie Stephen at Trinity Hall

Moving on had been more painful, if also liberating, for Leslie Stephen, who had become a fellow of the college, where he had also been an undergraduate, at the age of twenty-two in 1854. He taught mathematics, participated enthusiastically in the college boat club—he was a pioneer of the closer relationship between dons and students—and climbed mountains in the vacations. He thus went some way to disprove the view of Burnand, founder of the Amateur Dramatic Club, that "There is no such creature, properly speaking, as a young Don. If any man is a Don by Nature, he is never young." Dons who helped the ADC, of course, were an exceptional class, not "Dons by Nature".

As required by his job, and out of deference to the views of his father Sir James Stephen, Professor of History at Cambridge, Leslie Stephen was ordained deacon in 1855 and priest in 1859. The unusually long gap between the two stages suggests a certain reluctance, although it seems only to have been after 1859 that Stephen began to become aware of his own lack of religious belief. In 1860 he decided that he could no longer conduct chapel services, although the college managed to keep him on as a fellow. He left for London, literary criticism, and agnosticism at the end of 1864, although he did not formally renounce holy orders for another decade.

Religion, however, was only one factor in Stephen's comparative disillusionment with Cambridge. Soon after his departure he published a series of "Sketches from Cambridge", by "a Don", in the *Pall Mall Gazette*. These sketches, reissued as a book later in 1865, amount to a fairly outspoken attack on the university education of the time, although the pill is sugared by the ironic and often humorous tone. A don in old times "was allowed professedly to confine his labours to the consumption of port. It was a sufficient and a creditable occupation." But "if you wish at once to do nothing and to be respectable nowadays, the best pretext is to be at work on some profound study; it is not necessary that your performance should ever get beyond a publisher's list... An intention to write a book on classics or on theology makes a don fancy himself, and be supposed by others, to be hard at work." Later Stephen concedes that some college fellows, and more private tutors, are working hard at their teaching. But what they are teaching, he makes abundantly clear, is not worth the effort. Mathematics has its own appeal—its "special merit is that you can sit in your own room and spin it like a spider out of your own inside without ever even looking out of the window"—but this is not the reason given by the university for making it a compulsory subject. Mathematics and Classics are, it is claimed, good training for young minds; after three years of hard labour on these subjects, students will find anything else comparatively easy. But, says Stephen, most students' studies are actually motivated by tradition, the desire for glory, and the desire for money (a career as a lawyer, or a college fellowship for instance). What is studied at Cambridge is of direct use only to those few who "reach the top of the tree"; most of the rest aim simply to be "last among those not actually disqualified". Their tutors cram them with material they will soon forget. Teaching them is like "putting a cart-horse in training for the Derby."

Even with its faults, however, Cambridge retained attractions for Stephen. The last sentence of *Sketches* claims that he has enjoyed so many pleasant hours in the university "under its present constitution, that I feel a conservative shrinking from any proposals of change." Of course, the sentence further draws attention to the problem: reform is moving too slowly, not least because even the anonymous, liberal-minded "Don" who is purportedly writing the sketches finds change difficult. Stephen's attitude to Cambridge remained ambivalent; visiting for the annual college audit in December 1866 he told his future wife Minny Thackeray, the novelist's daughter, that he wanted to get away from "this dreary, foggy flat". But his continuing ambivalence was as much about his own probably manic-depressive nature as about Cambridge. In London he edited the *Cornhill Magazine* and the *Dictionary of National Biography* and wrote such authoritative works as *The English Utilitarians,* but rarely found personal happiness for long—not helped by the early death of Minny in 1875 and of his second wife, Julia Duckworth, in 1895. In some moods he became the Mr Ramsay of *To the Lighthouse,* by his and Julia's daughter Virginia Woolf: overbearing, selfish, morbidly sensitive about his own feelings and ruthlessly insensitive to the feelings of others; a sad contrast with the young and popular fellow of Trinity Hall.

CHAPTER FIVE

Cambridge Churches and Religion

The Venerable Bede's Latin *Ecclesiastical History* (c. 731) tells the story of an early excursion to Cambridge. Æthelthryth, wife of King Ecgfrith of Northumbria, but so holy that she would not consummate the marriage, persuaded him that she should withdraw from her queenly duties and enter a convent. Soon she became Abbess at Ely (she was of East Anglian stock), where she built a monastery. When she died, in 679, she was buried, like any other of her nuns, in a wooden coffin. But sixteen years later her sister Seaxburh, now Abbess, decided to move her bones into the church. Seaxburh sent out a group of monks to find blocks of stone to make a suitable container. (Ely, Bede explains for the benefit of those accustomed to less soggy lands, "is surrounded by waters and marshes and has no big stones.") And so they got into a boat and went "to a certain small, deserted fortress... which, in the English tongue, is called *Grantacæstir*"—Cambridge—where, near the walls, "they soon found a coffin made beautifully of white marble," complete with lid. It was very probably a Roman sarcophagus. Realizing that the Lord had directed their trip, the monks returned to Ely. The coffin fitted the miraculously uncorrupted body of Æthelthryth to perfection.

Once the "fortress" or "small city" (the *Civitatula* that gives its name to John Holloway's long poem about Cambridge of 1993) had developed into a thriving market-town, it supplied Ely, where a cathedral grew up around the tombs of the Saxon abbesses, not merely with marble containers but with a good income. The Bishops of Ely exercised considerable authority over the medieval town, and Cambridge remains, much bigger than Ely though it now is, part of its diocese. Trading success and the availability of more dry land early made parish churches a commoner feature of Cambridge. At St Bene't's

(Benedict's) Church the tower and its arch survive from about 1040, and the otherwise Victorian St Giles', on Castle Hill, has re-used the original chancel arch of about 1092 in the south aisle. Roughly opposite St Giles' is the small, plain St Peter's, near enough collapse to be almost completely rebuilt in the late eighteenth century, but containing an eleventh-century font, carved with double-tailed fish-men or tritons. As Nicholas Ray says in his guide to Cambridge architecture, the tritons are "representative of that combination of wild imagination and geometrical discipline which characterises the best of medieval art."

Church-building went on apace. A fifteenth-century Scot called John Major would, as a student at Cambridge, lie awake most of the night during the great festivals to hear the melody of the bells. Among the churches were St Botolph's, built near the Trumpington Gate (Botolph was a patron of travellers), whose present nave is mostly fourteenth-century, and St Clement's and St Michael's, dating, with later additions, from roughly the same period. (St Michael's now houses the Michaelhouse Café but also preserves intact the chancel or Hervey de Stanton Chapel, named after the founder of Michaelhouse, a college later absorbed into Trinity.) A Norman building that was the chapel of a leper hospital survives mostly unaltered off Newmarket Road, once well outside Cambridge. The Leper Chapel, or St Mary Magdalene, then served as a local church before becoming—the reason for its survival—a storehouse and servery for the annual Stourbridge Fair. The Augustinian canons were granted extensive lands at Barnwell—the name comes from a well where pagan worship had once taken place—in the twelfth century. Barnwell Priory was capacious enough to accommodate Richard II and his parliament in 1388. What remains is the restored thirteenth-century Abbey church of St Andrew the Less on Newmarket Road; stone in the walls and grounds of Abbey House (completed in 1678) in Beche and Abbey Roads; and, alone on a small green mound amid much later housing, a squat thirteenth-century building with bricked-up windows, known traditionally as the Cellarers' Chequer, on the corner of Priory and Beche Roads. (As some of the names suggest, the Priory became, in local memory, an abbey.)

Cambridge was significantly involved in the Reformation: all three of the future Protestant bishops and martyrs Cranmer, Latimer and

Ridley spent their early career here. They died at Oxford; in Cambridge itself the Marian persecution was visited on John Hullier of King's College, who in 1556 was condemned to burn on what is now Jesus Green. According to John Foxe, his friends tried to shorten his suffering by giving him bags of gunpowder, but it ignited only after his death. This at least, says Foxe, gave him a chance to die the death of a true Protestant martyr: books were cast into the flames "and by chance a communion book fell between his hands, who received it joyfully, opened it, and read so long till the force of the flame and smoke caused him that he could see no more."

Other Christian movements came and went; some of them are talked about in the sections which follow. There was a synagogue in Cambridge by 1778. The congregation, whose numbers increased greatly once the Religious Test Acts of 1871 enabled Jews, along with other non-Anglicans, to take degrees, met at various addresses until 1937, when the present synagogue in Thompson's Lane was completed. The mosque in Mawson Road, the Abu Bakr Siddiq Islamic Centre, was established in 1982; the number of Muslims in Cambridge rose from under a hundred in the early 1970s to over 20,000 by 2000. Other religions are represented by various community groups and university societies.

The Round Church

The Church of the Holy Sepulchre, known as the Round Church, was based originally, in about 1130, on the Holy Sepulchre in Jerusalem. It was extended in the fourteenth and fifteenth centuries. Early antiquarians were interested by the unusual shape of the church—there are few other round churches in England—but found it on the whole not to their liking. In 1781 the architect James Essex told the Society of Antiquaries that whoever designed the building "knew something of proportions though he wanted taste"; lacking that judgement vouchsafed to men of a later age, he gave such proportions "as were calculated to make it appear more like a castle than a church on the outside, and heavy and gloomy within."

By the early 1840s attitudes had changed markedly. The reformers of the Cambridge Camden Society dreamed of restoring the building to what they saw as its original twelfth-century purity. Their opportunity came because the church was in a state of near-collapse. Externally the most conspicuous aspect of the early Victorian overhaul, undertaken for the society by Anthony Salvin, was the replacement of the fifteenth-century sixteen-sided tower with a conical roof, which makes it, for Anne Stevenson, like a mushroom in a forest "of Gothic and traffic" ("Coming Back to Cambridge", 1971). More controversial at the time, however, was the substitution for the wooden communion table, in the absence and against the will of the traditionally Protestant incumbent, of a stone altar and credence table. These were, Rev. Faulkner pronounced, "abominable pieces of superstition and Popery".

Nicholas Ray argues that, rebuilt or not, the interior of the Round Church remains a good place to admire "the space and structure of Norman architecture... [T]he ring of vaults held on massive masonry is weighty, solid and reassuring, while at the same time, because of the circular plan and the changing diagonal views that that permits, spatially complex and subtle."

Great St Mary's and Market Hill

There has been a church on this site in the middle of Cambridge since the thirteenth century or earlier. The extant building is mainly late fifteenth- and early sixteenth-century and was designed very probably, like much of King's College chapel, by John Wastell. The tower, begun in 1491, was finished after many delays, and without the intended spire, in the early seventeenth century. The spectacular view takes in most of Cambridge. The interior, built in clunch stone and darkened by galleries put up in the eighteenth century, has had fewer admirers than the light Weldon limestone exterior. Many

Victorian alterations including a heavy reredos were removed in the 1950s, rendering the chancel, as Lynne Broughton says in the useful book about the church co-edited by the present vicar, Rev. Dr John Binns, "uncluttered and austere, some might say bare and unsympathetic; it is unquestionably a work of the 1950s." Its most striking feature is the golden *Majestas* or Christ in Majesty, designed by George Pace and made by Alan Durst in 1959-60.

Great St Mary's, although it functions as a parish church with its own congregation and services, is also the University Church. University sermons are delivered here during term-time. Until the building of the Senate House in the eighteenth century disputations and many public ceremonies took place in the church, and for centuries the main university chest and documents were kept here. (The chest was looted in the town uprising of 1381. In Susanna Gregory's medieval detective novel *An Unholy Alliance* (1996) Matthew Bartholomew of Michaelhouse must find out who fitted it with a fiendish poisoned blade.)

One of the most infamous public episodes at St Mary's was the exhumation in January 1557 of the body of the leading German Protestant Martin Bucer, who had died in 1551 after a brief period as Regius Professor of Divinity. Under Mary I the Catholic authorities decreed that while Bucer was buried here and his fellow reformer Paul Fagius nearby at St Michael's, parishioners could neither take communion nor bury their own dead. The offending dead were condemned to be burnt for heresy. Foxe's *Acts and Monuments* (or *Book of Martyrs*) records that the reformers' coffins were taken to the market-place and there tied to a stake with a long iron chain. It was market day and so "a great multitude of country folk" were present. Learning that the condemned men were already dead, the country folk "partly detested and abhorred the extreme cruelty of the commissioners toward the rotten carcases, and partly laughed at their folly in making such preparature," for, they said, treating the commissioners to some of their rustic Tudor irony, "it was not to be feared that they would run away." Once the Elizabethan regime was established there was a solemn service of restitution during which "many of the university... beset the walls of the church and the church porch on both sides with verses" in Latin, Greek and English, "in the which they made a manifest declaration, how they were minded both toward Bucer and Phagius." People attached less formal prayers and thoughts to the railings outside the church during the run-up to the Iraq war in the early months of 2003.

After the upheavals of the 1550s life at the church returned to a more even keel. Among those buried here were not just doctors and divines but, in 1614, Michael Woolf, churchwarden and landlord of the Rose, whose memorial wall-brass in the north aisle is aptly illustrated with a rose. Later, concerts of sacred music began. "Never tumble from a church window, during service" was the moral Byron extracted from the experience of trying to get down in the middle of *The Messiah* in 1807, tearing, in the process, "a woeful rent in my best black silk gown" and damaging "an egregious pair of breeches".

The market-place, where the reformers' bodies were burnt and where many of Michael Woolf's customers must have traded, has always stood close to Great St Mary's. It was much larger then than now, L-shaped and including markets for cheese, butter, meat, fruit and vegetables (whence the street-name "Peas Hill"). A fire in 1849 destroyed much of the area and allowed its remodelling. The bag issued by the market traders more recently proclaims—a veritable poem in plastic—the variety of goods available today:

Antiques Bags Boots Vegetables Bicycles
Tea & Coffee Boaters Cakes Shoes Fish
Furniture Socks Apples Apricots Shirts Old Books
New Books Sweets Leather Goods Pet Food
Ethnic Clothes Fashionable Clothes Boxers 2nd
Hand Clothes Wicker Work Beefeaters Bacon
Policeman's Helmets Hats Scarves Craft Flowers
Wholefood Puppets Pottery Bike Repairs CDs
Tapes Thermal Vests Records Coats Sweaters
Hand Made Jewellery Kippers Rucksacks Posters
Knickers Vests Moccasins Woolly Jumpers
Cheese Dolls' Houses Games Flowers Sausages
Suitcases Old Clothes Baskets Sheepskin Rugs
Indian Throws T Shirts Jogging Bottoms
Monkfish Daffodils Pot Plants Old Phones
Organic Food Yams Sunglasses...

At one end of Market Hill (S. C. Roberts' explanation of this surprising term is probably the best: "'Hill' signifies simply a rise in the ground above the level of the adjoining fen") looms the Guildhall. It was built, on the site of its predecessors, in 1938-9, when it was rather mysteriously hailed by the Cambridge Preservation Society as "an important contribution to the dignity of the town". It might politely be described as "of its time". Some pleasant older buildings survive, however, on the east side of the square.

Little St Mary's

The anonymous preface to Richard Crashaw's collection of 1646 explains that:

> We style his Sacred Poems, Steps to the Temple, and aptly, for in the Temple of God, under his wing, he led his life in St. Mary's Church near St. Peter's College. There he lodged under Tertullian's roof of angels; there he made his nest more gladly than David's swallow near the House of God; where like a primitive saint, he offered more prayers in the night, than others usually offer in the day; there, he penned these poems, Steps for happy souls to climb heaven by.

Some saw his activities in a different light. Another anonymous author says that his reported Popish veneration of an icon of the Virgin is "the rather probable because his practices in Little St Mary's, where he is Curate, are superstitious." When the iconoclast Dowsing visited the church in 1643, "We brake down sixty superstitious pictures, some popes and crucifixes, with God the Father sitting in a chair with a Globe in his hand."

The decorated tracery of the east window of the church, installed just before the original St Peter's Church was re-consecrated as St Mary the Less in 1352, is one of the features which survived Dowsing. There is a small crypt, now the chapel of the Holy Angels and All Souls, on the south side near the altar. The body of the church is unusually whole and harmonious; there is, exceptionally, no division between nave and chancel. It was restored by Sir George Gilbert Scott in 1857-62. The rather heavy carved wooden reredos installed by his son the younger George Gilbert Scott now stands at the west end; at the east end it was replaced by Sir Ninian Comper's lighter work in 1913.

Crashaw is commemorated in his own verse, inscribed on the doors of the South Chapel:

Let hearts and lips speak loud; and say
Hail, door of life; and source of day!
The door was shut, the fountain seal'd,
Yet light was seen and life revealed.

Little St Mary's is, the poet would no doubt have been pleased to know, the principal High Anglican or Anglo-Catholic church in the city.

St Edward's

The Church of St Edward, King and Martyr, built mostly in the fourteenth and fifteenth centuries, has one of Cambridge's quiet, small garden graveyards. (Another runs beside St Botolph's and there is a particularly attractive example behind Little St Mary's.) But the associations of the church have not always been peaceful. The eponymous Edward met a violent death, if one resulting from Saxon political intrigue rather than religious difference. And three sixteenth-century reformers, who can more reasonably be called martyrs, preached from the small, dark oaken pulpit, constructed in about 1510. Robert Barnes, Thomas Bilney and Hugh Latimer, while far from agreeing with each other on every doctrinal detail, had strong enough beliefs to bring each of them to the stake. Barnes, an Augustinian friar turned Lutheran, was burned at Smithfield in 1540. Bilney perished in the same way in Norwich in 1531, as would Latimer, under Mary Tudor's Catholic regime, at Oxford in 1555.

It was in Cambridge that, in happier days, the reformers came together. Latimer, who was a fellow of Clare, remembered in a sermon preached many years later how his relationship with Bilney, then a fellow of Trinity Hall, developed. (The church had been designated a "peculiar" of these two colleges in the fifteenth century; the south and north aisles of the chancel functioned originally as their chapels.) Until 1524 Latimer "was as obstinate a papist as any was in England." Bilney, hearing him speak publicly against Protestantism, with, it seemed to him, more zeal than knowledge, came to Latimer's study and asked him to hear his confession. "I did so; and, to say the truth, by his confession I learned more than before in many years. So from that time forward I began to smell the word of God, and forsook the school-doctors"—St Thomas Aquinas and his ilk—"and such fooleries". The two men subsequently worked together in hospitals and prisons and, according to Foxe's *Book of Martyrs*, "used much to confer together, insomuch that the place where they most used to walk in the fields was called long after them Heretics' Hill." The fields in question remain unidentified, but the White Horse, one of the main places where, says Foxe, the "learned in Christ flocked together in open sight" in the 1520s, occupied a site between King's and St Catharine's, roughly where King's Lane is now.

At St Edward's in December 1529 Latimer preached his famous "Card Sermon". Like the occupants of many a modern pulpit, he had a metaphor to hand: "whereas you are wont to celebrate Christmas in playing at cards," he told his congregation, "I intend... to deal unto you Christ's cards... The game that we will play at shall be called the triumph [the name of a game like whist], which if it be played well at, he that dealeth shall win; the players shall likewise win, and the standers and lookers upon shall do the same..." The theology of the cards is developed in a manner (and at a length) little to modern taste. But the main thrust of the sermon was evidently anti-Catholic. Dr Robert Buckenham of the Dominican friars came to St Edward's to preach in refutation of Latimer's points; he made use of some handy metaphorical dice. Latimer in turn delivered a second "card" sermon virtually in Buckenham's teeth: the friar sat "directly in the face of Latimer underneath the pulpit", and had to endure some pointed comments about the "figurative signification ... when they paint a fox preaching out of a friar's cowl." Buckenham, declares Foxe, "with this sermon... was so dashed that never after he durst peep out of the pulpit against Latimer."

Twenty-six years later, as Latimer faced his appalling death, he turned to his fellow sufferer with words that resonated much longer than his attacks on foxy friars: "Be of good comfort, Master Ridley, and play the man. We shall this day light such a candle by God's grace in England, as I trust shall never be put out." As Latimer was aware, "one suffering for the Truth turneth more than a thousand sermons."

In the twentieth century St Edward's commemorated Latimer and Bilney in the south aisle windows. In keeping with the church's Reformation credentials there is also a 1940s slate memorial, in the south aisle of the chancel, to two of the translators of the 1611 Authorised or King James version of the Bible, Edward Lively (Regius Professor of Hebrew) and Richard Thompson (fellow of Clare). Earlier memorials, however, record members of a wide range of professions outside—although often no doubt ministering to—the colleges. The "speaking stone" of the lawyer William Beck, who died in 1614, offers counsel as once he did in life, although now it is in verse and has a Christian tenor. There are several instances of increasing social mobility by the late eighteenth and early nineteenth century. A memorial near the restored fifteenth-century font records Lydia Gillam, whose father was a London solicitor and whose husband was Edward Gillam, "Cheese-Factor of this parish". Edward's second wife, Mary, was the daughter of a clergyman. Another member of the family was a saddler. Edmund Lunn, one might unkindly conclude, was above such activities: he goes down to posterity as only "many years a respectable inhabitant of this parish". ("Respectable", when Lunn died in 1813, was for the most part a term of simple praise—worthy of respect.)

College Chapel

During nineteenth-century services college "markers" went round with attendance registers, pricking the names of those present with a pin. Non-attenders were subject to fines. In fact, J. M. F. Wright maintains in his Trinity memoir *Alma Mater* (1827), the whole point of weekday chapel is "to see that all men are in college." Nobody, even the truly devout, goes there to pray. "In the morning," the students "muster with all the reluctance of a man going to be hanged; and in the evening, although now awake, and enlivened with the convivialities of the bottle, there is much the same feeling." Fellows, at least in the eighteenth and early nineteenth century, rarely felt obliged to join their charges at these musters. Clearly this attitude did not foster religious devotion or respect for the church; it encouraged, in at least some of the many undergraduates who would go on to be ordained, a cynical or perfunctory approach to their own ministry. "Be wise," counsels William Wordsworth, who was at St John's in the late 1780s,

> *Ye Presidents and Deans, and to your bells*
> *Give seasonable rest, for 'tis a sound*
> *Hollow as ever vexed the tranquil air;*
> *And your officious doings bring disgrace*
> *On the plain steeples of our English Church,*
> *Whose worship, 'mid remotest village trees,*
> *Suffers for this.*

Presidents and Deans were slow to take the point. In most colleges compulsory chapel survived until at least the First World War.

Theological Colleges

In the later nineteenth century a new seriousness about the training of the clergy resulted in the setting up of institutions by various denominations. Ridley Hall, next to Newnham College, opened in 1881 and caters for Evangelical Anglicans, serving, according to its Deed of Trust, the Protestant Reformed Church of England. It works closely with other members of the Cambridge Theological Federation, including the Anglican Westcott House, which was founded in 1881 by Brooke Foss Westcott (1825-1901), Regius Professor of Divinity and later Bishop of Durham; since the 1890s it has been based in Jesus Lane, around an attractive garden maintained by the Principal and students. One of the best known tutors at Westcott is a Roman Catholic, Lavinia Byrne, who in 2000 left the Institute of the Blessed Virgin following the hostile Vatican reaction to her book *Woman at the Altar*. Other members of the federation are Wesley House, for Methodists, on the other side of Jesus Lane (founded in 1921) and Westminster College (United Reformed) in Madingley Road, which was founded as a Presbyterian college in London in 1844 and moved to Cambridge in 1899.

St Edmund's College, formerly St Edmund's House, began in 1896 as a hostel for Roman Catholic priests and students. In 1965 it became a graduate college of the university (with full collegiate status from 1985). Catholic services continue in the chapel, but students are now drawn from a wide range of faith backgrounds. A huge tower (1992) is the most prominent feature of the already rather military-looking St Edmund's.

Three Nineteenth-Century Churches: Christ Church, All Saints, St Andrew the Great

The 1868 edition of the *New Cambridge Guide* lists the new churches built for the growing population of Barnwell, which was increasingly red-brick and no longer the spacious land of Priory buildings, fish-ponds and fields. Christ Church (consecrated 1839) in Newmarket Road, was "a spacious building of very peculiar outline and appearance, and erected more with a view of accommodating a large number, than with any regard to architectural taste or ritual propriety." But, the author concedes, it "has proved a great blessing to the thickly populated district in which it is situated."

As new churches appeared, the old were often remodelled or even demolished. All Saints in the Jewry, opposite St John's, impeded traffic because it projected too far into the street and was accordingly removed in 1865. (It was also felt to be too small.) What was once the graveyard, where now a regular craft market takes place, is marked by Basil Champneys' memorial cross of 1882 and is rendered strikingly beautiful, especially in winter, by the white trunks of its silver birches. Next door Champneys was also, in 1878-9, the architect of the red-brick, much-statued and currently disused Selwyn Divinity School. The congregation transferred to the new All Saints in Jesus Lane, now maintained by the Churches Conservation Trust, a superb example of the work of George Frederick Bodley. He wanted to create something like an Early English church of the fourteenth century. With this aim in mind, he employed Morris and Company, his fellow enthusiasts for the medieval (as conceived in the 1860s) to decorate the church. Bodley himself and other like-minded artists were also involved, then and later. The walls are stencilled in patterns (canopies and crowns below, pods and flowers of *planta genista* or broom above) of deep green, dark yellow, blue, and a range of reds—a darker, more sober equivalent to the Morris wallpapers. There is a pulpit (c.1875) painted with saints in gold and blue, and a wood-ribbed painted ceiling. And there is some good stained glass, both from the 1860s and later. The east window, designed mainly by Edward Burne-Jones, includes some work by Ford Madox Brown and by William Morris himself. Morris' vigorous, bearded St Peter (centre, second row up) has a distinct resemblance to the artist. The church also possesses what Edward Baty, taking up a familiar Oxford term, has called "Cambridge's sole spire worthy of the adjective 'dreaming'".

St Andrew the Great, unlike All Saints, remained on site, but it was rebuilt in 1842-3 by Poynter in what the *New Cambridge Guide* considered "the poorest and most unsatisfactory modern perpendicular style". The interior is more congenial than the undistinguished outside may suggest. As at All Saints, a number of memorials were transferred from the old church. The most noticeable, near the west end, states the sad facts of the life of Elizabeth, widow of Captain James Cook, the explorer. She not only outlived her husband by fifty-six years but also, over a period of fifteen years, lost three of her sons. Two died at sea and one, of scarlet fever, as a student at Christ's College.

Nonconformists

One day in 1646 George Fox was walking in a field when "the Lord opened unto me, 'that being bred at Oxford or Cambridge, was not enough to fit and qualify men to be ministers of Christ'." Fox "stranged" at this information, "because it was the common belief of people." But he soon saw the Lord's point, especially given the unhelpful response of the clergy, including his local man "Priest Stephens", to his "sorrows, grief and troubles" over the last few years. "What then should I follow such for?" Instead, he decided, he would rely "wholly on the Lord Jesus Christ". Having followed that vocation for nine years, founded the Society of Friends, travelled widely and endured much persecution, in 1655 Fox spent a night in Cambridge, joint-breeder of the Anglican priesthood. His reception was, in a sense, warm: "when I came into the town the scholars were up hearing of me: and were exceeding rude: but I kept on my horseback and rid through them in the Lord's power... The miners and colliers and cart men could never be ruder." When, amid continuing jeering and roughness from the young gentlemen, he reached his inn:

> the people of the house asked me what I would have for supper as is the usual way of inns. "Supper?" said I. "Were it not that the Lord's power was over [us], these rude scholars looked as if they would make a supper of us: and pluck us to pieces": for they knew I was so against their trade: which they were there as apprentices to learn the trade of preaching [and

therefore they] raged as bad as ever Diana's craftsmen did against Paul [Acts 19:24-41].

Slipping through the streets unrecognized ("it was darkish"), Fox managed to have a "fine meeting", the Quaker equivalent of a service, at the house of the mayor, Samuel Spalding. He spent the night there and took the precaution, whether divinely or practically inspired, of ordering "my horse to be ready saddled by the sixth hour in the morning and so we passed out of town and the Lord's power came over all: and the destroyers were frustrated the next morning for they thought I would have stayed in the town and they thought to have done mischief." The sixth hour was, apparently, too early for students even with such a good excuse to run riot.

Persecution of Quakers continued with such incidents as soldiers being sent to smash up the meeting house—a private house in Jesus Lane, thought to be on the site of the present Meeting House—and beat the Friends with "swords and staves" in the spring of 1660. Imprisonment was frequent. In somewhat more tolerant times (1777) a permanent Meeting House was built, although lack of numbers caused it to be used for other purposes from 1795 until meetings began again in 1884. The building was extensively altered in 1926-7.

Other Nonconformist churches appeared as the population swelled: the Unitarian chapel (1928) in Emmanuel Road; Wesley Methodist Church (1913); Emmanuel Congregational (now United Reformed) (1875) Church with its broad nave and timber ceiling and gallery. The glass at Emmanuel represents such Cambridge-educated Protestant heroes as Henry Barrow and John Greenwood (both hanged at Tyburn in 1593), a not particularly warty Cromwell, and an angelic long-haired Milton. The Baptist Church in St Andrew's Street (1903), shows externally, as Edward Baty puts it, George Baines' trademark of "random stonework which is best described as 'vertical crazy-paving'."

King's College

Gaining credit in Heaven was at least one of King Henry VI's motives for founding King's College, although this may have been little consolation to the many townspeople whose houses were swept away to make room for it. But the author of *An Account of King's College Chapel, in Cambridge* (1779) attributes to him an Enlightenment sensitivity to his inelegantly medieval people in building this "magnificent monument for himself for the ornament of succeeding ages":

> *Sensible of the rough, uncultivated genius of his nation, Henry established in his kingdom seats of erudition, enriched them with ample endowments, and distinguished them by privileges and immunities: thus inviting his subjects to forsake their ignorance and barbarism, and reform their turbulent and licentious manners.*

Some of the "privileges and immunities" survived into the nineteenth century: the students were exempt from university examinations until the early 1850s, and they and the fellows were drawn almost exclusively from Henry VI's earlier foundation, Eton College, until the early 1860s. But subjects turbulent and licentious enough to prolong the Wars of the Roses, and eventually to depose the king, helped prevent the full realization of his plan for a college in which the chapel would be only one among several monumental constructions. For nearly three centuries the collegians, few in number, all lived in one of the courts of the Old Schools (sold to the university in 1829), reached through the gatehouse opposite the entrance to Clare College. This situation changed only when James Gibbs' fine Portland stone neoclassical Gibbs or Fellows' Building went up in 1724-32. William Wilkins added the emphatically neo-Gothic gatehouse and screen on King's Parade, and the hall, in the 1820s. Other buildings are of the late nineteenth and twentieth century.

Even the chapel, which was built as the king willed, made its appearance only gradually. Work began in 1446, but the war, and especially the king's deposition in 1461, halted progress for the best part of half a century. The Yorkist kings Edward IV and Richard III revived the project after 1476, but it was only after a visit to Cambridge by Henry VII that, in 1508, a concerted effort to complete the work began under John Wastell. Henry, who lobbied unsuccessfully for Henry VI to be made a saint, determined now, with the aid of great numbers of masons and other workers, "by the Grace of Almighty God incessantly to persevere and continue till it be fully finished" as his kinsman devised. This he made practicable by providing £5,000, cannily requiring the Provost and scholars to agree to spend "every parcel" of the money on the chapel, and having them provide, for its "safeguard and sure keeping", "a strong chest bounden with iron"—now on show in the exhibition in the side chapels on the north side.

Most of the work on the exterior was finished by 1515, six years into the reign of Henry VIII. The famous fan vaulting dates from about 1512-15. The lectern with small statue of Henry VI was made at about the same time but achieved international familiarity only in the age of television, since readers use it in the festival of Nine Lessons and Carols broadcast each Christmas Eve by the BBC. (Eric Milner-White, Dean and former chaplain, devised the service in 1918 and its first radio broadcast was ten years later.) The glass is the work of Flemish, Dutch or German craftsmen including Bernard Flower (d. 1517) and, continuing until the 1540s, Galyon Hone. The east window shows Christ's Passion and the west shows the Last Judgement (added in 1879). In the intervening windows the lower sections present scenes from the life of the Virgin and of Christ, while the upper give Old Testament typological equivalents: God reveals himself, for instance, to Moses in the burning bush and to all humankind in the Nativity beneath it; Jonah is cast up by the whale and Jesus, at the Resurrection, by the grave. The magnificent oak screen between the ante-chapel and the choir, and the choir-stalls, were finished between 1533 and 1536, the years of Henry VIII's marriage to Anne Boleyn. Her initials are intertwined with his on the screen. Tudor symbols are also prominent in stone: "the tedious repetition of roses and portcullises" which failed to impress William Gilpin in his *Observations* on the eastern counties (1809).

A much later and more controversial addition was Rubens' *Adoration of the Magi*, painted in 1634 for the church of the White Nuns of Louvain, a work in which, as Michael Jaffé put it 1984, the painter keeps a "dynamic equilibrium" between "a tide of courtly magnificence"—the splendidly accoutred royal Magi—and "a response of unadorned dignity and unaffected warmth of greeting" from the Holy Family. After various changes of hands the *Adoration* was donated to the college by Major A. E. Allnatt in 1961. Allnatt had bought it two years earlier for £275,000, the highest sum ever, at the time, paid for a painting. At first it was displayed in the ante-chapel, and the decision to place it permanently beyond the high altar was unpopular in many quarters, mainly on the grounds that the dramatic baroque sweep and colour of the Rubens was completely at odds with the more subtle effects of the sixteenth-century glass in the east window. But, Jaffé argues, the change of focus at the altar is no less assimilable than the changes earlier introduced by the work of the Flemish glaziers or the late seventeenth-century organ-case. To minimize competition between painting and windows black shutters were fitted either side of the painting, the floor levelled, and some panelling removed.

King's College Chapel impresses partly by sheer size. It is 289 feet long, 94 feet high and 40 feet wide. On early maps it dwarfs all other structures. The television presenter Cornelius Carrington, in Tom Sharpe's *Porterhouse Blue*, feels that it dwarfs even his inflated personality. This, together with the sense that the chapel is "too well-known, too hackneyed" to serve as a television background for him, has him fleeing King's to seek "the less demanding atmosphere of Corpus Christi". John Betjeman professed himself more reasonably daunted

when in 1947 he told Kenneth Harrison, fellow and Lay Dean at King's, that "the building, music and glass" of the chapel "are so much too great to be effable in verse or prose." Nevertheless he enclosed a copy of his poem "Sunday Morning, King's Cambridge", and other commentators have found at least some of their responses "effable".

The four turrets and the other intervening pinnacles have attracted much notice. In the 1820s J. M. F. Wright of Trinity compared the pinnacles to "so many gigantic pepper-boxes". From Grantchester Meadows one morning in

February 1957 they looked, to Sylvia Plath, like "glistening pink sugar spikes on a little cake". For Richard Holmes, in his essay on M. R. James, they are more simply "mace-like". The ever-original John Ruskin wanted the pinnacles removed: "What a host of ugly church towers have we in England, with pinnacles at the corners, and none in the middle! How many buildings like King's College Chapel at Cambridge, looking like tables upside down, with their four legs in the air!" ("Mais," Joseph Aynard comments dismissively in *Oxford et Cambridge* (Paris, 1909), "il était d'Oxford.") D. H. Lawrence, too, was no fan of this sow on its back without its piglets.

The compulsion to compare extends to other parts of the chapel. From the Gibbs building George Santayana could see "the buttresses standing in file, like soldiers with shields, lances, and banners, or like the statue-columns of Karnak." The ceiling, says Thomas Fuller, is "a Stonehenge indeed, so geometrically contrived, that voluminous stones mutually support themselves in the arched roof, as if art had made them to forget nature, and weaned them from their fondness to descend to their centre." In Betjeman's poem it is "a shower that never falls." "It is held up, lifted up, as if it could move, like a baldacchino over a procession," says Santayana. And in one of his sonnets Wordsworth, more succinctly, celebrates "that branching roof/Self-poised".

It is difficult to sum up the impact of King's College Chapel as a whole. "Fine building, remarkably fine building," persistently repeated an uncle of E. M. Forster when he showed him round; the uncle was a man of few words at the best of times, but many people have felt similarly reduced. Santayana locates its distinctive quality in its singleness, as compared with the multiple vistas and levels, the forest of columns, of a cathedral: "This is a Gothic hall, a single chamber, and in that respect like the Pantheon, St. Sophia and the Sistine Chapel." Earlier he called it "a Gothic Parthenon in dignity". And, in what he sees as true Gothic spirit, "It is narrow, long, lofty: it draws you on, towards the goal of your pilgrimage... It is a throne room for the Risen Christ, to be present in the Sacrament." Coleridge, too, saw King's as a good example of Gothic, and Gothic as "infinity made imaginable".

Few people at King's itself spent their time imagining infinity in the chapel. In 1833, the same year in which Coleridge philosophized the Gothic, the author of an open letter to the Duke of Gloucester on *The Present Corrupt State of the University of Cambridge* declared that "If ever Gothic grandeur was thrown away, it is on this fraternity who fatten ingloriously in Gothic apartments; who take degrees... without any examination; who are privileged to be ignorant and nurtured to be careless." Even after the reforms of the 1860s Kingsmen retained their reputation for indifference or hostility to religion, less now because the fraternity were busy fattening ingloriously than because its general liberalism was out of tune with the Anglican church of the day.

Supernatural interests, meanwhile, were represented most famously by Montague Rhodes James, Provost between 1905 and 1918, who first composed many of his ghost stories for the group of friends gathered in the Provost's Lodge at Christmas. The annual ritual was that he would emerge from his bedroom armed with a newly completed manuscript, blow out all but one of the candles, and read. The horror of the tale was increased both by its beginning in some normal, seemingly trivial occurrence and by the impassive manner of the respectable, middle-aged reader (an authority on medieval manuscripts) behind his round spectacles. James makes a brief appearance as Dr Matthews, Provost of St James's, in Penelope Fitzgerald's *The Gate of Angels* (1990). "[S]o many things walk, you know," he tells Fred Fairly as they approach the Provost's Lodge one night, "when they seem to be buried safely enough." "What a strange face was his," comments the narrator, "protective and fatherly in the light, then again, as his head turned and his black-rimmed spectacles glittered, a blank."

E. M. Forster and King's

James, though friendly enough to individual undergraduates, was reluctant to engage in serious discussion with them, and held generally conservative views. Among the more personable and broad-minded dons were two of the people who taught and befriended Morgan (E. M.) Forster, who came up to King's in 1897: Nathaniel Wedd, a classicist, atheist, and foe of all college cliques, summed up by P. N. Furbank in his life of Forster as "small, thick-set and ferrety, a warm-hearted, pugnacious, hypochondriacal character, militantly egalitarian, and with a passion for bad language"; and the more peaceable

Goldsworthy Lowes Dickinson, recalled by F. L. Lucas as "an ivory-yellow mandarin in his black-silk Chinese cap, whose despair would suddenly relieve itself in a smiling handshake, a little crackling laugh, and a wave of his hands at the diabolical irony of things." Under such influences Forster discovered a new confidence in himself and in the possibility of real connection between human beings. (Wedd suggested to Forster that he might become a writer, probably at least confirming half-formed intentions). Not unlike Rickie in Forster's *The Longest Journey,*

> *He had crept cold and friendless and ignorant out of a great public school, preparing for a silent and solitary journey, and praying as a highest favour that he might be left alone. Cambridge had not answered his prayer. She had taken and soothed him, and warmed him, and had laughed at him a little, saying that he must not be so tragic yet awhile.*

Forster found, especially after moving into college in his second year, that "people had insides"—this time the eponymous hero of the posthumous *Maurice* is speaking—whereas:

> *Hitherto he had supposed that they were what he pretended to be—flat pieces of cardboard stamped with a conventional design. But as he strolled about the courts at night and saw through the windows some men singing and others arguing and others at their books, their came by no process of reason a conviction that they were human beings with feelings akin to his own.*

At Cambridge he also went some way, as fictionalized in *Maurice*, to admitting and tentatively exploring his homosexuality.

"King's stands for personal relationships," Forster wrote to Malcolm Darling, an old college friend, in September 1924, "and these still seem to me the most real things on the surface of the earth." But personal relationships were, he now felt, more difficult than they had seemed. *A Passage to India* (1924) exposes some of the difficulties. "The 'King's' view over-simplified people: that I think was its defect. We are more complicated, also richer, than it knew, and affection grows more difficult than it used to be, and also more glorious." Nevertheless, he was prepared to remain fairly closely involved with the college. Having delivered the 1927 Clark Lectures (published as *Aspects of the Novel*), he was offered and accepted a three-year "supernumerary" fellowship, and in 1946 he became a permanent honorary fellow and came to live in Cambridge, principally, until his death in 1970, in rooms in the front court. There he installed the mantelpiece and writing-table that had accompanied him to each of his homes since Rooksnest in Hertfordshire, the original Howards End. In these last years some visitors found Forster crusty, pusillanimous, or disconcertingly silent. Raymond Leppard appreciated his "charmingly exaggerated modesty", but in J. G. Ballard's *The Kindness of Women* (1991) he is a "whiskery old gent with sad eyes, like a disappointed child-molester". But inwardly, no doubt, he still dwelt on the Cambridge he described in his biography of Goldsworthy Lowes Dickinson:

> *Body and spirit, reason and emotion, work and play, architecture and scenery, laughter and seriousness, life and art—these pairs which are elsewhere contrasted were there fused into one. People and books reinforced one another, intelligence joined hands with affection, speculation became a passion, and discussion was made profound by love.*

Emmanuel College

King's College traditionally has its cows and Magdalen College in Oxford its deer-park. Emmanuel, however, is noted for its ducks. They swim on the long pool fringed with bamboo and gunnera, once the fishpond of the Dominican priory which occupied the site until the Dissolution. They waddle across the grass of the surrounding Paddock. They dabble too in the second college pool, in Chapman's Garden, once the domain of the Hebrew scholar Arthur Chapman.

This being a seat of learning, they are not common mallards only but a fine selection of mandarin, Carolina, tufted and pintail ducks and widgeons. And the pool itself is said to have done its bit for science: the patterns of ripples made on it by swans are supposed to have inspired the polymath Thomas "Phenomenon" Young to work on the wave theory of light in the late 1790s. In the same period the small pool in the Fellows' Garden was already in use for the more everyday activity of bathing. The fellows' modesty would now be amply protected by the wide spreading branches of the two-hundred-year-old oriental plane-tree that dominates the pool end of the garden. This is the Edenic "canopy" of Luís Cernuda's "El árbol" (1945), written by the exiled Spanish poet during his time as a lector at the university. A more recent arrival, in the Paddock and next to the Fellows' Garden, is the joyous, leaping green and gold loop of Wendy Taylor's sculpture "The Jester" (1994).

Jesters (and ducks) were probably not dear to the heart of the college founder, Sir Walter Mildmay (1520-89), Chancellor of the Exchequer and a man of strong Puritan leanings. But a court fool might have approved of the rather equivocal answer which, according to Thomas Fuller, he made to Elizabeth I when she asked him about Emmanuel. "Sir Walter, I hear you have erected a puritan foundation." "No, madam," he replied, "far be it from me to countenance anything contrary to your established laws; but I have set an acorn which, when it becomes an oak, God alone knows what will be the fruit thereof." Between the foundation in January 1584 and the middle of the seventeenth century, Emmanuel did indeed grow into a powerfully Protestant oak. The openness with which it declared its Puritan allegiance at times enraged the Church establishment. According to an anonymous list of "public disorders as touching Church causes" drawn up in 1603, the fellows and scholars did not wear their surplices or hoods at services. They engaged in their own "private course of public prayer, after their own fashion", rather than following the Book of Common Prayer. They did not " refrain their suppers" on Fridays and other fasting days; in fact, says their assailant, they always had supper in hall on such days, "yea upon Good Friday itself". (To make one day more special than another smacked, to some Puritans, of popish superstition.) Even their chapel had to point north, not, like everyone else's, east. The old Dominican chapel had been oriented east, but what was left of it by the 1580s was converted into the college dining-hall; James Essex converted it further in the eighteenth century.

Faced with so much hostility at home, many people went abroad in pursuit of freedom of worship. As much as a third of the first hundred graduates to settle in the American colonies were from Emmanuel. Among them were Thomas Shepherd, in whose honour Newtown, Massachusetts, was renamed Cambridge, and John

Harvard, benefactor of Harvard College. The novelist Hugh Walpole (1884-1941), who remembered his "shabby furtive career at Emmanuel with no honour and much timidity", must also have felt like emigrating at times. It was therefore "flattering to my vanity" to be given a tumultuous welcome by the audience at the Senate House when he came back to lecture on the English novel in 1925.

After the Restoration, under the mastership of William Sancroft, soon to become Dean of St Paul's and then Archbishop of Canterbury, the religious climate of the college changed. So, partly reflecting this, did its architecture, most visibly the new, east-aligned chapel which, at Sancroft's instigation, Christopher Wren designed in the mid-1660s. (The old chapel became the library, now the Old Library.) The new building, in Ketton stone, completely transformed Front Court. Wren's biographer Adrian Tinniswood is moved to celebrate the "uncompromisingly classical façade" of the chapel:

> *dominated*—totally *dominated*—*by the centrepiece, which breaks outwards and upwards in a giant Corinthian order topped with a pediment, broken to take a great clock, behind which is a square block that carries a round cupola... If there is a certain naïveté to the thing, an overconfident handling of classical decoration and an absence of restraint or due proportion, we shouldn't be too hard on the architect. His immaturity is more than offset by his sheer excitement in the joy of making.*

Religious debate in the twentieth century sometimes took forms that Mildmay and Sancroft would have found equally objectionable. William Chawner, Master since 1895, in 1909 announced that he had lost his Christian faith and caused a great scandal by distributing his questioning pamphlet *Prove All Things* to undergraduates as well as fellows. Initially at least, he also argued against that bastion of the establishment, compulsory chapel. The crisis was resolved only by Chawner's sudden death in 1911. In the 1980s Rev. Don Cupitt, fellow and Dean, caused more widespread controversy—and some healthy debate—with his views on "the end of the old realistic conception of God as an all-powerful and objective spiritual Being independent of us and sovereign over us". In the absence of such a being "it is we ourselves who alone make truth, make value, and so have formed the reality that now encompasses us."

Sidney Sussex College: Cromwell's Head

The founding statutes of Sidney Sussex were based on those of Emmanuel. Here, too, a proudly Protestant college was built on the site of a medieval religious house, this time Greyfriars (a common name for Franciscan houses, as Blackfriars was for the Dominicans). Greyfriars consisted, from the mid-fourteenth century, of a church and cemetery where Cloister Court is now (skeletons were unearthed during the building of the court in the late nineteenth century), a cloister on the site of Hall Court, a refectory and several other buildings. After the Dissolution Trinity College removed much of the stone—three thousand cart-loads in 1556 alone—for its chapel and appropriated the friars' conduit. It still supplies the fountain in Trinity Great Court.

Lady Frances Sidney, wife of the Earl of Sussex and aunt of Sir Philip Sidney, provided the name of the new college and, in her will, money to establish it (only just enough money, it turned out). She died in 1589 but it was not until 1596, after a prolonged struggle by her executors to obtain possession of the site from Trinity, that building began. The one surviving Greyfriars building, thought to be the refectory or kitchens, was converted into the college chapel, which, like that at Emmanuel, was oriented north-south. (Fragments of glass from the friary church have been incorporated in windows in the present ante-chapel.) The new buildings of Hall Court are the work of the master mason Ralph Simons, who also worked at Emmanuel and on the second court at St John's and the Great Court at Trinity. Externally the structure remained largely unchanged, apart from the addition of Francis Clerke's Building in 1628, until the 1820s. Internally James Essex redesigned the chapel to suit classical tastes, and Burrough did the same for the hall, in the eighteenth century.

The inadequate size and facilities of Simons' college, as well as early nineteenth-century preferences, eventually told against it. While Giles Fletcher the Elder (1546-1611) had celebrated late Elizabethan Sidney for its pinnacles as white as snow and "rose-red walls", *The Railway Traveller's Walk Through Cambridge* (1880) took the view that it had been "a gloomy, irregular pile, of the later Elizabethan period, in red brick and stone". Not everyone, however, liked the replacement, which was the work of Sir Jeffry Wyatville, scion of the architectural dynasty of the Wyatts who changed his name with royal approval, remodelled Windsor Castle for George IV and was knighted by him in 1828. He had in those days, in the opinion of Charles Henry Cooper in *Memorials of Cambridge* (1866), "a great but undeserved reputation as an architect". Cooper gives particulars of what Wyatville did to Sidney:

> *The brick walls were faced with cement, a number of insignificant turrets were erected, porches were added, and one of the wings of the original structure was converted into a low tower, surmounted with stepped gables. The gateway was removed and a new entrance formed under the low tower. These alterations have wholly destroyed the congruity and venerable appearance of the fabric.*

The earlier gateway that Cooper mentions was repositioned in what is now a peaceful corner of the garden next to Jesus Lane. (The garden, skilfully fitted into the relatively small space available, has attracted the sort of enthusiasm usually denied to the buildings.) The gateway is an elegant mid eighteenth-century piece; in removing it, as in most of his other alterations, Wyatville thought, difficult though it is to believe now, that he was restoring the college to its essential Elizabethan design. An earlier, rejected design does bear a more obvious resemblance to Simons' original. The use of the conspicuously un-Elizabethan cement was a matter as much of financial necessity as of aesthetic preference. Money was found, however, to face the tower in stone.

The chapel, already altered by Essex, was rebuilt in the early 1920s in a more imaginative neo-baroque style suited to the High Church complexion of religious life in the college at the time—a far cry from the Puritan simplicity of the original chapel. An oval plaque in the ante-chapel is a reminder of an earlier time: "Near to this place was buried on 25 March 1960 the head of Oliver Cromwell, Lord Protector of the Commonwealth of England, Scotland and Ireland, Fellow Commoner of this College 1616-17." Very little is known of Cromwell's year at Sidney, and indeed of his life before 1640, much of which was spent as a farmer and minor official in Huntingdon, St Ives and Ely. (There are small museums in his grammar school in Huntingdon and his house in Ely, which now also contains the information centre.) Even his entry in the college admission register cannot be read without reference to much later events, since soon after the Restoration in 1660 someone added an emphatic Latin explanation beginning "Hic fuit grandis ille impostor, carnifex..." ("this was the great impostor, the butcher") who, after the good King Charles I had been done to death, usurped the throne and inflicted his despotism on the three kingdoms for nearly five years. Accounts of his college career are similarly coloured. In 1663 James Heath, in *Flagellum, or the Life and Death of Oliver Cromwell, the Late Usurper*, has him "more famous for his exercises in the fields than in the schools... being one of the chief match-makers and players at football, cudgels, or any other boisterous sport or game"; his lack of a degree reflected his lack of "worth and merit". Even more unlikely is the Cromwell who excelled in mathematics, Latin and other studies in Samuel Carrington's *History of Oliver, Late Lord Protector*, published in 1659, the year after the great man's death.

Cromwell probably left Sidney after only a year because of the death of his father. As the only surviving son he went home to take charge of family affairs in Huntingdon. He eventually re-entered Cambridge life when he was returned as one of the town's two MPs in 1640. In August 1642, just before the outbreak of the Civil War, he acted decisively to prevent most of the colleges' plate being sent to the king at York. (Sidney, whose Master and fellows supported the king in spite of the college's earlier Puritan tradition, had already succeeded in getting £100 to him. Dons with more acceptable views were soon installed.) Cromwell also seized the arms and ammunition stored in the Castle, and strengthened its defences. But royalist forces never attempted to capture Cambridge, and Cromwell was increasingly needed elsewhere. His next important contact with his old college was posthumous.

When the Protector died in 1658 he was accorded a splendid funeral based closely on that of James I in 1625. He was embalmed and buried among the kings in Westminster Abbey. But the Restoration regime reburied him by the gallows at Tyburn and then, in 1661, once more exhumed the body and decapitated it. The head was displayed on a spike on the top of Westminster Hall until the 1680s. It passed, after this, in gruesome but recognisable shape, from owner to owner until Dr H. N. S. Wilkinson gave it to Sidney in 1960. An earlier owner offered it to the late eighteenth-century Master, Dr Elliston, who refused it in fear of exciting "prejudice". He did, in 1766, accept from the republican Thomas Hollis the portrait of Cromwell by Sir Peter Lely or his studio, which still hangs in the Hall.

Dr Johnson and Sherlock Holmes at Sidney

Dr Samuel Johnson's brief association with the college was more convivial. When he visited Cambridge between 16 and 19 February 1765 he was entertained chiefly by a young fellow of Sidney, John Lettice. Lettice had been primed on certain of Johnson's habits by his friend Dr Robert Levet; he remembered, over half a century later, how one night,

> *our distinguished visitor shone gloriously in his style of dissertation on a great variety of subjects. I recall his condescending to as earnest a care of the animal as of the intellectual man, and after doing all justice to my College bill of fare, and without neglecting the glass after dinner, he drank sixteen dishes of tea. I was idly curious enough to count them, from what I had remarked, and heard Levet mention of his extreme devotion to the teapot.*

Another distinctive figure, devoted more to opium than to tea, has become associated with Sidney: Sherlock Holmes. Dorothy L. Sayers first made the connection, with the aid of some ingenious Holmesian deduction, in 1934 ("Holmes' College Career", in *Baker-Street Studies*, edited by H. W. Bell). She teases her evidence from remarks about Holmes' youth in two Conan Doyle stories, "The *Gloria Scott*" and "The Musgrave Ritual". She concludes that he must have been at Cambridge not Oxford since he appears to have been living out of college as a freshman, which was against Oxford regulations in the 1870s but normal enough in Cambridge. He took the Natural Sciences tripos, probably specializing in Chemistry and Comparative Anatomy and Physiology. This fits with his evident interests and, in a time when there were few such students, with his remark to Watson, in "The *Gloria Scott*", that his "line of study was quite distinct from" that of his colleagues. He held a scholarship, Sayers argues, at "one of the smaller and less expensive colleges." When he first meets Watson he cannot afford the Baker Street rent, and that college may, "in default of more exact information", be identified tentatively with Sidney Sussex, not only inexpensive but possessed, unusually, of a laboratory. It was built between Cloister Court and Sidney Street in about 1870 and ceased to function in 1908.

"Unhappily," continues Sayers with resolutely straight face, "the name of Sherlock Holmes does not appear in the Cambridge History of Triposes for 1874, or for any other year." Either he missed his exams or "the lists were compiled with a lack of accuracy very far from consonant with the dignity of an Academic body." She floats another and darker possibility in a footnote: could "the malignant influence of Professor Moriarty" have "extended as far as Cambridge" and brought about "an extensive and retrospective falsification of the published lists"? But "it is better to assume carelessness than venality."

Holy Trinity Church

Holy Trinity is indelibly associated with the leading Evangelical churchman Charles Simeon, who was vicar throughout 1784-1836. In the vestry his chair is still in use and his umbrella, like some practical Protestant version of a relic, is displayed in a glass case. The umbrella— a great rarity in Cambridge when he first used it—was one of his familiar attributes; like his humanly unascetic love of fine clothes and good horses and his prominent chin, it was especially beloved of caricaturists. Sir James Stephen, in *Essays in Ecclesiastical Biography* (1849), is irresistibly unkind about the Simeon whom one might have taken for

> some truant from the green-room, studying in clerical costume for the part of Mercutio, and doing it scandalously ill. Such adventurous attitudes, such ceaseless play of the facial muscles, so seeming a consciousness of the advantages of his figure, with so seeming unconsciousness of the disadvantages of his carriage—a seat in the saddle so

> *triumphant, badinage so ponderous, stories so exquisitely unbefitting*
> *him about the pedigree of his horses or the vintages of his cellar.*

Stephen goes on to admit, nevertheless, that Simeon's virtues outweighed his faults. But for much of his career he was slighted or jeered at by people other than his dedicated followers, the "Sims" or "Simeonites". When, at the age of twenty-three, he was appointed to Holy Trinity, he faced the outright opposition of the church wardens and other parishioners who had wanted the curate, John Hammond, to become the new vicar. Those who wanted to protest against the new man (imposed on them by the Bishop of Ely), stayed away when he was due to preach and attempted further to sabotage his sermons by leaving their private pews locked. People who did want to hear were forced to do so from the sides and back of the church. Simeon tried to improve the situation by bringing in extra seats, and the church wardens promptly threw them out. Hostilities went on for several years before Simeon gained full control of his own church.

He had even fewer sympathizers at King's, where he was a fellow. But it was here, mainly in rooms on the top floor of the Gibbs Building, that he held his famous "conversation parties" for up to sixty students at a time. (Almost all of them came from outside King's.) As he realized himself, he could be rather pernickety, exploding for example when guests trod gravel into his carpet, but few allowed themselves to be put off. What they gained, if they stayed, was religious discussion and training in an age when the Church offered no such facility. Some of the instruction was practical: Simeon believed that preaching should come from the heart but was also aware that it had to communicate clearly. His disciple Abner Brown remembered his advice: "To get ease, read parts of your sermon to an ideal person (any object, as your inkstand, or candlestick)... and repeat this, till you perceive (as it were) that your ideal person clearly understands you." It is perhaps fortunate that Sir James Stephen did not witness this technique in action.

By the end of his career Simeon was preaching to huge congregations, sought out as a guru, an unignorable figure in both Cambridge and the national Evangelical movement. Stephen praises the way he struggled on, ignored or ridiculed for much of his career.

"His whole life was but one labour of love—a labour often obscure, often misapplied, often unsuccessful, but never intermitted, and at last triumphant." At King's, where once they laughed at him, he was honoured in 1836 by a grand funeral procession.

Selwyn College

"The contrast between Selwyn and King's is not hard to make photographically, or indeed in any other way," we are reminded in Frederick Raphael's *Oxbridge Blues* (1980). Selwyn has sometimes been cast as a poor relation of the older colleges. Originally there was some truth in this. The college was founded in 1882, named after George Augustus Selwyn, a graduate of St John's College, first Bishop of New Zealand and then Bishop of Lichfield, who had died in 1878. Its aim was specifically to educate Church of England students, charging them lower fees than other Cambridge colleges. Many of them became clergymen or lay missionaries. At first there was some hot opposition to what a Trinity undergraduate described, in *The Cambridge Review* for 29 October 1879, as this "strictly sectarian seminary". But in 1923 it became an Approved Foundation of the university and in 1958, by this time providing a wide range of non-theological tripos possibilities, achieved full collegiate status. The statutes of 1956 decreed that students need no longer be Anglican; neither, by the revised version of 1989, need the Master or Mistress do more than "respect the Anglican tradition of the college."

The red-brick main court, by Sir Arthur Blomfield, is especially attractive in autumn thanks to its Virginia creepers. Sir Hugh Casson likes the "loosely Jacobean style" of the hall and its "attractive larky outside staircase". Pevsner concedes that the chapel has a "not bad" front but declares that the inside lacks the "gravity" of the chapel of the same period at Queens'. Probably he did not appreciate the inventive, often contorted figures on the choir-stalls, including a comically malevolent griffin and a cartoonish bear chewing at the wood of its stall: a spirited late tribute to the Gothic grotesque.

Our Lady and the English Martyrs

Our Lady and the English Martyrs is known generally as "the Catholic church" or simply "the Catholic", partly because of its considerable bulk and prominent position by a crossroads near the station, partly perhaps because of the town's strong Protestant tradition; Roman Catholics themselves often call it by the acronym "OLEM".

The first post-Reformation Catholic church in Cambridge was St Andrew's, Union Road, built by Pugin in 1842. When it was superseded by OLEM it was dismantled and rebuilt at St Ives in Huntingdonshire in 1890. The new church, begun in 1885, was intended as a dramatic statement of faith. The drama was made possible by the wealth of Yolande Lyne-Stephens, a former ballerina who had married an immensely rich landowner. The lantern tower of the church is 118 feet high and the bell-tower with its spire—the "lupin spire" of Anne Stevenson's poem "Coming Back to Cambridge" (1971)—214 feet high. Outside and inside exuberant, full-blown neo-Gothicism prevails: everywhere, in stone and in glass, are representations of angels, saints, the Virgin and Child, English martyrs from St Alban onwards and including Saints John Fisher, Thomas More and Edmund Campion. The Rood (1914) features a striking pinewood Christ in Majesty—robed and crowned on an oaken cross which, in early medieval tradition, is also the Tree of Life with its vine leaves and grapes. Beyond, on the baldacchino over the high altar, inspired by the tomb of King Robert the Wise in Naples, white-robed angels with golden wings adore Christ while on the columns to left and right, surmounted by the archangels with their wings pointing upwards, are tabernacles containing figures of the martyrs.

Monsignor R. H. Benson (1871-1914), the best-known priest associated with the church—he was a curate here in 1905-8—disliked the baldacchino and claimed to be "quite sure", his Jesuit colleague and biographer Father Martindale records, "that his prayers caught its corners and could not mount beyond its roof." At first he found the whole church, indeed, "a little too gorgeous, and complete". But distrust of the over-decorated did not extend to his rooms next door at the Rectory; some people who, Martindale insists, knew the rooms only by repute, asked "How should zeal, self-sacrifice, unworldliness go with enormous oaken candlesticks, ancient madonnas smothered in rosaries, pictures of art-nouveau, and innumerable photographs of friends?" His brother A. C. Benson recalled also "green hangings, above which he set the horns of deer, which he had at various times stalked and shot... I told him it was too secular an ornament, but he would not hear me." He was also a keen designer of vestments.

Benson made a powerful, on the whole favourable impression on those, especially young people, whom he invited to talk to him among the candlesticks and rosaries in his green sanctum. Another priest, Prior MacNabb, remembered "an interesting living being, seated but by no means rooted on a sofa, smoking endless cigarettes and pouring out or drinking in stories, thoughts, ideas, with the energy of a fledgling taking food from its mother's beak." Benson's own passion for people and ideas was one reason why this zealous convert to Catholicism (his father had been Archbishop of Canterbury) found his congregation "as good as gold... but oddly cold". He campaigned against such coldness by delivering what Martindale calls his "alternately mystical and controversial, seductive and denunciatory sermons". So great was his influence on undergraduates that the Cambridge Anglican establishment became quite worried and even asked A. C. Benson if he could persuade him to leave.

Among those whom Benson influenced was the novelist Ronald Firbank (1886-1926), whom he received into the Catholic Church at OLEM in December 1907. Firbank's decadent habits—filling his rooms at Trinity Hall with white flowers, for instance—sound close to some of Benson's; and Brigid Brophy in *Prancing Novelist* (1973), her study of Firbank, argues that the priest "was an almost entirely Firbankian personage", a "high camp" figure who was an involuntary spur to satire. (There are elements of Benson in Firbank's Cardinal Pirelli.) His brother, with whom he had cycled, walked and argued around Cambridge, took a more sympathetic view, feeling that "his religion was one of artistic values."

Artistic, holy or both, the Catholic church "watches over the apostate city," says E. M. Forster in *The Longest Journey*, "taller by many a yard than anything within, and asserting, however wildly, that here is eternity, stability, and bubbles unbreakable upon a windless sea."

CHAPTER SIX

Cambridge Women

Women would not need a chapter of their own if Cambridge had not, for many years, attempted to segregate them. The university wanted to shut them out. Colleges employed female servants or "bedders" to tend to the young men, but attempted to recruit only those deemed old or unattractive enough not to lead them astray. In 1635 the Vice-Chancellor and heads of houses decreed that they must be over fifty years old. Inevitably, given the lack of alternative possibilities, some women became prostitutes; many also were wrongfully arrested as prostitutes because they were young, lower-class and in Cambridge. The proctors had the power to make such arrests and incarcerate women in the so-called Spinning House, a house of correction (and originally a workhouse) provided for by the will of Thomas Hobson the carrier. Until the early nineteenth century the inmates worked at spinning. Such "lewd and disorderly" people as were arrested were allowed no legal representation, were liable to be whipped, and could be imprisoned for several weeks in cramped and unhealthy conditions.

Town feeling against such uses or abuses of university power ran high. In 1860 there was an outcry over the arrest of a group of seven young women. *The Daily Telegraph* covered the case, and printed a letter that declared that until such arbitrary proceedings are ended "we have little room to denounce the Virginian slave-holders"; women, the letter argued, deserve "as large a share of the law's benefits as is accorded to thieves and murderers." This national airing of the problem resulted in a decline in the number of arrests. But it was the case of Jane Elsden, a seventeen-year-old locked up for street-walking in 1891, which spelled the end for the Spinning House. She escaped, was recaptured, was the subject of another public outcry, and was released by order of the Home Secretary. One result of this affair was the decision that legal representation would now be granted to those apprehended. University authority was further diminished by the Cambridge University and Corporation Act of 1894. The Spinning House was demolished in 1901 and replaced by a police station; in the 1960s this became City Council offices.

Progress by Degree

The idea that women might participate in the university was strongly resisted, whether out of misogyny, vested interest, or the genuine belief that women lacked the capacity to learn. When in the 1860s the Local Examinations run by Cambridge were opened to females, Professor Adam Sedgwick dismissed them, notoriously, as "nasty forward minxes". And when in the 1870s women's colleges finally came to Cambridge, progress towards full membership of the university was fraught and slow. At first women were allowed into lectures only at the lecturer's discretion and had no official right to take the tripos examinations. (Entry into lectures did not guarantee good treatment by the rest of the audience. A student who went up to Newnham in 1918 remembered how, as the women went down the steps to their customary places at the front, "every man behind them clumped and stamped in time with each of their steps.") Their social life, for fear of confirming misogynist suspicions, was limited, carefully chaperoned. To be so close to, yet excluded from, Cambridge life was, said the Newnham classicist Jane Harrison, like being "a peri outside Paradise".

In 1881 the Senate voted in favour of allowing women to enter for university examinations. Class lists were to be issued, and certificates given to successful candidates. This made possible the situation in which Agnata Ramsay of Girton was the only student listed in the first class for the Classical Tripos in 1887 and Philippa Fawcett of Newnham was listed "above the Senior Wrangler" in Part One of the Mathematical Tripos in 1890. Fawcett was awarded much praise, satire, and a certificate, while the Senior Wrangler and lesser male beings duly took their degrees. Some felt that Ramsay spoiled the effect of her triumph when, soon afterwards, she entered the university establishment by marrying Montague Butler, Master of Trinity. He was, at least, a strong supporter of the women's cause.

Opposition to the granting of degrees remained widespread, as was demonstrated most clearly by the events of 1897, when it was proposed that women should be given the "titles" of their degrees—titular qualifications, in other words. Since all Cambridge MAs had the right to vote on the matter, special trains were organized to bring them up from London. Undergraduates met the trains and escorted the voters to the Senate House, outside which there was a party atmosphere: crowds assembled and firecrackers were thrown. A comical effigy of a woman in blue bloomers on a bicycle was suspended above Bowes and Bowes bookshop (now the Cambridge University Press shop), and another of a woman in cap and gown was lowered from Caius. When the results were announced (1,713 against, 662 in favour) a mob of undergraduates rushed to Newnham but were turned back by the closed gates. Later they went wild in the marketplace, throwing fences and furniture onto a great bonfire. In 1921, a year after the first Oxford women were awarded degrees, "titles" were granted, but still not the substance. This time the rioters used a hand-cart to stove in the fine bronze Pfeiffer gates at Newnham, a memorial to the first Principal, Anne Jemima Clough. Apologies and repair money came from a number of undergraduate groups the following day, but the campaign for degrees had been dented more decidedly than the gates.

Seven years later, therefore, Newnham and Girton provided appropriate audiences for the talks on female inequality which Virginia Woolf revised and expanded as *A Room Of One's Own* (1929). Not everyone was impressed at the time; Muriel Bradbrook, who heard Woolf speak at Girton to the splendidly named society "Odtaa" ("One Damned Thing After Another"), says that "we undergraduates enjoyed Mrs Woolf, but felt that her Cambridge was not ours." At Newnham at least one student fell asleep while listening, in near-darkness, to Woolf's "mellifluous, cultivated voice" and there was some irritation at her description of the poor fare available at a women's college—thin soup, unexciting beef and vegetables, custard and prunes, no wine— compared with a men's college. (The quality of the food was not enhanced, apparently, by Woolf's late arrival.) But the finished essay was a highly influential polemic on behalf of women. Its main thesis— advanced too subtly and variously to seem as dull or abstract as a thesis—is that women have been prevented from succeeding as writers not because they have less ability than men but because they lack economic and physical opportunity: they need £500 a year and a room of their own. The contrast in meals—in the quality of the food and the concomitant quality of the conversation—is one illustration of the point. If Woolf does not express an opinion on "the comparative merits of the sexes even as writers", that is because

> *even if the time had come for such a valuation—and it is far more important at the moment to know how much money women had and how many rooms than to theorize about their capacities—even if the time had come I do not believe that gifts, whether of mind or character, can be weighed like sugar and butter, not even in Cambridge, where they are so adept at putting people into classes and fixing caps on their heads and letters after their names.*

The classes, caps and letters do, however, give self-respect and improved employment opportunities. Eventually, following a new vote in 1947, the first women were awarded Cambridge degrees in 1948. Slowly, integration began. A third college for women, New Hall was established in 1954. Lucy Cavendish College, named after an aristocrat with an interest in women's education, began in 1965, in 1970 moved into a house in Lady Margaret Road, gradually acquiring and extending neighbouring properties, and in 1997 achieved full collegiate status. Originally for female graduate students only, Lucy Cavendish has also admitted mature female undergraduates since the early 1970s. Two colleges for teacher training, Homerton, which came to Cambridge in 1894, and Hughes Hall, founded as the Cambridge Training College for Women Teachers in 1885, also remained single-sex until the 1970s.

Attitudes were slow to change: many men, as *Varsity* observed in 1961 were, beneath "civilised veneers", "prehistoric creatures, prepared only to see women as useful ornaments, and ready to strike out blindly in defence of their caves." This analysis was prompted by Union members' uncouth behaviour when women invaded the chamber as part of a campaign for female membership. This was at last achieved two years later. But the real decline of the cavemen came only with co-education. Clare, Churchill and King's led the way in 1972. Magdalene was the last male college to change in 1987. Girton, meanwhile, has accepted men since 1979; Newnham and Lucy Cavendish remain female; New Hall has women students but a mixed fellowship.

Girton College

In 1869 Emily Davies established her College for Women at Hitchin in Hertfordshire, near enough to Cambridge for lecturers to come for the day, but well away from the distractions of a male university. When the college moved to its permanent home in 1873 it was to a site more than two miles from the town-centre, up the then countrified Huntingdon Road, near the village of Girton. The distance, and a strong awareness of propriety, remained a defining feature of college life: Muriel Bradbrook, Mistress of Girton between 1968 and 1976,

recalls, in *'That Infidel Place': a Short History of Girton College 1869-1969*, the advice given to new arrivals in 1927 by the then Mistress, Miss Major. She recommended them "to put on gloves and hats at Storey's Way, the half-way line to Cambridge—'and remember, my dears, that the eyes of the Cambridge Ladies will be ever upon you.'"

Although Davies preferred to keep men and women physically separate, she aimed consistently for full integration of women into the university rather than their own separate institution. As Bradbrook says, she "kept absolute standards; for her 'Different means lower'... Miss Davies had to be a perfectionist, because the prejudice and assumption of the inherent inferiority of women's intellectual capacity must be exposed in an unambiguous fashion... Justice must be done and must be seen to be done." This single-mindedness could seem overdone. "The student was a mere cog in the wheel of her great scheme," felt Louisa Lumsden, a Girton lecturer who resigned following a disagreement with Davies. For many years she exercised a great deal of control over the college, dominating the governing body; Girton became truly self-governing only in the 1920s.

One still visible sign of Davies' determination is the large scale of the buildings designed by Alfred Waterhouse and his successors, on which she spent almost all the money she could raise. The second main building campaign of 1897-1902, including a massive new hall, "served as a silent protest to Cambridge," Bradbrook points out, following the refusal to grant women degrees in 1897: "what began as an anticipation of victory remained as a physical gesture of self-assertion and independence." A writer in *Varsity*, as late as 1977, saw Girton from a more blinkered point of view as "A large building, designed like a red-brick Mormon Tabernacle, which dominates the collective male psyche of Cambridge." At first there was enough space for students to have two rooms each. Rooms were arranged here not in the staircases traditional in colleges for men but in the long corridors which struck Virginia Woolf, in 1928, as "like vaults in some horrid high church cathedral—on and on they go, cold and shiny." Davies was sharply aware of "the power of being alone—it is perhaps the most precious distinctive feature of a college life." This was, as *A Room of One's Own* reminds us, foreign to the experience of most women.

C. S. Lewis compared Girton to Horace Walpole's Gothic "Castle of Otranto". Rosamond Lehmann was a student between 1919 and 1922 at what she calls, in her novel *Dusty Answer* (1927), this "solid red-brick barrack". But such impressions are much affected by mood, experience and weather. When Lehmann's Judith Earle is faced with the prospect of leaving, even the barrack, "caressed with sunset", looks "motherly and benign, spreading its sheltering breast for the last time above its midgets." The letters home which form the basis of Gwendolen Freeman's memoir of Girton in 1926-9, *Alma Mater* (1990), emphasize the physical as well as emotional warmth of the college for windswept young cyclists returning from town. For Kathleen Raine, another late 1920s student, arriving with high expectations, Girton's *proportions, its architecture... imposed certain intangible values and standards. On those lawns, in those cool corridors, I found myself conforming my behaviour to the architecture and the spacious scale of buildings and garden; walking with a prouder poise, with a sense of being visible to others of my own kind.*

Perceptions go on changing. When Lehmann's Judith comes back to visit, the place is "terrible—a Dark Tower... How had she been deluded for three years into imagining it friendly and secure?" In fact, "under its politeness," Cambridge had "disliked and distrusted her and all other females." Having made the mistake of making one person, her friend Jennifer, into "all poetry", and made some similar mistakes in her relationships with men, "she had nobody now except herself; and that was best." In real life, however, Freeman's experience was perhaps more representative:

The departure did take away for ever the ideal life of the scholar, though in time of course there were compensations. Looking back now over the plains of life, I see the three Cambridge years as a walled garden separated from the rest—a garden full of voices, freedom and some intimations of immortality.

Freeman was equally keen on the non-metaphorical grounds, the extensiveness of which is one benefit of the out-of-town site. They are, she wrote home, "perfectly gorgeous, lots and lots of trees and flowering shrubs and little paths running through them, and... lots of laurustinus and honeysuckle and almond and hawthorn and lilac and winter jasmine and privet and millions of other things." Emily Davies might not have approved: "Is this the way you do your work in the morning?" she once demanded, chancing upon a student gazing out of a corridor window at the garden. When examinations loom, it is true, the time for such gazing is short, as Judith in *Dusty Answer* knows:

Soon, Midsummer term was back with unprecedented profusion of blossom on the fruit trees, buttercups in the meadows, nightingale choruses in the cedars and limes. But now it seemed neither exciting nor delightful to be kept awake till dawn by nightingales; for sleepless nights lowered your examination value... Almost you resented the flowery orchards and meadows with their pagan-like riot of renewal. You noted them with a dull eye from behind the stiff ponderous academic entrenchments of your mind. But sometimes in the night, in dreams, the orchards would not be denied: they descended upon you and shook out fragrance like a blessing; they shone in pale drifts, in clouds, in seas,—all the orchards of England came before you, luminous and stirring beneath the moon.

Newnham College

Newnham was founded by the efforts of Henry Sidgwick, an enlightened fellow of Trinity who became Professor of Moral Philosophy in 1883, Anne Jemima Clough (sister of the poet Clough) whom he brought in as the first Principal, and Eleanor (Nora) Balfour, sister of the future Prime Minister, who married Sidgwick in 1876 and later succeeded Clough as Principal. The first five students lived in a house at 74 Regent Street from 1871-2 and then at Merton House, in the grounds of St John's. The first of the present buildings, Newnham Hall (subsequently Old Hall), opened in 1875 on a site much nearer the town than Girton but still, as a student of 1880 noted, "in the midst of open country with hedgerows all about".

The difference between Newnham and Girton in the early years was a matter of more than location. While Emily Davies fought for full equality of male and female students—they must take the same examinations, in the same building—the Newnham founders preferred a more flexible approach to study and a more gradual approach to reform. For some years it was possible to enrol at Newnham without intending to study for university examinations. The difference between the two colleges is also apparent in the architecture: Newnham has often been seen as "feminine", in what some at least would agree to be a positive sense: relaxed, elegant, suited to its purpose rather than aggressively proclaiming it. Particularly in the early days, before the separate houses of Newnham (once divided by a public lane) were linked, there was a strong contrast with the long corridors of Girton. The buildings, in "Queen Anne" style, look remarkably unified because everything put up between 1874-5 and 1910 was the work of one architect, Basil Champneys. The effect, especially of Clough Hall with its tall cylindrical bays or oriels, has been generally admired. Nicholas

Ray, in *Cambridge Architecture: a Concise Guide*, describes the "playful version of classicism" in Clough:

> *High buttresses or plinths support stumpy engaged Ionic columns. The capitals, architraves, friezes and decorative swags are all made of red terracotta. The decorative mouldings run around the bays, where they are translated into white painted timber. Above the cornice are scrolls and each pier ends in a terracotta pinnacle. The character is exuberant, but at the same time precise.*

In the Pfeiffer building, at the Newnham Walk entrance to the college, Champneys "revels in the asymmetry"—or, as Mark Girouard has put it, "the approximate symmetry"—of the two towers.

The gardens contribute significantly to the general effect of well-designed informality, the proportion and atmosphere, as A. S. Byatt says in *Still Life*, of "a comfortable country house". (But Byatt's Frederica finds it, in 1954, less attractive: "It was a setting for cocoa, toasted crumpets, tea parties. Frederica wanted wine, argument, sex.") There is a sunken pond; a generous provision of seats and benches; paths among the trees, half-hidden in summer, away from the main buildings; wild flowers flourishing in the Old Laboratory area; substantial yews, larches and horse-chestnuts. Outside the college, Sidgwick Avenue was planted with plane-trees in the 1890s, at Nora Sidgwick's wise suggestion, to moderate the dominance of red brick.

In *A Room of One's Own* it is on the terrace, glancing at the garden, that Virginia Woolf imagines seeing the "bent figure, formidable yet humble, with her great forehead and her long shabby dress" of the recently deceased Jane Harrison (1850-1928). In life this most charismatic and colourful of Newnham students and scholars certainly used the garden. In *Reminiscences of a Student's Life* (1925) she describes how, having been brought up "in a narrow school of Evangelicalism... with sin always present, with death and judgement before you," she was released by one of her set books at Newnham, Aristotle's *Ethics*: "I remember walking up and down in the College garden, thinking could it possibly be true, were the chains really broken and the prison doors open?" Inside, the walls of her room in Newnham Hall were decorated with what she later considered "dolorous" William Morris paper. When George Eliot visited the college, she "came for a few minutes to my room" and "said, in her shy, impressive way, 'Your paper makes a beautiful background for your face.'" Such was the "ecstasy" at the great author's remark that Harrison fainted. More characteristically robust was her response—at least as she tells it fifty years later in *Reminiscences*—when another famous visitor came to call. Helen Gladstone, daughter of the great Liberal statesman, was "a college friend of mine, or rather, more exactly, a friendly enemy." Harrison, as "a rigid Tory in those days", did not join in the general rapturous welcome of the "Grand Old Man" when he visited Newnham:

> *I shut myself up in my room. Thither—to tease me—she brought him. He sat down and asked me who was my favourite Greek author. Tact counselled Homer, but I was perverse and not quite truthful, so I said 'Euripides'. Aeschylus would have been creditable, Sophocles respectable, but the sceptic Euripides! It was too much, and with a few words of warning he withdrew.*

Harrison returned to Newnham in 1898 to take up a post with an unusually generous allowance of time for research. She was becoming established as an authority on myth; her influential *Prolegomena to the Study of Greek Religion* and *Themis: a Study of the Social Origins of Greek Religion* were published in 1903 and 1912. When she lectured, according to Francis Cornford, her "rather low voice vibrated with the excitement that had been working in her for many hours of preparation. The hushed audience would catch the nervous tension of her bearing, even before the simple conversational tones began to convey the anticipation of some mystery to be disclosed." In college she struck Frances Partridge, who came up as Frances Marshall in 1918, as wanting "to know everything and everybody" and "treated the young absolutely as equals." Since Harrison's charisma worked so well, it is difficult to obtain an objective impression of her; Mary Beard's *The Invention of Jane Harrison* (2000) attempts to deconstruct the myth. Harrison herself liked the image in the portrait Augustus John came to Newnham to paint in 1909: "a fine distinguished prize-fighter who has had a vision and collapsed under it."

The average Newnham don was, not surprisingly, less evidently remarkable than Jane Harrison. To student eyes in the 1950s many of them still seemed—as to Dody Ventura in Sylvia Plath's novel-fragment "Stone Boy With Dolphin"—"Victorian-vintage dons". Eleanor Bron, also at Newnham in the late 1950s, describes a "bizarre and lamentable" College Feast at which speeches were delivered "by women who were not at ease to women who were not very interested."

Plath's so-called Victorians dine on "apples, chunks of cheese and dietetic biscuits". (This was perhaps a wise choice; the students meanwhile are consuming "sodden dinners of spaghetti, turnips and slick fried egg, with purple raspberry fool for dessert".) Assuming a demure expression, Dody glides past the high table, away from "the scrolled white-painted hall with its gilt-framed portraits of Principals in high-necked gowns, leaning altruistic and radiant from the walls", to scrape the snow off her favourite statue. Plath, who lived across the grounds on the third floor of Whitstead, a house for foreign students at Newnham, records in her long journal entry for 19 February 1956 walking alone in the moonlight to see her "bronze boy", a copy of Verrocchio's *Boy With Dolphin.*

In the journal the statue begins a string of thoughts about children, women, and hatred of weakness. In the fiction its significance remains somewhat more elusive. Dody is going to a party, a version of the *St Botolph's Review* party at which Plath met Ted Hughes, with "safe, slow Hamish". The Leonard/Hughes whom she will encounter is not safe or slow, nor keen on dietetic biscuits. Dody chose men carefully, "with care and a curtsey to the stone figure in her garden". The statue returns several times in the story, like an object in a Plath poem—central, perhaps symbolic, but shifting, difficult to pin down to a single meaning. She tells Leonard that she has "this statue to break". He stamps, and "in the center of the maze, in the sanctum of the garden, a stone boy cracked, splintered, million-pieced." Yet when she gets back to the house she sees

> *the unbreakable stone boy in the garden, ironic, with Leonard's look, poised on that sculpted foot, holding fast to his dolphin, stone-lidded eyes fixed on a world beyond the clipped privet-hedge, beyond the box borders and the raked gravel of the cramped and formal garden paths. A world of no waste... a world love-kindled, love-championed.*

New Hall

The third college for women was founded in 1954 and was based originally at the Hermitage, now part of Darwin College. The move to the present site off Huntingdon Road began in 1962 and most of the buildings were finished in 1965. Even before their completion, *Cambridge New Architecture* concluded rather patronizingly that "In architectural history the line between grandeur and folly is a thin one. Is a poverty-stricken college of learned women the place to indulge in Byzantine whims?" It was the domed hall that attracted particular attention; Pevsner, too, is suspicious of the "shades" of Agra and Byzantium, and suggests that the architects Chamberlin, Powell and Bon probably "thought that for girls the easy beauty of this court was more appropriate than, say, the hardness of Churchill... The total whiteness was also probably chosen as something feminine." P. D. James' investigator Cordelia Gray, in *An Unsuitable Job for a Woman* (1972), also notices "the obtrusive femininity of its white brick" and is unsure about "the mannered prettiness of the shallow pools where the goldfish slipped like blood-red shadows between the water lilies." The dome makes her, like Pevsner before her, think of a peeled orange, and the whole place reminds her of "a harem; admittedly one owned by a sultan with liberal views and an odd predilection for clever girls, but a harem nevertheless."

Most people strolling in the light corridors and agreeably countrified grounds of the college, or coming upon Barbara Hepworth's bronze "Ascending Form (Gloria)" will find it difficult to be quite so suspicious. The Hepworth is part of the college's growing collection of women's art, built up mainly since 1986. There are also regular temporary exhibitions by women artists.

CHAPTER SEVEN

Cambridge Poets

In 1254 the clergy of the fledgling University of Cambridge accompanied the Bishop of Ely to Somersham in Huntingdonshire. Here they heard Michael of Cornwall's inventive verse attack on the frivolity, ignorance and dubious social standing (an ex-swineherd who now cleans sewers and works as a hangman, claims Michael) of his fellow Anglo-Latin poet Henry of Avranches. The flyting extended over three sessions in 1254-5, the other two taking place in Westminster or London. Later official occasions usually elicited less full-blooded verse. In June 1751 Horace Walpole told Sir Horace Mann that "We have been overwhelmed with lamentable Cambridge and Oxford dirges on the Prince's [Frederick, Prince of Wales'] death." But such occasions did provide poets with a concrete challenge; George Herbert's first published poems (in Latin) appeared in the Cambridge volume of "lamentable ... dirges" for Prince Henry in 1612 and Milton's *Lycidas*, more improbably, in a volume of tributes to Edward King of Christ's in 1638. The Chancellor's Medal for English poetry, first awarded in 1813, has called into being some fairly mediocre poems but also some more promising work like Tennyson's winning entry on the prescribed subject of "Timbuctoo" in 1829 or Edward Upward's on "Buddha" in 1924.

Yet most poets operate outside such formal parameters. In 1789 Wordsworth refrained from attaching verses to the coffin of the Master of St John's because he had not known the deceased; Tennyson, after his "Timbuctoo" victory, said that "Prize Poems... are not properly speaking 'Poems' at all, and ought to be forgotten as soon as recited." Poetry or more general student magazines provided a more informal opportunity for twentieth-century poets, as did poetry societies and readings—less university-dominated and now happening in houses, churches, halls and "cybercafés" as well as college rooms. Some poets actually wrote against the university and its formalities: Tennyson fired his youthful salvo against the whole useless place in "Lines on Cambridge of 1830". The communist poet John Cornford (1915-36) wrote unambiguously anti-establishment pieces—and a few love poems which register the personal cost of political commitment—when he was at Trinity. (In pursuit of the cause he was killed in the Spanish Civil War on his twenty-first birthday or the day after.)

There is, however, a tradition of Cambridge—the place and its surroundings more than the university as an institution—as a home of poetry, or at least to a succession of poets. In Book Three of *The Prelude* Wordsworth looks back to Chaucer, whose tale "of amorous passion" *The Reeve's Tale* is set in Trumpington, and to Milton, in whose supposed rooms at Christ's he "Poured out libations, to thy memory drank." In "The Old Vicarage, Grantchester", Rupert Brooke invoked Chaucer, Byron and Tennyson.

The poetic tradition also helped attract outsiders. In 1894 Stéphane Mallarmé spoke on "La Musique et les lettres" to twenty attentive people, mostly dons, in a candle-lit, wood-panelled room at Pembroke College. His larger, more general Oxford audience had been somewhat less receptive, but he was enthusiastic about both of the "collegiate towns" with their shaded greens and palaces, their life mixing the cloister, the school, and sport, where people, chosen and paid simply because they are charming, "live like peacocks to be the ornament of a garden." In fact, democracies—he felt that France provided nothing similar—ought to create such places for the benefit of poets. Dylan Thomas' response was less rarefied. In 1937 he came to read at St John's but was so drunk that he soon, with a cry of "I am a Dionysiac poet, a Dionysiac poet," collapsed. Usually better-behaved poets come to such events as the annual Cambridge Conference of Contemporary Poetry.

Grantchester Meadows: Sylvia Plath and Ted Hughes

Between autumn 1956 and summer 1957 the recently married Sylvia Plath and Ted Hughes rented the ground floor of 55 Eltisley Avenue, a Victorian terraced house near Grantchester Meadows. While living here Hughes taught at the secondary modern school that has now become Coleridge Community College and wrote poems including

"Thrushes" and "View of a Pig". Plath wrote poems such as "Hardcastle Crags", worked hard for her Cambridge tripos, and perseveringly typed and despatched copies of both Hughes' poems and her own to magazines and competitions. She scored a signal success for him when, in February 1957, the poems she had typed as *The Hawk in the Rain* won a competition sponsored by the American publishers Harpers and judged by the poets W. H. Auden, Marianne Moore and Stephen Spender.

Plath believed completely in Hughes' poetry: in *The Hawk in the Rain*, she wrote to her mother, "he combines intellect and grace of complex form, with lyrical music, male vigour and vitality, and moral commitment and love and awe of the world. O, he has everything!" In personal terms, too, there were few signs of how mutually destructive the poets' relationship would later become. But in "55 Eltisley" (published in *Birthday Letters*, 1998) Hughes sounds a somewhat foreboding note. All that seems to remain of the previous inhabitants of the house is a bloodstain on a pillow, probable evidence of the last illness of the man whose widow was moving out; the death and the bereavement are the only house-warming guests. But the time at 55 Eltisley was, once they had cleaned it, repainted the yellow walls grey, and moved their books in, mostly fulfilling. Plath rose early to write amid what she calls, in a journal entry for 11 March 1957, "A silvern burble and twit and blither of myriad birds outside secret in the blue misted light." And they often walked in the meadows, the subject of her "Watercolour of Grantchester Meadows". On 8 February 1957 she walked alone at morning by fields "shining bright silver-wet in the sun, and the sky a seethe of grey clouds and egg-shell blue patches, the dark bare trees along the river framing brilliant green meadows," allotments, the bare ploughed land. "I felt myself," she assured her mother and herself, "building up a core of peace inside." On 8 April 1957 she was up for the sunrise: "First, the luminous blue light, with big stars hanging [like the big planets of Hughes' "Horses"]; then pinkness, spreading translucent," the birds in the brambles, owls flying home, water-rats "skipping into the water." She also (Chaucer was her special subject for the coming exams) took the opportunity to stand on a stile and declaim from *The Canterbury Tales*—"Whan that Aprill with his shoures swoote..."—"to a pasture of cows". "I never had such an intelligent, fascinated audience," she told her mother. "You should have seen their expressions as they came flocking round me." She recited endlessly, unstoppably, Hughes remembers in "Chaucer". She had taken up one of her metaphorical "bumpers of champagne".

In February they had taken out into the fields a clay head of Plath made by a fellow-student at Smith College, Massachusetts. She told her mother that she had developed "a strange fondness for the old thing", but the poem she sent with her letter, "The Lady and the Earthenware Head", expresses darker feelings. Although the head is not even a good likeness she finds it difficult to "junk", fearing to break the traditional bond between self and effigy. (The poem, much worked over, reads like a brilliant parody of the earlier literature she was reading at the time— perhaps suitably in a piece so aware of old superstitions. It lacks the concentrated power of her more successful, mostly later work, and she came to dislike it.) At Hughes' suggestion they left it "high up on a branch-platform in a gnarled willow... like a monument at rest in the midst of nature." Later in "The Earthenware Head" Hughes puzzles over the profound uneasiness it caused her, the "perverse rite" of its disposal, and what happened to it afterwards: preserved like the "cold pastoral" of Keats' Grecian Urn, or smashed by boys as feared in Plath's poem, or fallen with the tree, or lost in the river-mud. Like many of the poems in *Birthday Letters*, this piece seeks to engage in dialogue with Plath, her poems, the past and the nature of memory rather than coming to firm conclusions.

Probably Plath would have taken her head elsewhere, addressed other cows, were it not for the activities of the Cambridge Preservation Society, which, formed in 1928, scored an early victory for environmentalism in 1931-2 when it defeated a planned by-pass across Grantchester Meadows. Some 110 acres of the land were secured from such development, and the most popular Cambridge walk continued. In university circles the walk was once known as the Grantchester Grind. A wider audience heard of the "lazy water meadow" from Pink Floyd's "Grantchester Meadows" (1969).

Grantchester: Rupert Brooke

The destinations of the modern Grind include the village's four public houses, the smallest of which, the Blue Ball, is famous for its ancient simplicity—no music, five tables, two sorts of beer both approved of by the Campaign for Real Ale—and the Orchard tea garden, which prided itself, in the early twentieth century, on selling no ale at all: a notice proclaimed that it had no connection with any public house and was patronized by Varsity Men. The respectability of the establishment is further stressed in a photograph (reproduced in the Orchard's souvenir booklet) of the staff standing ready in their long white aprons. The older woman in the picture, Mrs Stevenson, who lived in Orchard House, first served tea to some undergraduates beneath the apple trees in 1897. Although there is now a fair amount of indoor seating, the orchard itself, with its deck chairs and, in season, abundant blossom or fruit, is still very popular.

Next to the orchard a small free museum now documents the life of Rupert Brooke (1887-1915). The orchard might have been lost, and Mrs Stevenson forgotten, had Brooke not been her tenant at Orchard House in 1909 and 1910. She herself becomes almost part of the place: "an old lady like an apple (especially in face)" who fed him on honey, eggs and milk, in Brooke's letter of July 1909 to Noel Olivier, later for a time his unofficial fiancée. The landlady and the diet both suggest the wholesome rustic Englishness that Brooke would later, at least half seriously, celebrate in "The Old Vicarage, Grantchester". His room at the Stevensons', he told a friend, Erica Cotterill, "opens straight out onto a stone verandah covered with creepers, and a little old garden full of old-fashioned flowers and *crammed* with roses. I work at Shakespeare, read, write all day, and now and then wander in the woods or by the river."

He had come here, ostensibly, to escape from the distractions of Cambridge, and did succeed in putting in some work for his dissertation on Puritanism in English Renaissance drama. But "the apple blossom and the river and the sunsets have combined to make me relapse into a more than Wordsworthian communion with nature, which prevents me from reading more than 100 lines in a day, or thinking at all." He was also much visited by friends for tea, conversation, and (usually naked) swimming expeditions. The list of Bloomsbury and other friends who came—Russell, Woolf, Keynes and Forster among them—remains good advertising for the Orchard. When visitors arrived he would, he assured Cotterill, "mock them and pour the cream down their necks and roll them in the rose-beds or push them in the river, and they hate me and go away." On 1 May 1910, he told Olivier, "a great many people ... decided to breakfast with me"; although it rained, "they all turned up, thousands of them, men and women, devastatingly and indomitably cheery." When the rain stopped they "put on goloshes and gathered cowslips in the fields" and engaged in the mock-pagan ritual of worshipping a mandrake. People still punt from Cambridge to Grantchester on May Morning. And bright if by this time bedraggled young things have also, traditionally, poled here after their May Balls.

Whether or not the Stevensons knew about the mandrake worship, Brooke's and his friends' way of life was not, it seems, entirely acceptable to them. "The village 'talked' because of bare feet," he told his friend Dudley Ward on 10 May, and later in the summer he found that his old rooms had been let. Instead, he moved next door and rented, as on a longer-term basis from May 1911, two ground-floor and one first-floor rooms at the Old Vicarage. Built in about 1685, the house had been the vicarage until the 1820s. From the early 1850s it belonged to Samuel Page Widnall (1825-94), a Grantchester notable who wrote a history of the village and built the Castle Ruin—a folly in the Old Vicarage garden. In the church the distinctive (rather quaintly home-made) candelabra and the model of the building before its extension in 1875-6 are Widnall's work. By Brooke's time the Neeve family lived in the house; their beehives supplied the Orchard and were doubtless one reason for the much-quoted and much-parodied final question of "The Old Vicarage, Grantchester": "And is there honey still for tea?" (Tea is interrupted because the honey attracts hornets in Nevill Willmer's illustrated poem "The New Heritage Grantchester" (1981). In a Peter Sellers sketch of the 1950s Brooke's yearning question is answered by a waitress who tells her customer that honey, like everything else he has asked for, is "off, dear.")

Brooke's mother bought the Old Vicarage after his death. In 1931 she left it to Dudley Ward. In 1979 it was bought by Jeffrey and Mary Archer, the first of whom, popular and much-mocked novelist, former Deputy Chairman of the Conservative Party, and imprisoned for perjury in 2001-3, has often been described as "notorious". Mary Archer, a university chemist who works on solar energy, has been doomed to bear the epithet "fragrant" since Mr Justice Caulfield first saluted her "elegance, fragrance and radiance" at the end of her husband's libel action against the *Daily Star* in 1987. But the house remains indelibly associated with its earlier occupant. Often sitting on the "soft lawn with a sundial and tangled, antique flowers", Brooke worked here on his second dissertation, on the Jacobean playwright John Webster, and wrote some of the poems published in the first Georgian anthology (1912). He wrote the famous Grantchester poem, however, in a café in Berlin in May 1912 in a very different state of mind from the one he had enjoyed in his "Arcady". By this time he was in emotional crisis, swinging between love of several women and wild misogyny, his letters full of irrational hatred for friends and for himself. Gone were the days of acting in student plays, cycling around Grantchester to deliver Fabian pamphlets, basking in the adoration of male and female followers; his posthumous transformation into a heroic epitome of Englishness required the suppression of everything that was most flawed and most interesting about him. But, give or take some racist or misanthropic muttering against the "*Temperamentvoll* German Jews" in the café, the poem makes contact with, or further idealizes, the Grantchester idyll: the lilac in bloom, the chestnuts making "a tunnel of green gloom", the May fields all golden:

Ah God! To see the branches stir
Across the moon at Grantchester!
To smell the thrilling-sweet and rotten
Unforgettable, unforgotten
River-smell, and hear the breeze
Sobbing in the little trees.

Nowhere but Grantchester will do. But it comes as a relief, to anyone expecting the poem to concentrate only on the golden land of honey and the clock for ever stopped at ten to three, that the point is made through humour. Lesser local settlements are rejected because

At Over they fling oaths at one
And worse than oaths at Trumpington,
And Ditton girls are mean and dirty,

> *And there's none in Harston under thirty,*
> *And folks in Shelford and those parts*
> *Have twisted lips and twisted hearts,*
> *And Barton men make Cockney rhymes,*
> *And Coton's full of nameless crimes,*
> *And things are done you'd not believe*
> *In Madingley on Christmas Eve.*

The exaltation of Grantchester is a poetic exaggeration, a rhetorical ploy—itself almost funny—but with an edge also of desperation for a world that may be lost, that probably never existed.

There is, of course, no trace of irony in the quotation from the poem—"men with Splendid hearts"—on the war memorial by the village church. Brooke's name is more worn than the others on the memorial, rubbed away by the devoted or the curious. Among the early pilgrims were Scott and Zelda Fitzgerald, who came here briefly towards the end of their European tour of 1921.

The church has, unusually, several graveyards. The first, by the building, has marked graves from the 1690s onwards. Several fellows of Corpus Christi College are commemorated by a column surmounted by a pelican, symbol of the college and of Christ's sacrifice. Inside the church the seventeenth-century pulpit, transferred in 1835, was the Master's stall in the old chapel at Corpus. Beyond a wall lies the second churchyard, begun in 1872. Those buried here include Anne Jemima Clough (1820-92), first Principal of Newnham College and sister of the poet Arthur

Hugh Clough. A third yard was consecrated in 1910 and a fourth in 2002.

Byron's Pool

In Ravenna in January 1821 Byron read the invocation to the goddess of the river Severn in Milton's *Comus*: "Sabrina fair/Listen where thou art sitting/Under the glassy, cool, translucent wave..." This song, says Byron in his journal, "has brought back upon me—I know not how or why—the happiest, perhaps, days of my life... when living at Cambridge with Edward Noel Long, afterwards of the Guards" and lost at sea in 1809. The two Trinity undergraduates "were rival swimmers",

fond of riding—reading—and of conviviality... The description of Sabrina's seat reminds me of our rival feats in diving. Though Cam's is not a very 'translucent wave', it was fourteen feet deep, where we used to dive for, and pick up—having thrown them in on purpose—plates, eggs, and even shillings. I remember, in particular, there was the stump of a tree (at least ten or twelve feet deep) in the bed of the river, in a spot where we bathed most commonly, round which I used to cling.

By the time Rupert Brooke came to Grantchester this "spot" had long been identified as a pool a quarter of a mile off the road between Grantchester and Trumpington, where the river Rhee is joined by Bourn Brook and becomes the Cam. Brooke imagines, in "The Old Vicarage", that "His ghostly Lordship" still swims here and "tries the actions, essays the tricks,/Long learnt on Hellespont, or Styx." Brooke himself often swam in Byron's Pool. His passion for cool immersion suggests his belief (later verging on the obsessive) in cleanliness as a physical manifestation of inner wholeness and wholesomeness. "In Grantchester their skins are white;/They bathe by day, they bathe by night" (uncomfortable lines, of course, when taken in conjunction with the racism elsewhere in the poem). But there was a simpler appeal to such summer expeditions as the one recalled by Brooke's friend David "Bunny" Garnett:

[At midnight] we went out of the garden of the Old Vicarage into the lane full of thick white dust, which slipped under our weight as we walked

> *noiselessly in our sand-shoes, and then through the dew-soaked grass of*
> *the meadow over the mill-wall leading to the pool, to bathe naked in the*
> *unseen water, smelling of wild peppermint and mud.*

The Reeve's Tale

Once Byron's Pool had a more practical purpose. Until the late fifteenth century it adjoined Trumpington Mill. (This should not be confused with Grantchester Mill, on the edge of the village, the wall of which Garnett mentions and which burned down in 1928. The tall mill-house was rebuilt as a private residence.) Here Geoffrey Chaucer set the third of his *Canterbury Tales*, the Reeve's Tale. Nobody knows whether Chaucer visited the area, but the topography is plausible and he knew the local landowner Sir Roger de Trumpington. Sir Roger's crusader forebear and namesake, who died in 1289, is commemorated by a brass, one of the earliest in England, in Trumpington church.

Chaucer's Miller has just told a tale at the expense of an Oxford carpenter who is made a complete fool of by his young wife Alisoun and her lover, the "clerk" or student Nicholas. Bad feeling between the Miller and the Reeve has already been indicated; the Reeve is a carpenter by trade, and reeves and millers were proverbial enemies— while the former strove to provide the maximum yield for their lords, the latter had a reputation for sharp practice. The Reeve's Tale is partly an act of revenge (although as in most of *The Canterbury Tales* the identity of the pilgrim speaker soon becomes less important than the demands of genre—fabliau, in this case—and the particular tale to be told.) The revenge consists of making the miller of Trumpington fall victim, even more spectacularly than the Oxford carpenter, to clerkly ingeniousness and sexual vigour; possibly this is also an early example of Oxford v. Cambridge competition.

The students, Aleyn and John, northerners whose speech includes such dialectal variants as "sal" for "shall" and "banes" for "bones", have come from Soler Hall, almost certainly a name for King's Hall (later absorbed by Trinity College), which had a noticeable number of solars or upper rooms and of northern students. They have come to have the college wheat ground. The college Manciple, the official who is usually in charge of such business, is ill and the miller has been taking the opportunity to cheat the college even more outrageously than usual.

The students have persuaded their master or "wardeyn" to lend them his horse, promising that "The millere sholde not stele hem half a pekke/Of corn by sleighte."

At first, the miller, "deynous Symkyn"—"scornful Simon"—seems to have all the advantages on his side: bristling with weaponry, he evidently bullies everyone as he insists on the high status of his proud wife, who is the illegitimate daughter of the supposedly celibate village priest. (In 1343 a real Rector of Trumpington was succeeded by his son, although he was removed from office soon afterwards.) The clerks intend to watch the miller closely, alert for any malpractice, but he distracts them simply by going off to untie their horse; the stallion makes off for the fen where the wild mares run, calling to them with an enthusiastic "wehee". J. A. W. Bennett, in *Chaucer at Oxford and at Cambridge* (1974), concludes that the fen in question was the area between the Rhee and Bourn Brook still called Lingay Fen. While Aleyn and John chase the horse around the fen with desperate cries of "Keep! Keep! Stand! Stand! Jossa," the miller purloins enough of the college flour for his wife to make a "cake" or loaf. At last the wayward mount is captured in a ditch. When the students, "wery, and weet, as beest is in the reyn", finally arrive back at the mill, it is too late to ride back to Cambridge. Symkyn grudgingly grants them what lodging he can—they all have to sleep in one room—and sends his daughter Malyne out to buy ale.

During the night, the clerks wreak their unexpected revenge, the sort of crude revenge which fabliau relishes. The strong ale has knocked Symkyn out; one stage beyond mere snoring, he "fnorteth" like a horse. His wife and daughter snore too, and this "melodye" keeps their guests awake: awake enough for Aleyn to decide on the best way to get his own back on the corn-pilfering miller: "yon wenche will I swyve." John urges caution—out of fear of the miller, not moral scruple—but Aleyn crosses the room and "shortly for to seyn, they were aton" ("at one"). John is still unhappy with his colleague's conduct, this time out of envy and because when this "jape" is recounted people will hold him "a daf, a cokenay!" (a fool, a weakling). Rather than that, he will try his own luck. Malyne's baby brother is sleeping in a cradle at the foot of the parents' bed. Inspired by native wit and the folk-tale tradition, John moves the cradle to the foot of his own bed. Soon the miller's wife stops snoring and goes "out to pisse." When she comes back she misses the cot, gropes about in the dark, finds it, and gets into bed with the clerk, cheerfully reflecting on how dreadful it would have been if she had done just that. Soon her bedfellow—her husband, she thinks—proves more vigorous than usual.

The concise, brutal farce draws towards a close as Aleyn also picks the wrong bed and tells Symkyn, not John, what he has been doing. In the ensuing fight the miller's wife grabs a staff and smashes it down on what, by the glimmering of the moon through a hole, she takes for Aleyn's nightcap but is actually her husband's bald head, earlier well "varnished" by the drink. The clerks beat him up, dress, and on their way out collect the stolen loaf which Malyne, who enjoyed Aleyn's attentions, had told him about. And thus, triumphantly concludes the Reeve, "have I quyt the Millere in my tale."

Trinity College

Henry VIII's foundation of Trinity College in 1546 was a characteristically large and absolute project: he amalgamated three earlier institutions, King's Hall (established by Edward II in 1317), Michaelhouse, and Physwick Hostel and enriched the college with the revenue of some twenty-six dissolved religious houses. The royal connection has remained, in spite of the *lèse-majesté* of the chair-leg, which, at an unknown date, replaced the sceptre held by Henry's statue of 1601-15 on the Great Gate (built between 1490 and the 1530s as a gatehouse for King's Hall). On the other side of the gate the statues are of James I, Anne of Denmark and their son the future Charles I (1615). Elizabeth I (1597) is on the gatehouse in the south range of Great Court and a seventeenth-century Edward III on the tower by the chapel—an earlier, relocated gatehouse of King's Hall. Safe as yet from chair-legs, the belligerent monarch in his bulging breastplate thrusts his sword through the three crowns of England, Ireland and France. Edward VII, George VI and Prince Charles were Trinity undergraduates. The Mastership is still a Crown appointment.

But Trinity has not collected only royal scalps. Partly because it was always one of the larger colleges, its alumni include many Nobel Prize-winning scientists, the historians Macaulay and Trevelyan, Sir J. G. Frazer, author of *The Golden Bough*, philosophers from Bacon to

Russell, and an implausible-sounding list of poets including Herbert, Marvell, Dryden, Byron and Tennyson.

With the power, size—the Great Court measures 340 by 288 feet—and wealth of Trinity came a reputation, sometimes deserved, for luxury. Inevitably when the *Daily Worker* published the menu of a college feast in 1932 it was Trinity's. The student weekly *Granta*, flippantly taking up the communist daily's "cooking hints", suggested that "maybe there is a moral attached, such as 'Stop being one of the workers. Become a Trinity Don instead.'" Twenty years earlier A. A. Milne, light-heartedly looking back at his time at Trinity in his poem "Golden Memories", maintained that his most powerful Cambridge recollection was not of sport, work, the river or even the editorship of his beloved *Granta*, but Salmon Mayonnaise and—its only possible rival, revealed at the climax of the poem—Crème Brûlée.

For students who overdose on crème brûlée there is the drastic digestive option of the Great Court Run. Traditionally (the details vary) the aim is to run round the perimeter of the court, in full evening-dress and after a lavish Trinity feast, while the clock chimes its twenty-four strokes at midnight. Harold Abrahams was one of the more famous athletes to undertake this feat; in the 1981 film *Chariots of Fire* (where Eton stands in for Trinity) he succeeds—as in reality did the Olympic hurdler Lord Burghley, descendant of the Elizabethan statesman and Cambridge Chancellor. His time, on 7 June 1927, was 42.5 seconds. The run has continued to attract professional athletes—in 1988 Sebastian Coe beat Steve Cram, at noon and not in evening dress—as well as less practised and often inebriated participants. Up to 2,000 runners, the great majority of them sober, take part in the annual Chariots of Fire charity relay race, which usually goes through part of Trinity grounds.

Most of the time the court is more peaceful. The Master's Lodge and Combination Room glow warmly red at evening. Water runs, or occasionally is spectacularly frozen, in the central fountain. The Jacobean fountain-head (restored in 1715) was put up by Thomas Nevile, Master 1593-1615, who was responsible for much of the remaining lay-out and appearance of the college but was by no means the last incumbent of the Lodge to have a powerful impact on his contemporaries. Much the most famous or notorious is Richard Bentley (1662-1742), the great classical scholar and less great reviser of Milton who, in spite of his colleagues' best efforts to remove him, remained in position from 1699 until his death. The many bones of contention included his introduction of tough new tests for prospective fellows, his lavish restoration of the Lodge—and especially the splendid new staircase—and his high-handed treatment of the fellows, most of whom he clearly regarded as inferior creatures. Macaulay said that his was "a spirit daring even to rashness, self-confident even to negligence, and proud even to insolent ferocity." Once, just when his enemies seemed to be about to succeed in getting him removed, he was saved by the sudden death of the Bishop of Ely, John Moore, who, as Visitor of the college, had been about to pronounce the sentence of deprivation. In 1718 he was stripped of his degrees by the university Senate, before which he had refused to appear, but six years later they were restored by the Court of King's Bench. In 1734 those enemies who survived seemed at last to have obtained his dismissal but he simply refused to go, seizing on the fact that it was laid down in the statutes that the Vice-Master must carry through the business of removing him. The loyal Vice-Master, Richard Walker, could be relied on to do no such thing; his complaisance in bringing the great Bentley's hat when called earned him a place beside him in Pope's *Dunciad*:

> *His hat, which never vail'd to human pride,*
> *Walker with rev'rence took, and laid aside.*
> *Low bowed the rest: He, kingly, did but nod.*

Finally in 1735 the Master and fellows reached a compromise by which he ceased actively to run the college but was allowed still to reside in the Lodge. Here he continued his scholarship and his surprisingly harmonious domestic life, as fondly remembered in the memoirs of his grandson, the playwright Richard Cumberland, who was born at the Lodge in 1732.

Bentley, in spite of his prominence in college history and the "daemonic energy" with which, in Lytton Strachey's words, he "revivified... the whole domain of classical scholarship," was not granted the Trinity accolade of a statue in the chapel. Bentley himself had, in 1706-17, transformed the interior of the Tudor chapel (the main survival of which is the wooden carvings in the ante-chapel), installing the grand screen and reredos. But the first statue, Roubiliac's Newton, was put into this setting by Robert Smith, Master 1742-68, as part of his campaign to establish the intellectual reputation of the college. Roubiliac accordingly presented, Patricia Fara points out in *Newton: the Making of Genius* (2002), "an Enlightenment gentleman engaged in public discourse and inspired by God." By contrast, William Wordsworth responded to the statue with "Romantic perceptions of a solitary genius detached from normal life". From his bedroom in neighbouring St John's in the late 1780s he could see, "in moonlight nights"

> *The antechapel where the statue stood*
> *Of Newton with his prism and silent face,*
> *The marble index of a mind for ever*
> *Voyaging through strange seas of Thought, alone.*

(The first two lines are included in the 1805 version of The Prelude but the last two were added, in a rare late moment of insight or felicity, in about 1840.)

The Victorian college added four more statues to the pantheon. Henry Weekes' Bacon of 1845 commemorated a Trinity man with an earlier claim to be considered the founding father of modern science, or who, from the perspective of the period as encapsulated in George Pryme's "Ode to Trinity College" (1812), caught

The first faint gleam of manly thought,
That broke on that benighted age
To guide the wanderings of the sage.

The ruffed Bacon (derived closely from a monument in St Albans) looks like one of "the sage", but is perhaps less convincing than the more contemporary statues. The same is true, to a degree, of Matthew Noble's bewigged Barrow of 1853. (Isaac Barrow, first Lucasian Professor of Mathematics from 1663 until he resigned in favour of his pupil Newton in 1669, was Master of Trinity 1672-7). Thomas Woolner's Macaulay (1868) honours the historian who, in 1822-4, occupied rooms in Great Court, Staircase E. (Newton had lived on the same staircase.) Macaulay was known as a prodigious and retentive reader; his nephew Sir G. O. Trevelyan says that he would pace the court each morning, "reading with the same eagerness and the same rapidity, whether the volume was the most abstruse of treatises, the loftiest of poems, or the flimsiest of novels." Woolner's Whewell (1872) portrays the formidable polymath—philosopher of science, geologist, astronomer, theologian and much else—who was Master from 1841 to 1866 and who is often unfairly typecast by Sydney Smith's epigram: "science was his forte and omniscience his foible."

The last statue, Sir Hamo Thorneycroft's Tennyson (1909) is, in Pevsner's opinion, "like the prima donna's noble father in Italian opera, characteristically Edwardian, compared with Woolner's dignified simplicity." Tennyson himself, it is true, might have laughed at such laureate nobility. When he was an undergraduate at Trinity his feelings for the Cambridge establishment had been far from reverent. "Lines on

Cambridge of 1830" thunders, with youthful ardour, against halls and ancient colleges, "Your portals statued with old kings and queens", "Wax-lighted chapels, and rich carven screens,/Your doctors and your proctors and your deans." But the university reformed and Tennyson became embarrassed by the poem's "spirit of undergraduate irritability". Thorneycroft's statue is true to the public face of the older Tennyson. This is not someone who can be imagined inventing the anguished speakers of "Mariana" or *Maud*; but he can just about be imagined writing "Ulysses"—"strong in will/To strive, to seek, to find, and not to yield." All the statues, however, are to be seen at their best when they punctuate, and seem to entertain dialogue with, a crowd of living people during the interval of a concert in the chapel.

Nevile's Court and the Wren Library

Beyond Nevile's magnificently decorated Jacobean hall with its hammer-beam roof and screen (covered, as Pevsner puts it, in a "barbarous profusion of strap-panels, caryatids, etc."), the Master built, at his own expense, a cloistered court (completed in 1612). The conception was sufficiently classical for John Evelyn, who thought Great Court overrated, to acknowledge Nevile's Court in 1654 as "cloistered and well built". Nevile's Court feels particularly tranquil at dusk; it no doubt seemed all the more so in the pauses of Bertrand Russell's and his friends' conversation as they walked and talked here until the early hours after Apostles' meetings. It was just outside the college walls, however, that Russell experienced one of his most dramatic early realizations: "I had gone out to buy a tin of tobacco, and was going back with it along Trinity Lane, when suddenly I threw it up in the air and exclaimed 'Great God in boots!—the ontological argument is sound!'"

Byron's "*Super*excellent rooms" were almost certainly in Nevile's Court, probably on staircase I (where Russell later had rooms when he was a fellow) in spite of a tradition which put him on staircase K in Great Court. The attraction of that location was the presence of a turret in which Byron's bear could be imagined living. The bear, who did at least briefly reside in college, excited—was obviously expected to excite—questions. When "they asked me what I meant to do with him... my reply was 'He should sit for a fellowship.'" Byron, as a nobleman with an allowance of £500 a year, could afford to be contemptuous about the fellows. Exempted by his status from anything as tedious as examinations, he spent much of his time at Cambridge (off and on in 1805-7, when not enjoying gambling and sex in London) riding, swimming, boxing, drinking, or being with the Trinity choirboy John Edleston, two years his junior, whom, Byron said in 1807, he loved "certainly... more than any human being."

But painstaking academic work was not to be expected when, as he told the family solicitor John Hanson with only some exaggeration, "Study is the last pursuit of the Society; the Master eats, drinks, and sleeps; the Fellows drink, dispute and pun, the employments of the undergraduates you will probably conjecture without my description." Byron developed such impressions in two early satirical poems. "Thoughts Suggested by a College Examination" has "Magnus" (William Lort Mansel, Master since 1798), exalted like Milton's Satan:

> *Plac'd on his chair of state, he seems a god,*
> *While Sophs and Freshmen tremble at his nod.*
> *As all around sit wrapt in speechless gloom,*
> *His voice, in thunder, shakes the sounding dome;*
> *Denouncing dire reproach to luckless fools*
> *Unskill'd to plod in mathematic rules.*

"Granta: a Medley" surveys satirically, from "St Mary's spire", a university of fellows who, being "sage, reflecting men" are happy to trade votes for advancement; the candidates for college prizes, "Deprived of many a wholesome meal;/In barbarous Latin doom'd to wrangle" while their colleagues dice and drink; and a college choir who are such "a set of croaking sinners" that

> *If David, when his toils were ended,*
> *Had heard these blockheads sing before him,*
> *To us his psalms had ne'er descended,—*
> *In furious mood he would have tore 'em.*

"The Cornelian", in more sentimental vein, was inspired by Edleston's parting gift of a cornelian heart; with some financial aid from Byron he was "to be stationed in a mercantile house of considerable eminence in the Metropolis."

By Byron's time Nevile's Court, originally three-sided, had long been closed by the Wren Library, that "baroque hovercraft on fire" once observed in spring sunshine by Clive James. The court was lengthened, and the library erected, between 1676 and 1695. Much attention was lavished on the interior, including armorial bearings, grasshoppers and vegetation, carved in limewood by Grinling Gibbons: "miracles," as David McKitterick says in *The Making of the Wren Library* (1995), "of undercutting and sculptural delicacy". Most of the busts, however, arrived later as part of Robert Smith's plan to celebrate and promote Trinity through its notables. Between 1751 and 1757 Roubiliac produced some of his finest and most various portrait sculpture. The subjects include Bacon, Bentley—placed less controversially in the library than he would have been in the chapel—and the great seventeenth-century jurist Sir Edward Coke. Several other eighteenth-century artists including Rysbrack contributed busts. Giovanni Battista Cipriani designed the window in which Bacon presents Newton to George III, a conception admired in its own day but often ridiculed later; the 1835 guidebook *Ambulator* censors it as "surely a strange anachronism" and "a gross violation of propriety and truth". And there is Thorvaldsen's seated statue of Byron—here the noble poet, for whom quips about fellows and bears would surely be unthinkable.

The Wren Library was, before the Fitzwilliam opened, the nearest thing the town had to a public museum. Here you could see not only books or manuscripts but, as *A Concise and Accurate Description of...Cambridge* explained in 1790,

> *a dried human body of one of the original inhabitants of the Madeiras; a curious Chinese pagod, a lock of Sir Isaac Newton's hair, head of Newton in wax, an universal ring dial, quadrant and compass of Sir Isaac Newton's; a large lizard, the greatest in the kingdom; a quiver of arrows fought with by King Richard III against Henry VII at the memorable battle of Bosworth; a curious skeleton of a man in miniature, cut out by a shepherd's boy; a stone taken from the wife of a locksmith at St Edmund's Bury after her death...*

There are still some Newton relics but at present the main objects on display are manuscripts: the only surviving volume of autograph Milton; Tennyson's *Maud*; one of Byron's letters about his feat of swimming the Hellespont, Housman's *A Shropshire Lad*; a bright, surprisingly new-looking fifteenth-century Book of Hours owned later by Anne of Austria; the letter in which Michael Faraday accepts Whewell's suggested new terms "anode", "cathode", and "ion".

The Avenue and the Fellows' Garden

In 1838 Tennyson came to muse on the scenes of his and Arthur Hallam's youth:

Up that long walk of limes I passed
To see the rooms in which he dwelt.

Another name was on the door;
I lingered; all within was noise
Of clapping hands, and boys,
That crashed the glass and beat the floor;

Where once we held debate, a band
Of youthful friends, on mind and art,
And labour, and the changing mart,
And all the framework of the land.

Hallam (who lived on the first floor of William Wilkins' 1820s New Court) shone beyond everyone else—in fact "the God within him" lit his face—in those debates as remembered or idealized in Tennyson's *In Memoriam* (1850). The avenue still patterns or formalizes the approach to Trinity from the Backs.

On the other side of Queen's Road is the Fellows' Garden (rarely open to the public), substantially larger and more wooded than most others. Here on a warm Sunday in June 1889 Robert Browning, who was visiting Cambridge, was unusually confiding to Edmund Gosse about himself and his work. They sat, says Gosse, "under the shadow of a tree, in a garden-chair... The blue sky was cloudless above, summer foliage hemmed us round in a green mist, a pink mountain of double-may in blossom rose in front." Apparently oblivious to these surroundings, Browning talked for two hours. He briefly sketched out a plan for a poem with a characteristically "non-obvious or inverted moral", and he marvelled at "the audacious obstinacy which had made him, when a youth, determine to be a poet and nothing but a poet" and on the other hand at "the desolateness"—which he usually denied—"of his early and middle life as a literary man" in the face of hostile criticism.

Sixteen years earlier, when George Eliot came to Trinity, the weather was rainy and the garden conversation less personal but the interlocutor, F. W. H. Myers, a fellow of the college, was even more impressed. Eliot's text was the three words "God", "Immortality" and "Duty"; she

> *pronounced, with terrible earnestness, how inconceivable was the first, how unbelievable the second, and yet how peremptory and absolute the third. Never, perhaps, have sterner accents affirmed the sovereignty of impersonal and unrecompensing Law. I listened, and night fell; her grave, majestic countenance turned towards me like a Sibyl's in the gloom... And when at last we parted, amid that columnar circuit of the forest trees... I seemed to be gazing, like Titus at Jerusalem, on vacant seats and empty halls—on a sanctuary with no presence to hallow it, and heaven left lonely of God.*

How much of this is Myers rather than Eliot nobody knows. She had just finished exploring such ideas in accents interestingly less stern in *Middlemarch*.

Whewell's Court

Thom Gunn distinguishes "Nevile's Court for perfection, Great Court for show, and Whewell's Court for living in"—as he did in 1950-3. The college had expanded across Trinity Street, on the initiative of William Whewell, into Gunn's "fine example of heavy Victorian Gothic" in 1859-68. (The architect was Anthony Salvin.) Other well-known inmates have included the poet A. E. Housman during his years as the apparently dry and unpoetic Kennedy Professor of Latin; two students of rather different persuasion who overlapped with him were the communist student organizer James Klugmann and the then communist (he remained a Marxist) Victor Kiernan, according to whom the professor was "anchored by misanthropy to this out-of-the-way spot". But he occasionally revealed more sympathetic feelings. In the Leslie Stephen lecture of 1933 Housman told his large audience about poetry as emotion, appealing to "something in man which is obscure and latent, something older than the present organisation of his nature, like the patches of fen which still linger here and there in the drained lands of Cambridgeshire."

Not surprisingly in view of such sentiments, the rigorously logical Ludwig Wittgenstein, who lived above him in Whewell's Court, did not get on with Housman, who, as a "philosophical hedonist" notoriously denied him the use of his private WC in his hour of need. Wittgenstein was involved in a more public disagreement, again with both a physical and a theoretical dimension, at a meeting of the Cambridge Moral Science Club, in King's College, in October 1946. Karl Popper was the guest speaker and Bertrand Russell, who approved of Popper's *The Open Society and its Enemies*, was also present. As Popper remembered it in *Unended Quest* (1974), Wittgenstein, increasingly angry as he dismissed the philosophical "problems" raised by the speaker, started to use a poker "like a conductor's baton to emphasise his assertions." When the poker-wielder demanded an example of a moral rule, Popper replied, "'Not to threaten visiting lecturers with pokers.' Whereupon Wittgenstein, in a rage, threw the poker down and stormed out of the room, banging the door behind him." But Popper's version of events has been vehemently rejected by several witnesses. David Edwards and John Eidnow have investigated the incident and its background in *Wittgenstein's Poker* (2001), where they present—food for more philosophy and some psychology—"clear memories equally in conflict. The poker is red-hot or it is cold. Wittgenstein gesticulates with it angrily or uses it as a baton, as an example, as a tool... He leaves quietly or abruptly... Russell speaks in a high-pitched voice, or he roars."

Christ's College; John Milton
In the depths of the Fellows' Garden at Christ's is a deep rectangular pool, built principally for hardy bathing in the mid-eighteenth century, and supplied with water from Hobson's Conduit. There is a small pavilion and seat at one end, good for quiet contemplation. And around the pool are busts and urns commemorating great ones of the college, all contemplative in one way or another. The urns are for Joseph Mede, the seventeenth-century scholar and millenarian ("most learned in mystical divinity", as Thomas Fuller put it) and the novelist, scientist and administrator C. P. Snow (1905-80). The busts represent

Ralph Cudworth (Regius Professor of Hebrew 1645-88 and Master of Christ's 1654-88), the eighteenth-century mathematician Nicholas Saunderson, and John Milton, who took his BA at the college in 1629 and his MA in 1632.

Tradition says that Milton wandered poetically in the gardens. The venerable so-called "Milton's Mulberry" survived from three hundred such trees planted in the year of Milton's birth, 1608, in deference to James I's desire to produce silk. (The scheme proved short-lived since the wrong species of mulberry was chosen.) Possibly the poet did wander about composing verses in the orchard, but it is an image which fits rather well with other attempts, in the eighteenth and nineteenth centuries especially, to make him into a safely poetical figure only—not a republican controversialist or an independent Puritan.

On the whole Milton was too busy, and sometimes too frustrated, to pace the college greensward. He studied hard, as he had since boyhood. But in 1628 or 1629, under the guise of taking one side in a Latin debate, he took the opportunity to question the value of a curriculum which consisted of "the trivial disputations of sour old men". There were also, in his first year or two, more personal problems. The pale, long-haired youth, sixteen at the time of his arrival in Cambridge, soon became known as "the Lady of Christ's". His dedication to work, virtue and high ideas no doubt contributed to this image. Although the death of one of his college contemporaries, Edward King, was later the occasion of *Lycidas*, he seems not to have known either King or anyone else in Cambridge particularly well. He also, for reasons unknown, fell foul of his tutor, William Chappell. Their quarrel may have been about Milton's problems with the "sour old men" or about politics or religion—Chappell approved of William Laud, future royalist Archbishop of Canterbury and arch-enemy of Puritans. Whatever the reason (perhaps just a clash between strong-willed teacher and strong-willed pupil), Milton was rusticated or temporarily sent down, probably in 1626. A more colourful version of his punishment originated either with his brother Christopher or with John Aubrey, the author of *Brief Lives*. Christopher told Aubrey, many years later, that Milton received "some unkindness" from Mr Chappell, and Aubrey at some point wrote "whip't him" above "unkindness". (Samuel Johnson expanded on this in his *Life of Milton*.) Such treatment was sometimes meted out to younger students, but is very unlikely in this case.

Milton's time at Christ's was not, however, all unhappy. After his rustication he was allowed to transfer to a more congenial tutor, Nathaniel Tovey. His relations with his fellow students may have improved; they chose him as "Father" of the vacation revels in the summer of 1628. No doubt they enjoyed the expected witty, in-joke-laden Latin oration which he delivered in this role, and were surprised and, one hopes, impressed, when he incorporated also an English verse tribute to the power of his native language, which he asks to

> *from thy wardrobe bring thy chiefest treasure;*
> *Not those new-fangled toys, and trimming slight*
> *Which takes our late fantastics with delight,*
> *But cull those richest robes, and gayest attire*
> *Which deepest spirits, and choicest wits desire.*

Definition through careful distinction remained one of the essential characteristics of his work. The clothing imagery, more immediately, probably complements the costumes that he and other participants wore for the revels. English duly obliged, during the years in which he was associated with the college, with some of his first significant poems: "On the Morning of Christ's Nativity" (1629), "L'Allegro" and its companion "Il Penseroso" (1631) with their antithesis, familiar to the author, of "Such sights as youthful poets dream" and "the lamp at midnight hour".

Ralph Cudworth (1617-88) had a longer and generally more equable relationship with the college, and wanted to "justify the ways of God to man" in very different ways from Milton. With his friends Henry More, who came to Christ's as an undergraduate in 1631 and was a fellow, refusing all promotion, from 1639 until his death in 1687, and Benjamin Whichcote, Provost of King's in 1644-60, he belonged to the group which came to be known as the Cambridge Platonists. They believed, in contrast to many of their contemporaries, in reason as the primary route to God; "for spiritual is most rational," as Whichcote declared. There is a common tendency, said More less pithily, "to be filled with high-swollen words of vanity, rather than to feed on sober truth, and to heat and warm ourselves rather by preposterous and fortuitous imaginations, than to move cautiously in the light of a purified mind and improved reason."

Milton's Christ's had consisted of one early sixteenth-century court and some outbuildings. He is said to have occupied rooms on the first floor, left of the entrance gate, but a likelier tradition has him in more spartan accommodation in a wooden building in the grounds known as "Rat's Hall". Lady Margaret Beaufort had, with the encouragement of John Fisher, re-founded God's House, which had occupied the site since the 1440s, as Christ's. Between 1505 and her death in 1509 she spent £1,625 on the court. Parts of God's House were retained and renovated, but the Master's Lodge and the hall were new. (The hall was largely rebuilt by George Gilbert Scott the Younger in the 1870s.) The magnificent gateway was also installed, with the same Beaufort and Tudor emblems as at her other foundation of St John's (see p.52), but with a presiding statue of Lady Margaret herself in place of the saint. Other early survivals are the late fifteenth- and early sixteenth-century glass in the windows on the north side of the chapel and the window connecting the chapel with the Master's Lodge. This was put in originally so that Lady Margaret, who lived for a time on the premises, could look down from her oratory during services. (The window, later blocked up, was re-opened in 1899.) Little else now looks as it did to her or to Milton. The change began in the time of the Platonists. The Fellows' Building, in the second court (looking towards the garden) was built in 1640-3. Eleven years after its completion John Evelyn, a connoisseur of the new style after his travels in France and Italy, admired the "exact Architecture" of this "modern part" of the college. The classical impression was furthered when, in the eighteenth century, the brick and clunch of the first court were covered with smooth stone and the chapel was "improved".

During C. P. Snow's long association with the college—he was a fellow in the 1930s and 1940s and remained actively involved as an honorary fellow—Third Court, begun in the late nineteenth century, was completed (1953) and the layered New Court, by Sir Denys Lasdun, architect of the Royal National Theatre, went up (1970). The college in Snow's novel *The Masters* (1951) is evidently Christ's—it "stands upon an existing site, and its topography is similar to that of an existing college"—and the novel is concerned with various college machinations and especially those preceding the difficult Master's election of 1936. One of the candidates, Paul Jago, becomes progressively more desperate to achieve his ambition:

> *He longed for all the trappings, titles, ornaments and show of power. He would love to hear himself called Master; he would love to begin a formal act at a college meeting "I, Paul Jago, Master of this college..." He enjoyed the prospect of an entry in the college history—"Dr P. Jago, 41st Master". For him, in every word that separated the Master from his fellows, in every ornament of the Lodge, in every act of formal duty, there was a gleam of magic.*

This attitude ill equips Jago to combat the subtle intrigue which awards the post to his rival. Jago hates the anxiety and humiliation that his ambition has brought upon him, but cannot escape his obsession. Snow maintained a somewhat more detached view from the vantage-point of his rooms in the first court—those in which tradition placed Milton.

Jesus College

Samuel Taylor Coleridge called Jesus "the very palace of winds". *Cantabrigia Depicta* (1776) describes its openness more positively: the college is "Situate out of the town, a little east of it, surrounded by groves, gardens, and fine meadows... There is a fine prospect of the country on every side." Jesus is no longer "out of the town", but its own groves and gardens and its views across the stream to Jesus Green and across Victoria Road to Midsummer Common provide a fine "prospect" still.

Trees have had an important place in college tradition. A great walnut-tree flourished in First Court between the late sixteenth and late eighteenth centuries. Laurence Sterne, as an undergraduate in the 1730s, is said to have studied in the shade of the tree with his lifelong friend John Hall-Stevenson, who in his *Crazy Tales* (1762) humorously maintains that it was the only thing at Jesus "folks went to see":

Being of such a size and mass,
And growing in so wise a college,
I wonder how it came to pass
It was not called the Tree of Knowledge.

In 1802, not long after the walnut was eventually felled, Edward Daniel Clarke, subsequently the first Cambridge Professor of Mineralogy, planted in the Fellows' Garden the seed of an oriental plane-tree which he had brought back from Thermopylae. In 2002 there was a party, with music, poetry and morris dancing, to celebrate its two-hundredth birthday.

Another form of celebration in the college grounds is Sculpture in the Close, a biennial summer exhibition of contemporary sculpture. Anthony Gormley and Anish Kapoor have contributed work, and the college acquires some pieces for its permanent collection. Barry Flanagan's "Bronze Horse" (1983), on long-term loan, stands with one hoof raised, in the traditional posture of such predecessors as the bronze horses of St Mark's but looking free to roam the grass of First Court. Sculpture in the Close was launched by the archaeologist Colin Renfrew (Lord Renfrew), who was Master of Jesus in 1986-97. The exhibitions are among the sources of his book *Figuring It Out* (2003), an exploration of "the parallel visions of artists and archaeologists".

Green tranquillity reflects the original function of the site, to provide a suitably reflective home for the nuns of St Mary and St Radegund. They arrived in the twelfth century, and parts of the chapel and cloister survive from soon afterwards. (A wall was removed in the nineteenth century to reveal the Early English arched entrance of the Chapter House, at the east end of Cloister Court.) By the late Middle Ages the convent was falling into disrepair; there were few nuns, and a legacy of scandalous behaviour—free coming and going, extravagance, suspicious intimacy with priests. John Alcock, Bishop of Ely, therefore decided, in 1496, to expel the two remaining sisters and set up a college instead. The refectory became the college hall and the Prioress' quarters the Master's Lodge. Alcock adapted the chapel for college use, lowering the roof and removing the aisles. He extended the cloisters, roofed the hall in its surviving Spanish chestnut, and installed a library above it. This, now the Old Library, was the main repository of college books until 1912. Jesus raised three million pounds for the larger and more luxurious Quincentenary Library (1996), by Eldred Evans and David Shalev.

Bishop Alcock's statue fronts the gatehouse—a restrained predecessor of the flamboyantly decorated gatehouses at Christ's and St John's of a few years later—approached by the long walled passage known as the Chimney. His presence is also asserted by the emblematic cocks—playing on his name—on the gatehouse and elsewhere, for instance on the nave and crossing roofs of the chapel designed by William Morris and painted in the 1860s. The aim of the Victorian restoration of the chapel as a whole, however, was to recreate its thirteenth-century appearance. As part of this programme Augustus Pugin in 1849-58 replaced Alcock's Perpendicular east window with his own window and glass, incorporating, as a mark of genuineness, some fragments originally from Chartres Cathedral. Edward Burne-Jones designed most of the glass for the nave and transepts in the 1870s.

Among the memorials in the south transept chapel is a low relief by Albert Bruce-Joy showing the familiar features of Thomas Cranmer—derived from the portrait in the hall—lips resolute or resigned, eyes more contemplative or troubled, a contrast with the sterner clerical figures on the bench-ends in the chancel. (At least they were probably intended to look dignified and devout when two Jesus fellows designed them in the 1840s. They seem, to a modern eye, a little self-conscious.) Cranmer came to study at Jesus at the age of fourteen in 1503, became a fellow in 1511, and maintained contact with the college during his time as Archbishop. The memorial at the west end of the chapel, possibly by Grinling Gibbons or by his associate Artus Quellin, is to another man with close relations with the monarchy, Tobias Rustat, Yeoman of the Robes, who loyally served Charles II during his years in exile as well as after the Restoration. Rustat, whose father was at Jesus, was buried in the chapel in 1694. Having obtained wealth, the inscription says, "by God's blessing, the King's favour and his industry", he bestowed much of it "in works of charity". These included the endowment of a scholarship at Jesus for the sons of deceased Anglican clergymen.

Coleridge at Jesus

Coleridge, who came up from Christ's Hospital in 1791, was admitted to a Rustat Scholarship. He moved into rooms on the right of Staircase D in First Court. Characteristically full of ideas, talk and good intentions, at first he worked hard, gratifying his elder brother George by winning a university prize for his Greek "Ode on the Slave Trade" at the end of the first year. There were also bouts of drinking, depression, running up debts, allegedly medicinal laudanum-taking, trips to London and general dissipation. And, as ever alternating between inactivity and energetic engagement, Coleridge also began to involve himself in the political issues of the day. His friend Charles Valentine Le Grice, who was at Trinity, remembered evenings of supper and conversation when Greek was pushed away "to discuss the pamphlets", which, in this time of revolutionary and counter-revolutionary fervour, "swarmed from the press" daily. Coleridge "had read them all" and could repeat whole pages of Burke verbatim, according to Le Grice.

Undergraduate political debate took on more immediate relevance in Cambridge when, in 1793, William Frend, a fellow of Jesus well known to Coleridge, was excluded from the college and then from the university as the author of *Peace and Union Recommended to the Associated Bodies of Republicans and Anti-Republicans*, a pamphlet calling for parliamentary and other reforms. (His 1787 piece advocating Unitarianism had already cost him his college tutorship.) Coleridge, who was influenced in the direction of Unitarianism by Frend, was one of the students most vociferous in his defence—one of those who, during his trial at the Senate House, were involved in what Vice-Chancellor Milner called "noisy and tumultuous irregularities of conduct".

By the beginning of his third year, in September, drink, mounting debts and self-doubt had overwhelmed his political and religious interests. In late November he disappeared from Jesus and, in desperation, enlisted in the 15th Light Dragoons under the name—preserving his initials—Silas Tomkyn Comberbache. After some months as an improbable and not very successful soldier he was bought out by his long-suffering brothers. Once more full of good resolutions, he returned to Cambridge in April 1794. But at the end of term he set off on a walking-tour which would direct his interests away, once more, from conventional study and a conventional church career. Back in Cambridge in September he wrote breathlessly about that summer to his new friend Robert Southey: "Since I quitted this room what and how important events have been evolved! America! Southey! Miss Fricker!... Pantisocracy—O I shall have such a scheme of it!" He enclosed a poem about Pantisocracy—his and Southey's ideal centred on establishing a commune "on the banks of the Susquehanna"—and spent much of the term arguing his case with anyone in Cambridge who would listen, among them even the horrified Master of Jesus and the unsympathetic mayor.

Still caught up with Pantisocratic idealism, soon to be replaced by a succession of other visions, Coleridge departed without a degree in December 1794. It was, he came to feel by the time he wrote *Biographia Literaria* (1817), "an inauspicious hour" in which "I left the friendly cloisters and the happy grove of quiet, ever honoured Jesus College, Cambridge." But if his studies were neglected his poetry was developing—his and Southey's play *The Fall of Robespierre* was published in 1794 by the radical editor of *The Cambridge Intelligencer;* "Pantisocracy" looks forward to the more assured poems of a few years later with its vision of

> *the cottag'd dell*
> *Where Virtue, calm with careless step may stray,*
> *And dancing to the moonlight roundelay,*
> *The wizard Passions weave a holy spell.*

More immediately Coleridge was launched on his career as a character, a talker, a passionate, dazzling pursuer of ideas and the ideal: on his improbable progress from the delight and despair of the fellows of Jesus to the "Sage of Highgate". A copy of the august portrait of 1814 by Washington Allston hangs in the college hall. Jesus also owns a mezzotint, after James Northcote's portrait of 1804, which shows the half-way stage—Coleridge as troubled but poetic fallen angel—and in the chapel, near Cranmer, a memorial of 1932 shows a slightly more idealized head, albatross above and "He prayeth best who loveth best..." below.

Pembroke College

Clive James came to Cambridge, after three years in London, as "a complete failure", author of a few poems which no-one wanted to publish. According to *May Week Was in June* he also failed, on arrival, to find Pembroke College. Lost in thick fog on the way from the station, he took a wrong turning and mistook the Fitzwilliam Museum for the college. At length, he claims, "the ashlared front wall of a college crustily identified itself to my fingertips. When stone became wood, I guessed it must be the front gate of Pembroke and turned towards an egg-yolk halo which materialized in the form of the Porter's Lodge." The porter treated him to the same repertory of Antipodean jokes as the man on the desk at the museum: kangaroos, koalas, walking upside-down. But he directed James to an unexpectedly fine set of rooms. When he applied to Pembroke he had mentioned that he would be practising his clarinet. Since then he had given up the idea of even learning to play; nevertheless he acquired a magnificent set of rooms with oak panelling; there would, he says, have been space for Benny Goodman and his whole band.

James' rooms, D6, were in Old Court, built soon after the foundation of the college in 1347 by Marie de St Pol, widow of Aymer de Valence, Earl of Pembroke. (The walls were ashlared in 1712.) A few years earlier Ted Hughes had lived on the same staircase. James, reflecting on the relative lenience of university discipline, tells the story of how the poet not only had women to stay the night but "advertised the fact by encouraging them to dry their stockings out of his window." The Senior Tutor finally plucked up the courage to confront Hughes, only himself to be confronted by the naked poet "with his arms thrown apart, shouting 'Crucify me!'" The tutor and the Dean had tea, says James, and agreed to pretend that nothing had happened.

Few at Pembroke saw Hughes in such revealing moments. Few knew him well. On the whole he held himself aloof from the often mannered life of the Cambridge literary fraternity. He was keen to keep his Yorkshire identity, his roots in the countryside, intact. Occasionally there were glimpses of intensity. For example, John Coggrave, an English student at Selwyn, told Hughes' biographer, the novelist and poet Elaine Feinstein (herself at Newnham at the time), about an occasion when Hughes read aloud from Blake's *The Island of the Moon* "with such intensity that we were riveted and when he finished he looked up with a ferocious glee that had us all in fits of laughter." But in spite of this ferocity of involvement, Hughes was not happy studying literature in the approved manner; in "The Burnt Fox" (*Winter Pollen: Occasional Prose*, 1994), he recalls how, late one night, getting nowhere with his attempts to write an essay, he gave up and went to bed. Soon he dreamed that, as he sat over his paper with its few lines written,

> *The door opened wide and down the short stair and across the room towards me came a figure that was at the same time a skinny man and a fox walking erect on its hind legs. It was a fox, but the size of a wolf. As it approached and came into the light I saw that its body and limbs had just now stepped out of a furnace. Every inch was roasted, smouldering, black-charred, split and bleeding. Its eyes, which were level with mine where I sat, dazzled with the intensity of the pain. It came up until it stood beside me.*

It said "Stop this—you are destroying us" and with its hand left a wet blood-print on the blank part of the page. In 1979 Hughes told Keith Sagar that

> *I connected the fox's command to my own ideas about Eng. Lit., & the effect of the Cambridge blend of pseudo-critical terminology and social rancour on creative spirit, and from that moment abandoned my efforts to adapt myself. I might say, that I had as much talent for Leavis-style dismantling of texts as anybody else... but it seemed to me not only a foolish game, but deeply destructive of myself.*

He therefore switched to Archaeology and Anthropology for Part Two of his degree in 1953-4.

Two years after the dream came the unburned fox and unbloodied printing of the page in his "Thought-Fox". In the meantime Hughes completed his degree. He did various jobs in London but was often, sometimes for long periods, still in Cambridge. He met friends to talk and sing at the Anchor, the pub overlooking Silver Street bridge and mill pond. (As an undergraduate he seems more often to have patronized the Mill, nearby in Mill Lane.) He published "The Jaguar" and "The Casualty" in the Cambridge magazine *Chequer* in November 1954. The title of another, smaller, one-issue magazine, *St Botolph's Review*, came out of Hughes' period living in the garden of St Botolph's Rectory, first in a hut—a former chicken-coop—and then in a tent. He and the main occupant of the hut, Lucas Myers, were among the contributors. Sylvia Plath, an American studying at Newnham who had also published in *Chequer*, bought a copy of the review and on 26 February 1956 came to its launch party in hired rooms on the second floor of the Women's Union in Falcon Yard (off Petty Cury; later demolished). Amid much alcohol and loud jazz the two poets met. In her journal Plath, writing soon after the end of the party, says that

> *that big, dark, hunky boy, the only one there huge enough for me... came over and was looking hard into my eyes... I started yelling again about his poems... and he yelled back, colossal, in a voice that should have come from a Pole, 'You like?' and asking if I wanted brandy, and me yelling yes and backing into the next room and then he kissed me bang smash on the mouth and ripped my hairband off... and my favorite silver earrings: hah, I shall keep, he barked. And when he kissed my neck I bit him long and hard on the cheek, and when we came out of the room, blood was running down his face... The one man in the room who was as big as his poems, huge, with hulk and dynamic chunks of words; his poems are strong and blasting like a high wind in steel girders. And I screamed in myself, thinking: oh to give myself crashing, fighting, to you.*

The tooth-marks branded Hughes for a month, he says in "St Botolph's" (*Birthday Letters*, 1998). But "The me beneath", he goes on in the last line of the poem, was branded for ever: branded both in the sense that he was marked as hers and that some people would "brand" him—in spite of her history of suicide attempts—as solely responsible for her death in 1963.

Ted Hughes had a number of poetic predecessors at the college. Edmund Spenser (1552-99) came up in 1569. Within a few months he had published his translations of Marot and Petrarch for Jan van der Noot's *Theatre of Worldlings*. But little is known about his time at Pembroke (he took his BA in 1573 and MA in 1576) except that he formed a stimulating friendship with Gabriel Harvey (c.1550-1631), who became a fellow in 1570. Together, in 1580, they published *Three Familiar Letters*, in which they discuss their experiments with classical syllabic metres—a dead-end for Spenser, soon abandoned—and promote themselves.

Harvey's energy, learning, considerable ambition (his social origins, like Spenser's, were fairly humble) and talent for stirring up controversy must have made a strong impression. For many of his colleagues, and for his later satirical opponent Thomas Nashe (a graduate of St John's), it was a strongly unfavourable impression. In 1573 the fellows prevented him from proceeding to take his MA and he wrote at great length to the mainly absentee Master, John Young, protesting at defamation by his enemies: "every thing, my going, my reading, my speaking, my behaviour argueth great and intolerable arrogancy... I suppose verily never bear was so baited at the stake with bandogs and mastiffs as some of them... have baited and tussled and chased me." When a letter failed to have any effect, Young put in a personal appearance, forced the fellows to enable Harvey's MA, and for good measure appointed him Greek Lecturer at Pembroke. Soon the Master had to intervene to stop the fellows deposing Harvey from his lectureship—which he was well qualified to hold. For a time his relations with his colleagues seem to have improved. He became university Praelector in Rhetoric, published his orations, presented Latin verses to the queen at Audley End ("ruffling it out, huffty-tuffty, in his suit of velvet," claims Nashe), and seemed on the brink of a career at court. But a brief period as secretary to the Earl of Leicester ended in Harvey being told that he was "fitter for the university than for the court". Back at the university, when his fellowship at Pembroke ran out in 1578 he moved to Trinity Hall. Many a battle—with colleagues, with censorship, with Nashe, with Nashe's fellow Johnian Robert Greene—lay ahead. Spenser moved more successfully to Leicester's household, went to Ireland as secretary to Lord Grey de Wilton, and produced *The Faerie Queene* (1590-6), with its brief reference in Book Four to "My mother Cambridge" and its "many a gentle Muse, and many a learned wit".

A "learned wit" less colourful than Harvey was his and Spenser's Pembroke contemporary Lancelot Andrewes, who became Master

(1589-1605), Bishop of Winchester, and one of the most notable preachers of his time. Andrewes was one of a succession of important churchmen connected with the college. Among them was Matthew Wren, who studied at Pembroke and became a fellow in 1605. Later his royalism as Master of Peterhouse and Bishop of Ely earned him eighteen years as a prisoner in the Tower of London; he built the new chapel at Pembroke in 1663-5 in fulfilment of a vow made during his imprisonment. (The medieval chapel in Old Court became the library some years later and is now the Old Library.) The architect was Wren's nephew, Christopher, Savilian Professor of Astronomy at Oxford, and this was his first completed building. It is also the first entirely classical building in Cambridge. The high west end, with its pilasters and hexagonal lantern, may have been based on an elevation in Sebastiano Serlio's *Architettura* for a temple at Tivoli. The mathematical precision of the chapel design was more evident before George Gilbert Scott the Younger extended it twenty feet east in 1880. Bishop Wren envisaged the work as his monument as well as a munificent gift to the college, and he was buried in a vault here, with all the pomp associated with the brand of religion for which he had suffered, in 1667. But the chapel also contains two reminders of earlier periods: near the altar, the fine ash-wood board-seated chair of Nicholas Ridley, who was Master in 1540-53; and, in the ante-chapel, a good fifteenth-century alabaster of St Michael weighing souls while the Virgin intercedes, rosary in hand. She protects someone under her cloak; at the other side a devil with animal's body tries, unsuccessfully, to weigh the balance down.

A few years before the new chapel the Hitcham Building was built: the south range of what is now Ivy Court. Thomas Gray moved out of Peterhouse (see pp.42-3) and into the Hitcham Building in 1756. From 1758 he occupied the rooms, now named after him, at the Hall end of the first floor. In 1773, two years after Gray's death, the fourteen-year-old William Pitt the Younger, a well-connected fellow-commoner, took up residence in the same suite. He was already something of a prodigy—it was said that "he seemed never to learn, but merely to recollect"—as befitted the man who, ten years later, became Britain's youngest Prime Minister. Pitt's statue reclines in a toga in front of the college library.

It was only occasionally and with some reluctance that Gray entered the public arena; the Duke of Grafton obtained his appointment as Regius Professor of Modern History in 1768, and when Grafton was elected Chancellor of the University the following year the poet obliged by providing an *Ode for Music* to be sung at his Installation. But Gray spent much of his time in his rooms with their large Japanese vases, harpsichord, and pervasive scent of pot pourri, working laboriously at crafting a few poems, writing letters and furthering his interest in natural history. Among the papers he bequeathed to the college is his Commonplace Book, which includes not only drafts of poems and lists of British poets but careful notes on such matters as the remedy for a viper-bite, the contents of a dead mole, and birdsong.

Gray's reserved life and small poetic corpus have often been contrasted with the inspirational wildness and prolific output of his acquaintance Christopher Smart, who entered Pembroke as a Sizar in 1739 and was elected as a fellow in 1745. In his early years at Cambridge Smart was already an accomplished Latin poet. He also wrote an English "Secular Ode" for the Pembroke Jubilee of 1743—held then because the foundation date was believed, incorrectly, to be 1343—in which he invokes Spenser and, buoyed up by college spirit, asserts that it was "in these pleasant groves" that the "peerless bard" had his first ideas for *The Faerie Queene* and "here first plann'd [his] works of vast emprize." Personally Smart was well known and, it seems, generally liked. Gray was much less forthcoming, but, even while he was still at Peterhouse, had enough contacts at Pembroke to know that Smart's future was less assured than it looked: in 1747 he told his friend Thomas Wharton about Smart's heavy drinking, daily increasing debts, vanity, and involvement in

a comedy of his own writing, which he makes all the boys of his acquaintance act... [H]is piece, he says, is inimitable, true sterling wit and humour by God; and he can't hear the Prologue without being ready to die with laughter. He acts five parts himself, and is only sorry, he can't do all the rest... All this, you see, must come to a gaol, or bedlam, and that without any help, almost without any pity.

The play, the subsequently lost *A Trip to Cambridge, or the Grateful Fair*, seems to have been performed successfully in the college hall, with the dramatist taking only one part. But Gray was right about gaol and Bedlam. Smart was first arrested for debt later in 1747. He suddenly left Cambridge for London in 1749. There, after a religious conversion experience when he was recovering from illness in 1756, he took to praying enthusiastically in public places. (He had earlier, in more conventional mode, written the poems on different aspects of God which made him five times winner of the university Seatonian Prize.) He was first placed in a hospital for the insane in 1757 and would die in debtors' prison in 1771. But amid the sufferings of these years he produced his best, strangest, most unconventional poems, visions far removed from Gray's more considered world.

The fabric of Pembroke changed little in the century after Gray's death. Then, as student numbers increased, between 1871 and 1878 Alfred Waterhouse designed Red Building, knocked down the old Master's Lodge and the south range of Old Court—not without controversy—and put up a new library and hall. The library, with its Flemish clock-tower, is one of Waterhouse's more generally valued creations. The Old Library was nearly demolished, but saved after the fellows voted to dispense with Waterhouse's services in 1878. His successor, George Gilbert Scott the Younger, built New Court as well as extending the chapel. The red-brick Pitt Building followed early in the twentieth century and Orchard Building in 1957. Finally, a more adventurous range of buildings, Foundress Court, partly in white Bath stone, was completed by EP (Eric Parry) Associates in 1997. Beyond a row of huge plane-trees, a pergola leads to the wing housing the new Master's Lodge.

The mixing of architectural styles does not jar, mainly because the buildings are separated, punctuated or softened by well designed gardens. There is still enough space for lawns, generous herbaceous borders, a small mound and pond, a great variety of evergreens. At times this is still A. C. Benson's "beautiful, embowered, bird-haunted place"; the descendant of the place to which Nicholas Ridley's thoughts returned a few days before he was burnt at the stake in Oxford in 1555. Pembroke has been "ever named since I knew thee, which is now thirty years ago, to be studious, well learned, and a great setter forth of

Christ's gospel"; he memorized the New Testament epistles "in thy orchard", whose "walls, butts and trees, if they could speak, would bear me witness."

CHAPTER EIGHT

Cambridge Science

William Whewell, polymath and Master of Trinity, coined the word "scientist" as late as 1840. But there were, of course, scientists in Cambridge long before this. William Gilbert (1544-1603) was educated at St John's and the better-known William Harvey (1578-1637) at Caius, although their main achievements—Gilbert's discovery of terrestrial magnetism, Harvey's of the circulation of the blood—came later. Sir Isaac Newton (1642-1727) was much more closely associated with Cambridge; he came up to Trinity in 1661, was elected a fellow in 1667 and was Lucasian Professor of Mathematics from 1669 to 1701. Indeed, he became a Cambridge cult figure; his death-mask is kept at King's, his walking-stick in the Wren Library at Trinity and his statue in the chapel. The mathematical institute founded in 1992, the computerized catalogue of the University Library, a trust fund at Trinity and the pub at the top of Castle Hill are all named after him.

Newton was, for much of his life, reclusive and fanatically hard-working, although as an undergraduate he was not, apparently, quite immune to mischief: one of his pocket-books, owned by the Fitzwilliam Museum, contains not only the Hebrew alphabet and later mathematical notes but a list of sins from 1662 including "squirting water on Thy day" and profaning Sunday even further by putting a pin in the hat of a certain John Keys with intent to "pick" him. During the Great Plague of 1665 and another outbreak in 1666 he returned to his family home in Lincolnshire, where he "had", he remembered later, "the direct method of Fluxions", or differential calculus, and "had entrance into the inverse method of Fluxions", or integral calculus. He also "had the Theory of Colours" and, possibly helped by the fall of a famous apple from a tree in his orchard, "began to think of gravity extending to the orb of the Moon" and "compared the force requisite to keep the Moon in her orb with the force of gravity at the surface of the Earth." (The apple tree planted at the front of Trinity in the 1950s is descended from one in the Lincolnshire garden.)

Back in Cambridge he continued to develop these ideas in his notebooks, letters and lectures. His experiments with prisms, lenses and mirrors contributed to the theories about light eventually expounded in his *Optics* (1704). Much of his important work on mechanics had appeared in the *Philosophiae naturalis principia Mathematica* (1687), known more pithily as the *Principia*. For long periods of his career, however, Newton was absorbed in the study of ancient chronology and of theology. (His heterodox views prompted him to obtain a special dispensation from Charles II by which the Lucasian Professor could keep his college fellowship without taking holy orders.) He was also interested in alchemy; so interested, J. M. Keynes concluded, that he was not so much "the first of the age of reason" as "the last of the magicians, the last of the Babylonians and Sumerians".

In the 1690s Newton also developed what now appear to be rather more practical concerns, some of which would have appealed to Keynes. He began to work for the Mint, becoming its Master in 1698 and actively supervising currency reform as well as the pursuit and punishment of forgers; it was his achievements at the Mint, rather than in science or mathematics, that won him a knighthood—bestowed by Queen Anne in the drawing-room of the Master's Lodge in Trinity— in 1705. Nevertheless, he continued some research and kept in contact with the work of others as President of the Royal Society from 1703.

Newton claimed that "I do not know what I may appear to the world; but to myself I seem only to have been like a boy playing on the seashore, and diverting myself in now and then finding a smoother pebble or a prettier shell than ordinary, whilst the great ocean of truth lay all undiscovered before me." Some people, of course, fail to find the special pebbles and shells. And some do not even reach the seashore: in 1769 Cock Langford of Trinity College is supposed to have been asked, during the Latin disputation for the degree of MA, whether the sun went round the earth or vice versa. After a pause for reflection he replied "Sometimes the one, sometimes the other."

Others in eighteenth-century Cambridge, assisted by the *Principia* and the Newtonian reflecting telescope, were, not surprisingly, more knowledgeable in such matters. In 1704 Thomas Plume had left nearly £2,000 to the university "to maintain a studious and learned Professor of Astronomical and Experimental Philosophy, and to buy him and his successors books and instruments, Quadrants, Telescopes etc." The ebullient Richard Bentley, Master of Trinity, was instrumental (with some help from Newton) in the appointment of Roger Cotes as the first Plumian Professor and the choice of Trinity gatehouse as the site of the first astronomical observatory in Cambridge. (Bentley also provided a laboratory at Trinity for the chemist Giovanni Francesco Vigani.) Robert Smith, who succeeded both his cousin Cotes as Professor and Bentley as Master, encouraged various sorts of scientific research and himself wrote *A Complete System of Optics* (1738), codifying, expanding and in some cases distorting Newton's *Optics*, and *Harmonics, or the Philosophy of Musical Sounds* (1749). Another astronomical college head was John Smith, Master of Caius from 1764 and Lowndean Professor of Astronomy from 1771, who installed a transit telescope above his college ante-chapel. His predecessor in the Lowndean chair, Roger Long, Master of Pembroke, imparted knowledge with the aid of a revolving copper "Uranium"—a celestial sphere or planetarium, large enough for thirty people to sit in.

The Cambridge stargazers made few original discoveries and their science, and science in general, seems to have become less fashionable later in the century. The observatory at Trinity was dilapidated by the early 1790s and removed in 1797. (The one at St John's survived into the 1850s.) But their observations and their enthusiasm helped prepare the way for the more systematic Cambridge astronomy practised from 1823 at the University Observatory off Madingley Road, a neoclassical building whose dome originally housed a telescope. In the twentieth century Arthur Eddington (1882-1944), who pioneered study of the structure of stars, was one of the most notable Directors of the Observatory. Other Cambridge astronomers were Sir Fred Hoyle (1915-2001) and Sir Martin Ryle (1918-84). Hoyle, a successful writer of science fiction, was a proponent of the steady state model of the universe; he coined the term "Big Bang" as a contemptuous description of the main opposing theory, which Ryle, the pioneer of radio astronomy, supported. (The "saucers" of Ryle's radio telescope are a familiar landmark to the west of Cambridge.)

The Old Cavendish Laboratory

"Here in 1897 at the old Cavendish Laboratory J. J. Thomson discovered the electron, subsequently recognized as the first fundamental particle of physics and the basis of chemical bonding, electronics and computing," proclaims a plaque in Free School Lane. The laboratory was part of the extensive science area (the Downing and New Museums sites) mostly built after 1850 and expanded rapidly in the first decades of the twentieth century. In the 1970s the Cavendish finally moved from this now increasingly cramped location to new premises at the West Cambridge science site.

Several generations of the "Cambridge school" of physicists worked or trained here. The laboratory itself was designed, in 1873-4, by James Clerk Maxwell (1831-79), first Cavendish Professor of Experimental Physics from 1871 and author of an important *Treatise on Electricity and Magnetism* (1873). His work in this field was, although they did not meet, an early inspiration to Sir Joseph John Thomson (1856-1940), who worked at the Cavendish from 1880, succeeding Lord Rayleigh as Professor four years later. Thomson (Nobel Prize for physics 1906, knighted 1908) built up the group of research workers who gave Cambridge Physics its formidable reputation.

Particularly significant among Thomson's associates was Ernest Rutherford (1871-1937), later Lord Rutherford, who arrived from New Zealand as a research student in 1895. He worked at McGill University in Montreal and then at Manchester before returning to Cambridge as Thomson's successor in 1919. Rutherford worked on radioactivity and presided over the "annus mirabilis" of science at the Cavendish, 1932. "Living in Cambridge," says C. P. Snow in *Variety of Men* (1967),

> one could not help picking up the human, as well as the intellectual, excitement in the air. James Chadwick, grey-faced after a fortnight of work with three hours' sleep a night, telling the Kapitsa Club [under the aegis of Piotr Kapitsa, Cambridge and Soviet physicist]... how he had discovered the neutron;... John Cockcroft, normally about as much given to emotional display as the Duke of Wellington, skimming down King's

Parade and saying to anyone whose face he recognised: 'We've split the atom! We've split the atom!'

Rutherford himself made a stronger impression on people than most of the physicists. Snow remembers "a big, rather clumsy man, with a substantial bay window that started in the middle of the chest", loud of voice, exuberant, childishly delighted by his own success (Snow overheard him telling his tailor that his shirt was too tight round the neck. "Every day I grow in girth. *And* in mentality"), but with a degree of well-hidden insecurity. His ideas, in keeping with his personality, were "simple, rugged material"; he thought of atoms as being like tennis balls, watched the way the smaller particles he discovered moved or bounced, and progressed from there, "as certainly as a sleepwalker, from unstable radiocative atoms to the discovery of the nucleus and structure of the atom". And he did it all with surprisingly simple equipment, with "sealing wax and string".

Paul Dirac (1902-84), who predicted the existence of anti-matter, was a research student at the Cavendish in the mid-1920s before becoming Lucasian Professor of Mathematics. One of his successors as professor is Stephen Hawking (b. 1942), a more widely known theoretical physicist who came to Cambridge to do postgraduate work in 1962. His fame relies on his work on space-time and black holes, his brave attempt to convey his ideas to a broader audience in *A Brief History of Time* (1988), and the progressive motor-neurone disease that was first detected near the beginning of his career. In 1985 he lost his speech, already much impaired, following a tracheotomy, and soon afterwards learned to communicate using a computer-generated voice synthesizer, controllable by small movements of the fingers.

From the Double Helix to the Human Genome

Francis Crick (b. 1916) joined the Medical Research Council Unit, which was then based in the Cavendish Laboratory, in 1949. The American James Watson (b. 1928) joined him there in 1951. Over the following two years they worked in close partnership, modelling possible structures for DNA. In 1953 they identified the structure as a double helix. In *The Double Helix* (1968) Watson says that Crick "winged into" the Eagle, the pub in Benet Street where they had lunch every day. Here, somewhat prematurely in his partner's view, he told "everyone within hearing distance that we had found the secret of life." Crick, in *What Mad Pursuit* (1988), says he has no recollection of this. (The Eagle is also famous for its RAF Bar, which preserves the names and squadron numbers British and American airmen burnt onto the ceiling with lighters and candles during the Second World War.)

The discovery was, of course, fundamentally important. It also became controversial, less because of the science than because of the attitude of some of the people involved. Rosalind Franklin (1920-58), a crystallographer and graduate of Newnham College, produced, at King's College, London, in 1952-3, X-ray data which were vital in proving that the double helix model was correct. As John Gribbin tactfully puts it in his history of science, "it was only much later that it emerged just how the crucial X-ray data got to Cambridge, what a vital role it had played in the model building, and just how badly Franklin had been treated both by her colleagues at King's and by Watson and Crick." Franklin died of cancer at thirty-seven in 1958, while Crick, Watson, and Maurice Wilkins, with whom she had worked unhappily in London, were jointly awarded the Nobel Prize for physiology or medicine in 1962. The impression of injustice is markedly increased by the notorious remarks in Watson's *The Double Helix*. Sometimes his account is hostile, sometimes it simply expresses the common prejudices of the period. Franklin was not interested in clothes. "There was never lipstick to contrast with her straight black hair, while at the age of thirty-one her dresses showed all the imagination of English blue-stocking adolescents." In view of the difficulties between her and Wilkins, "The thought could not be avoided that the best home for a feminist was in another person's lab." Creatures called "popsies" also make several appearances in the book.

In what the geneticist Steve Jones describes as "a curiously embarrassed postscript", Watson does pay tribute to Franklin and concedes that his first impressions of her were often wrong and that he and Crick realized "years too late the struggles that the intelligent woman faces to be accepted by a scientific world which often regards women as mere diversions from serious thinking"—as "popsies", perhaps.

Identification of the double helix structure of DNA was, with the Cambridge biochemist Fred Sanger's Nobel-winning work on the structure of proteins, a necessary step on the road to sequencing the human genome. (The genome is the complete DNA of an organism—the instructions that make the organism.) From 1962 work in this direction proceeded at the Medical Research Council Molecular Research Laboratory. Its director was the Austrian émigré Max Perutz, who in the 1950s had demonstrated the structure of haemoglobin, the protein of the red blood cell. The staff included Crick (who eventually moved to the Salk Institute in San Diego in 1977) and Sanger. It was Sanger who, in 1975, came up with a method of reading the sequence of DNA. As a result several teams were ready, by the 1990s, to begin the huge and ambitious task of mapping the genome. The British end of this operation was based, from 1992, at the Sanger Centre in Hinxton, near Cambridge. This led, through much further work in Britain and the United States, to the publication of a working draft of the sequence in June 2000, rushed out in order to defeat the attempt by the Celera Genomics company to achieve a monopoly on the information. The title of the 2001 book by Sir John Sulston, former director of the Sanger Centre, and Georgina Ferry, suggests some of the events and issues involved: *The Common Thread: a Story of Science, Politics, Ethics and the Human Genome.*

The Museum of Zoology
Sir David Attenborough, in his autobiography *Life on Air* (2002), remembers that his Cambridge Zoology course in the 1940s seemed

> *largely laboratory-bound. We were taught about the anatomy of animals and peered into the entrails of crayfish, dogfish and rats. We sat in lecture theatres while the complexities of animal classification were explained and illustrated with skeletons and stuffed skins... But there was no suggestion that we might ultimately, as qualified zoologists, watch elephants in Africa or crouch in a hide in the depths of a tropical forest watching some rare bird at its nest.*

The Museum of Zoology still displays many a dead beast—preserved or skeletal—but also has active links with researchers in the field. And its "type" specimens, a good number of them collected during the nineteenth and early twentieth century, are still essential to classification. DNA analysis, possible on some specimens up to a million years old, can be used to look at the earlier distribution of a species and help with re-population.

The collection (only about five per cent of which is actually on display) moved into its current light, airy galleries in 1973. A good general view from above can be seen by going up the steps at the front of the building, past a sizeable Fin Whale skeleton. The smaller whales suspended from the ceiling include an impressively tusked narwhal. Inside, among many other exhibits, are canine, feline, rodent and prehistoric giant sloth skeletons, corals, and the largest wasp-nest recorded in Britain—a pendulous, layered structure made from strips of wood pulp.

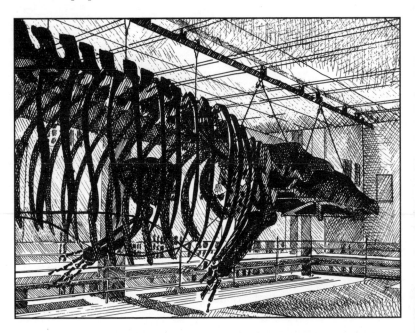

Some of the specimens owned by the museum were collected by Charles Darwin, including forty samples of South American fish from the voyage of the *Beagle*. There are also examples of his first serious passion in natural history: beetles. His years as an undergraduate at Christ's were, he felt in later years, "wasted, as far as the academical studies were concerned." He spent much of the time apparently confirming his father's fear that he would become an "idle sporting man"—shooting, hunting, riding. But his friend and second cousin William Darwin Fox, a final-year student at Christ's when Darwin arrived, influenced him in other directions. Janet Browne, in *Charles Darwin: Voyaging* (1995) describes

> *the eccentric 'museum' haphazardly lying around [Fox's] student rooms: stuffed swans, rare pine martens, day-old chicks, the pupae of moths to incubate through the summer, the corpse of a female goosander shot by Darwin... Every available surface was draped with things that had once flown or grown, to the despair of the gyp [college servant] who kept them clean and a Mr. Aiken who looked after the excess in bulging hampers in his cellar.*

It was Fox who also introduced Darwin to the more space-saving science of entomology. Darwin recalled his beetling, in his autobiographical fragment, as "the mere passion for collecting, for I did not dissect them and rarely compared their external characters with published descriptions, but got them named anyhow." He understates his achievements in what was, as Browne points out, a little-documented subject. But there was no doubting his "zeal":

> *one day, on tearing off some old bark, I saw two rare beetles and seized one in each hand; then I saw a third and new kind, which I could not bear to lose, so that I popped the one which I held in my right hand into my mouth. Alas it ejected some intensely acrid fluid, which burnt my tongue so that I was forced to spit the beetle out, which was lost, as well as the third one.*

Undaunted (and having at least held on to the specimen in his left hand) he displayed the persistence and ingenuity that would characterize his researches in other areas: not only pursuing beetles in person but hiring "a labourer to scrape, during the winter, moss off old trees and place [it] in a large bag, and likewise to collect the rubbish at the bottom of the barges in which reeds are brought from the fens." This methodical approach enabled him to catch some rare species, and "No poet ever felt more delight at seeing his first poem published" than did the future author of *The Origin of Species* "at seeing in Stephen's *Illustrations of British Insects* the magic words, 'captured by C. Darwin, Esq'."

Later in his Cambridge years Darwin learned much about botany and geology from Professors Henslow and Sedgwick. And even before the invitation to join the *Beagle* his head was "running about the Tropics," he told his sister Caroline. But the record of the earlier enthusiasm survives in the specimens which reached the museum collection, and in a cartoon by Darwin's fellow beetler Albert Way. At left the top-hatted naturalist bestrides a large beetle, net at the ready. This is "Darwin and his Hobby"—or hobby-horse—says the caption. The picture on the right shows the beetle more evidently in motion, Darwin still wielding his net, and in the background a milestone "To Cambr I". "Go it Charlie!" shouts the caption, encouragingly.

The Botanic Garden

The nesting-habits of the jackdaw are one reason for the present location of the University Botanic Garden. In 1762, after years discussing the idea of developing such a garden, the university acquired a five-acre plot off Downing Street, formerly the property of a Mr Mortlock. Wrought-iron gates, transferred to the Trumpington Road entrance of the new garden in 1909, adorned the entrance. Some 4,000 varieties of plant were grown and used primarily for the botanical education of medical students. But in the early nineteenth century the project began to run into difficulties, among them the jackdaws' habit of removing the wooden labels patiently positioned by the gardeners. And the plants themselves were increasingly overshadowed by new university buildings.

The solution came from John Stevens Henslow, the Professor of Botany, who in 1831 persuaded the university to move from the old plot—later used for the science buildings of the New Museums site— to a 38-acre cornfield owned by Trinity Hall. Henslow's greater claim to fame is that his lectures, conversation and field-trips inspired Charles Darwin to take up natural history as something more than a hobby. It was mainly through Henslow that Darwin got his place on the *Beagle* in 1831.

Tree-planting at the new Botanic Garden eventually began in the 1840s and several glass-houses were open by the mid-1850s. Funds were short. The eastern half of the site was given over to allotments until after the Second World War. The first annual report of the Botanic Garden Syndicate noted, in 1856, that "the formation of a collection of hardy plants was... preferred to one consisting of numerous tender species, which would have required the erection of extensive and costly plant-houses for their preservation." Nevertheless the report was satisfied that the existing glass-houses contained "a sufficiently numerous collection to be tolerably illustrative of the chief groups of the plants that inhabit the warmer regions of the earth." Henslow's ideal was being fulfilled: this garden was planned not as a medical aid—a "physic garden"—but as a larger scientific attempt to provide the raw material for systematic botanical study, the evidence of "those physical forces by which mere brute matter is regulated and arranged." It still provides the modern equivalent of that resource. From the beginning, however, there was also room for aesthetic considerations: although science must take priority, the syndicate explained that "in order to encourage a general taste for botanical studies, and to render the Garden an agreeable acquisition to the University, the designers consulted ornamental appearance, wherever it did not interfere with the main object." In keeping with this concession to rational pleasure members of the public were, if "respectably dressed" and prepared to leave their name and address, allowed in.

The Sedgwick Museum

When Adam Sedgwick (1785-1873) was elected Professor of Geology at Cambridge in 1818 he is reported to have said (exaggerating a little), "Hitherto I have never turned a stone; henceforth I will leave no stone unturned." Some of the stones he turned are on display in the museum founded in his memory. During his long tenure as professor he increased the collection begun by John Woodward (1665-1728) from about 10,000 objects to about half a million. (Woodward's study, with most of his collection in its four magnificent original walnut cabinets, is recreated at the museum.)

Sedgwick's industriousness as a collector was accompanied by a zealous desire to communicate his discoveries. His popular annual lecture series ran from 1819 to 1870. Noticeably more enthusiastic and informative than most contemporary lecturers, he demonstrated his points with the aid of specimens and diagrams from the collection. His field-trips in the country around Cambridge were equally famous and innovative. "The Woodwardian Professor," announces a paper of 1835 in the museum, "invites his class to meet him on horseback at the Barnwell Gravel Pits... precisely at ten o' clock... He will halt at Quy Hill, quarter before eleven; and Swaffham Hill and Reach, quarter before twelve; and at the Stone Pit, Upware, quarter before one." From there the party would proceed to the pits of greensand and Kimmeridge clay near Ely before returning to Cambridge along the turnpike (now the A10). A convivial meal at a country inn rounded off the more serious part of the proceedings; perhaps this is part of the reason the grooms who hired out the horses allegedly called the whole activity "jolly-gizing". Certainly Sedgwick's expeditions were the source of much digressive "exuberance of cheery reminiscence" in his lectures as remembered by one student of the 1850s.

It was Sedgwick's longer expeditions to North Wales that enabled him to establish the Cambrian system. (He took Charles Darwin on one of the early Welsh forays as part of a crash-course in geology before he left Cambridge.) He was also often in his native Dentdale in Yorkshire, for both family and geological reasons. He spoke at amateur scientific societies around the country and served as President of the recently founded Kendal Natural Historical and Scientific Society from 1838. He also worked closely with Prince Albert (Chancellor of the university from 1847) to advance reform more generally, and wrote the greater part of the report for the Royal Commission on universities in 1850-2.

Sometimes the strain of the work was too great. Sedgwick suffered periods of depression and listlessness and struck some people as a confirmed hypochondriac. Yet lecturing, field-trips, and Dentdale seem always to have reinvigorated him. With the advantage of hindsight one might feel that his sufferings were psychosomatic, a result of the suppressed strain of uniting geological inquiry with strong religious belief. But his faith, like that of most of his liberal scientific contemporaries, appears to have remained secure. It was clear to Sedgwick that geology confirmed, rather than questioned, God's controlling purpose. He subscribed to the "catastrophist" theory of periodic convulsion of the crust of the earth: the convulsions were clear evidence that "God has not created the world and left it to itself," for geology provides certain proof that "during successive periods there have been, not only great changes in the external conditions of the earth, but corresponding changes in organic life." Such views made him read his former pupil Darwin's *The Origin of Species* (1859) with, he told him, "more pain than pleasure. Parts of it I admired greatly, parts I laughed at till my sides were almost sore; other parts I read with absolute sorrow, because I think them utterly false and mischievous."

Personally Sedgwick was often described as "rugged", a quality traditionally linked to his origins in the Dales. "Nature cast me in a large mould, and gave me a very rugged countenance," he said in protest at a portrait by Thomas Phillips which, he felt, made him look too much of a dandy. The representations in the museum conform better to the professor's self-image. A statue shows the rough countenance directed, with concentrated curiosity, at a specimen held in his left hand and presumably just quarried out with the geological hammer he holds in his right. The intensity, the gleam in the eye, survive in the museum's two portraits of him in his later years; more tangible signs of his work are present in specimens he found or acquired, notes for his lectures, field-notebooks, his deerskin collecting bag and several of his hammers.

The museum opened in 1904. Since 1841 the collection had been housed in the Cockerell Building and before that many of the minerals and skeletons had simply been crammed into Sedgwick's rooms at Trinity. The older part of the museum, with its Sedgwick displays and cabinets of coprolites and dynamically patterned "Marston Marble" (ammonite shells packed together), is dominated by the skeletons of an iguanodon and a giant Irish Elk (its antler-span is over seven feet) which Sedgwick acquired in 1835 for £140. His other purchases, which were at least as important in building the collection as his own finds, include a fossilized ichthyosaurus. He bought it from Mary Anning (1799-1847), who

excavated on a professional basis at Lyme Regis and achieves the rare tribute, as a woman, of a portrait—bonnet, basket and hammer—in the museum.

A newly refurbished gallery is aimed more particularly at children, welcomed already by the stone bears and bison of the entrance steps. A fossil giant carnivorous spider, *Megarachne servinei*, is presented next to an enormous, hairy, squeal-provoking model of what it once looked like. Finally the small Whewell gallery shows minerals with rather more technical information. There are items on colour in minerals, jade and its various uses, fluorite including Blue John. Aesthetically this is a museum of remarkable range, from the whites and greys, bone and stone of the first area to the sparkling quartzite and lustrous reds and greens of the last.

The Whipple Museum of the History of Science
Robert Stewart Whipple (1871-1953) "little thought when I bought an old telescope, for the sum of 10 francs from an antique shop in Tours in 1913, that I was embarking on the slippery slope of collecting." Long before then, however, he had been involved with more up-to-date

instruments: he had joined the Cambridge Scientific Instrument Company as Horace Darwin's personal assistant in 1898 and went on to become Managing Director and Chairman. Darwin, youngest son of Charles Darwin and an expert in mechanical design, bought a half share of the recently founded precision engineering company in 1881.

In 1944 Whipple donated to the university his collection of about a thousand antique scientific instruments and a thousand related, often rare, books. Apparatus manufactured by the original Instrument Company was added when, in 1974, the company which had taken it over in 1968 was itself taken over. Since 1959, after periods in the Fitzwilliam and elsewhere, the museum has been in its permanent home in the former Perse School in Free School Lane. The main gallery is in the restored Jacobean schoolroom with its hammer-beam roof. (The school moved to Gonville Place in 1890 and then to its present site further out of town in 1960. After this the room became an engineering and then a physical chemistry laboratory.) Among the exhibits here are eighteenth- and nineteenth-century octants and sextants, brass astrolabes, a magnificently decorated Grand Orrery made in about 1750—a mechanical model of the solar system as then known, without Uranus, Neptune and Pluto—a compound achromatic microscope, made by James Smith in about 1846 for Charles Darwin (he declared it "a splendid plaything"), a ten-foot mahogany telescope constructed to William Herschel's design in 1790, and models of DNA in plastic, Lego bricks and origami.

Gonville and Caius College

Since the sixteenth century Gonville and Caius College has often been associated with the study of medicine. William Harvey was an undergraduate here in the 1590s, although his more important training came afterwards in Padua. Christopher Brooke, in his history of Caius (as it is usually known), notes that the college "attracted a galaxy of young physiologists" in the late nineteenth century, the great age of the subject under Sir Michael Foster, Praelector in Physiology at Trinity from 1870 and the first professor from 1883. Sir Vincent Wigglesworth, expert on the tsetse fly, read medicine at Caius and returned as a professorial fellow in 1946. Graduates of the college have been successful in many other fields, but the medical connection remains.

The founders of the original Gonville Hall, however, had no association with medicine. Edmund Gonville, the unusually wealthy Rector of Terrington St Clement in Norfolk, was licensed, in 1348, to set up his college in what later became Free School Lane. When he died in 1351 responsibility for the new foundation was taken over by the more powerful William Bateman, Bishop of Norwich, who had recently set up Trinity Hall. Two years later the bishop exchanged Gonville's site for a small plot with two stone houses nearer Trinity Hall; Gonville Court grew up around the two houses, but retains few traces of its medieval origins. It was re-faced in stone in the mid-eighteenth century, mainly under the auspices of Sir James Burrough, subsequently Master, and the north side was rebuilt. The medieval hall was transformed, in 1853, into Anthony Salvin's grander building with hammer-beam roof.

The medical connection begins largely with Dr John Caius (1510-73), student and fellow of Gonville Hall who later (1557) re-founded the college as Gonville and Caius (pronounced "Keys", as indeed the doctor often spelled his name before fashionably latinizing it). From Cambridge, like Harvey after him, he had moved on to the premier European centre for medical education, the University of Padua. There he had not only continued his medical studies but taught Greek Philosophy. And he had been taught by, and lodged with, Vesalius, "the father of modern anatomy". On his return to England in 1544, he prospered as a London physician, anatomical demonstrator, and medical administrator, several times President of the Royal College of Physicians. He was also the author of such works as a tendentious Latin work proclaiming the antiquity of Cambridge University over Oxford, a treatise on "the sweat or sweating sickness", and a pamphlet *De canibus Brittanicis* classifying the breeds of native dog. Brooke points out that there is no firm evidence for the traditional claim that he was successively personal physician to Edward VI, Mary I and Elizabeth I, but he evidently amassed, whether mainly as a city or a court practitioner, the considerable fortune needed to extend and re-launch the needy Gonville Hall.

When Caius arrived in Cambridge, after at least thirteen years' absence, in 1558, he expected to find the (no doubt highly idealized) university of his young days—all dedication to learning and deference to wise teachers. Instead, he was shocked, like many a returning graduate in middle age, to come upon what he considered a marked decline in manners, morals, and standards of dress. Accordingly the statutes he drew up for the college stipulate correct dress and ban such activities as archery and "hurling the axe". Students are allowed, graciously, to throw and catch balls if they can find some part of the college "where there is no fear of their doing mischief." But bear- and bull-baiting are out: they are not only dangerous but "extinguish the desire of study in youth," waste time and money, and (one of the clichés of the age) make the participants "brutes instead of men". As befits a medical man, Caius was also aware of health matters: Caius Court must have no buildings on its south side, "lest the air, being prevented from free movement, should be corrupted, and so do harm to us." The doctor prescribed and proscribed.

On the death of Thomas Bacon, last Master of Gonville and first of Gonville and Caius in 1559, Caius was himself elected Master. He insisted on taking the post unsalaried; there were already quite enough college debts to pay off. At first he continued to direct affairs from London; it was when he actually moved into college in the mid-1560s that his trouble, and the fellows', began. It was his wise belief, stated in the statutes, that "the duties of a master consist rather in the prudent conduct and arrangement of the college business than in the study of books," but his practical sense was not always apparent when it came to conducting and arranging people. He angered some of the fellows by his continual revision of the statutes, his suspected Roman Catholic leanings, and his occasional high-handedness. In 1566 two of his victims, Robert Spenser and Stephen Warner, wrote in desperation to the Chancellor, William Cecil (the future Lord Burghley) complaining, among other things, that the Master delighted in emptying the fellows' purses in costly lawsuits, had expelled more than twenty of their number, and even had his enemies "stocked [put in the stocks] or beaten". (The memory of his fieriness may have induced Shakespeare, a generation later, to name after him the choleric and rather rapier-happy French doctor in *The Merry Wives of Windsor*. They have little else in common.) A few days earlier Matthew Parker, Archbishop of Canterbury and closely involved in Cambridge affairs, "was informed of certain articles charged upon Dr Caius, not only sounding and savouring atheism, but plainly expressing the same." Cecil and Parker made some attempts at mediation between Master and fellows. Parker seems not to have pursued the charge of atheism. They were very reluctant to take any action against Caius because, as Parker wrote to Cecil, "I do rather bear with the oversight of the Master... in respect of his good done and like to be done in the College by him, than with the brag of a fond sort of troublous factious bodies. Founders and benefactors are very rare in these days." It would set a bad precedent.

It is improbable that Caius was an atheist. Continuing Catholic loyalties are perhaps more likely. Whatever the truth, dissident fellows obtained their best results so far when, in 1570, they reported to the Bishop of London that "he maintaineth within his college copes, vestments, albs, tunicles, censers, crosses, tapers, also all kinds of mass books" and was opposed to all true—Protestant—doctrine. This time the archbishop and Chancellor could not protect him. The offensive items were seized. "A bonfire was lighted in the first court, round which," as J. B. Mullinger's university history says, "for the space of three hours were to be seen, toiling resolutely and perspiring", the Vice-Chancellor, the Master of Trinity, and the Provost of King's, "as they brought forth the contraband properties and hurled them into the flames." Such "brazen saints and Cherubim" as would not burn were "pummelled with pious zeal" and hammers. This was especially humiliating for a man of Caius' evident pride. But he remained Master, working as usual at his statutes, until just before his death three years later. Most of the statutes were abandoned by his successors, but he established the college securely and had an indelible effect on its fabric.

By 1565 Caius had bought almost all the land now occupied by the main college site. He built the salubriously three-sided Caius Court and the three gates whose position and iconography enacted his ordered vision of student life—how, again, to "conduct and arrange" it best. The undergraduate enters the college through the Gate of Humility, proceeds into Caius Court through the Gate of Virtue, and leaves by the Gate of Honour. Humility, at the entrance which now leads into Tree Court, became so decayed—prompting quips about the decay of humility in modern times—that it needed extensive restoration by 1815 and was later removed to the Master's Garden. (The arch at the modern entrance is still inscribed "Humilitatis".) The more faithfully restored Virtue and Honour are still in place, examples of the Italianate style that Caius himself had seen at first hand in northern Italy and probably in France. Virtue is described by Christopher Brooke:

> *As one approaches it across Tree Court it is a delightful sample of panelled stonework, a peaceful renaissance composition in marked contrast to the formidable castellated gatehouse of Queens' or the ornate yet still militant gates of Trinity and St John's. Within, the Gate of Virtue is plainer, matching the extreme simplicity of the two wings of the court, only adorned with an inscription to Wisdom, the general dedication of the college.*

Honour is more noticeable and more mixed in style: "a singular and pretty example of florid ornament in the manner of the sepulchral edifices of the ancients, but with certain characteristic mixtures of mediaeval origin", according to Robert Willis and John Willis Clark in the nineteenth-century *Architectural History* of the university. David Watkin, in his history of western architecture, points out that this "fetching toy" derives, by way of one of the "festive gateways" which welcomed the future Philip II of Spain into Antwerp in 1549, from a design in Serlio's *Architettura* (1537). Pevsner feels that the whole composition is too small, but Brooke values it as "a miniature triumphal arch, on a scale suited to the modesty of the court and that of the little street which originally ran from it to the Schools." Certainly it is one of the more arresting pieces of small-scale architecture in the city. But the ease with which its two sides can be compared is affected by how often the college enforces Caius' pronouncement that the Gate of Honour should, if possible, be kept closed all day, "lest persons passing through the College should invade the privacy of students, and disturb them at their work; render the courts foul and muddy; injure the buildings; purloin articles of property that have been left lying about; and turn a private path into a public thoroughfare by the prescription of long use."

Finally Caius made his presence felt in the chapel. "Vivit post funera virtus," declares his large black, gold and mottled alabaster monument—"Virtue [or strength, or glory] lives on after death"; "Fui

Caius"—"I was Caius." (The tomb is the work of Theodore de Have or Haveus, who may also, working in close collaboration with Caius, have been the architect of the court and the gates.) Also in the chapel, on opposite walls and, unlike Caius', provided with effigies, are the tombs of his approved successor, Thomas Legge (d. 1607), and Legge's friend the fellow and physician Dr Stephen Perse (d. 1615): ruffed, gowned and bearded, solidly virtuous figures. Legge's Latin tragedy *Richardus III* was performed at St John's in 1579. It was a work powerful enough, supposed Sir John Harington, "to terrify all tyrannous-minded men from following their foolish ambitious humours." Perse, who made even more money than Caius (he worked in finance as well as medicine), was a great benefactor of the college and the city. His will set up and endowed the Free School (ancestor of the modern Perse School) and provided Caius College with money for building schemes, funds for fellowships and scholarships, legacies for the cook and the under-cook. The chapel was completed by 1375; major alterations in 1637 included the wooden-panelled ceiling; an apse and mosaics were added in 1870; but the Elizabethan and Jacobean monuments act as a continuing reminder of one of the great ages of the college.

The apse is the work of Alfred Waterhouse. A great increase in college numbers had led to his being commissioned to begin work, in 1868, on what Pevsner calls "his remarkably self-possessed and insensitive pile" for Tree Court. Criticism has been levelled particularly at the dominating, towered, statued—the founders Gonville, Bateman and Caius are represented—Trinity Street front. Its inspiration is the French Renaissance château, but to Pevsner it looks like "the municipal offices of a big commercial town in the North", and to Sir Charles Tennyson (*Cambridge from Within*, 1913) like a south-coast hotel. Yet once inside the court, even those sensitive souls who shudder at the Victorian grandeur of the exterior can usually enjoy the civilized atmosphere, the avenue of whitebeams, and the wisteria.

Further accommodation was built across Trinity Street—St Michael's Court, behind St Michael's church—in 1903 and expanded in 1934. Finally Harvey Court, named after the physician, was built beyond the Backs, off Queen's Road, in 1960-2. Michael Grant has characterized Sir Leslie Martin's and Colin St John Wilson's terraced tiers as "stern, pillared, windowless, Babylonian or Assyrian"; this is "a rigorously intellectual building which concentrates upon one idea and upon the single material of brick, offering a decided interpretation of how students should live—whether they agree with it or not."

The Scott Polar Museum

The Scott Polar Research Institute, in Lensfield Road, specializes in glaciology and the glaciomarine environment. Cambridge is one of the most important centres for such study. The institute was founded in 1920 and the British Antarctic Survey, founded in 1943, is based at High Cross, Madingley Road. The museum provides a more immediately accessible history of polar exploration, the necessary starting-point for such research.

Outside the museum a figure with powerful legs and short outstretched arms appears to welcome you: an Inukshuk or "cairn in the shape of a man" from Baffin Island, used by Inuit hunters to guide caribou in their direction. Inside is a remarkably various collection of equipment, photographs and documents from the main British Arctic and Antarctic expeditions. Sir William Parry (1790-1855) led four Arctic forays between 1819 and 1827. He made contact with various groups of Inuit, and several sketches of them by Captain George Lyon are shown; to the explorers the sight of "an Eskimaux creeping into the passage of a snow hut"—not even known in English, yet, as an igloo—was extraordinary. There is also a good selection of Inuit carvings in soapstone or whale and walrus ivory: a thickset black caribou with white antlers, small polar bears, two wrestlers pushing at each other's hands and feet, a walking-stick of narwhal tusk and walrus ivory. Somehow more unexpected now (although it is simply the early equivalent of taking your CD player) is the barrel organ that Parry took with him. Its five barrels held a total of forty tunes, including highland reels, "God Save the King" and—the native love of tea as well as of monarchy was exported to the frozen north—"Polly Put the Kettle On". Other Arctic material concerns the ill-fated last expedition of Sir John Franklin, searching for the North-West passage in the mid-1840s. His ships *Erebus* and *Terror* stuck fast in the ice and the entire party perished, either of disease or, having finally abandoned the ships, starvation. Relics include some spoons, daguerrotypes of the officers in their best uniforms before setting off, and a broken pair of spectacles.

The Antarctic displays focus mainly on Scott and Shackleton. Among the objects from Scott's expeditions of 1901-4 and 1910-12 are a pocket compass and barometer, an ice axe, medical supplies and a primus stove, wooden skis and, more sadly, Captain Lawrence Oates' reindeer-skin sleeping-bag, which, the label explains, is "cut along much of its length to ease the entry of Oates's badly frostbitten leg." From Shackleton's epic journey of 1914-16 the Scott Polar has Frank Worsley's journal of the voyage of the *James Caird*, the twenty-foot boat in which Worsley, Shackleton and four others somehow succeeded in sailing the 800 miles of ferocious sea between Elephant Island and South Georgia, and some of the instruments with which Worsley navigated.

A case of shiny gold and silver medals awarded to Nansen, Scott, Shackleton, posthumously to Edward Wilson, and others, seems remote from the harsh reality of early polar exploration. (How much conditions have changed is emphasized by examples of multi-layered modern clothing and a motorized sledge to compare with the wooden specimens.) But the icy splendour of the world the explorers saw is suggested by the cold blue and white rectangles of David Smith's painting *Tabular Iceberg in the Southern Ocean* (1976).

Chapter Nine

Cambridge Drama, Music and Art

In 1642, when one of John Milton's political and religious opponents sought to discredit him by saying that he frequented "Playhouses... and the Bordelloes", he counter-attacked with some energy. Clearly the upright Milton did not go near brothels; it was the comment about playhouses that angered him more; he contrives simultaneously to suggest that there is nothing wrong with watching plays and to condemn a particular sort of play. For the criticism is nothing but hypocritical, he says, when it comes from the sort of people—supporters of the court and the established Church—who encourage university drama. In the colleges "young divines" and such—most students went on to become clergymen—have often been seen

> *writhing and unboning their clergy limbs to all the antic and dishonest gestures of Trinculoes [drinkers or fools like Trinculo in* The Tempest*], buffoons, and bawds; prostituting the shame of that ministery which either they had, or were nigh having, to the eyes of courtiers and court-ladies, with their grooms and mademoiselles. The while they acted, and overacted, among other young scholars, I was a spectator; they thought themselves gallant men and I thought them fools, they made sport and I laughed, they mispronounced and I misliked, and... they were out and I hissed. Judge now whether so many good text men were not sufficient to instruct me of false beards and vizards without more expositors [i.e. without going to the theatre in London]; and how can this confuter take the force to object to me the seeing of that which his reverend prelates allow, and incite their young disciples to act?*

Today we can relish the idea of Cambridge actors—the young Jonathan Miller or John Cleese for instance, and the odd future bishop—"writhing and unboning" on a student stage. And although Milton's carefully directed outburst has its part to play in his anti-prelatical tract, it seems possible that he too enjoyed college drama back in the less fraught atmosphere of his time at Christ's in the late 1620s. (Elsewhere he speaks more tolerantly of theatre.) Acting had been encouraged by the college authorities for several centuries, and particularly in the sixteenth and early seventeenth century was often felt to have clear educational advantages. The playwright Thomas Heywood, who was at Cambridge in the 1590s, used this tradition in *An Apology for Actors* (1612) as part of his ammunition against Puritan attacks on the theatre. At Cambridge, one of the "well-springs of all good arts, learning and documents", he saw "tragedies, comedies, histories, pastorals and shows, publicly acted by graduates of good place and reputation":

> *This is held necessary for the emboldening of their junior scholars, to arm them with audacity, against they come to be employed in any public exercise, as in the reading of the Dialectic, Rhetoric, Ethic, Mathematic, the Physic, or Metaphysic lectures. It teacheth audacity to the bashful grammarian... and makes him a bold sophister, to argue pro et contra... to reason and frame a sufficient argument to prove his questions, or to defend any axioma, to distinguish of any dilemma, and be able to moderate in any argumentation whatsoever.*

Milton may have snorted at some of Heywood's "graduates of good place and reputation", but the rhetorical skills evident in his own polemic may have been sharpened by the words they spoke.

Heywood and others could the more easily claim worthy educational purpose for university plays because they were usually in Latin. Some ancient works were given—a play by Terence was acted at King's Hall, later incorporated in Trinity, in 1510/11—together with a good number of more modern Latin pieces by college fellows or associates. Among the best known of these works were the tragedy *Richardus III*, by Thomas Legge, performed at St John's in 1579, and *Pedantius*, a satire on Gabriel Harvey of Trinity Hall by Edward Forcett of Trinity College (1580 or 1581). At the progressive St John's earlier the same century (1534/5) Sir John Cheke had staged Aristophanes' *Plutus* in Greek, an idea that was not really taken up again in Cambridge until the nineteenth century. More often Greek plays were given in the more familiar Latin. One such occasion was enlivened when, in about 1547-8, Dr John Dee, fellow and "Under-Reader in the Greek Tongue" at the newly founded Trinity College, "set forth" the *Pax* (or *Eirene*, *Peace*) of Aristophanes. Dee proudly remembered his device for "the Scarabaeus his flying up to Jupiter's Palace, with a man and his basket of victuals on his back: whereat was great wondering, and many vain reports spread abroad, of the means how that was effected." These special effects, as well as his later career as an astrologer, did much to enhance his reputation for occult knowledge.

As the audience's wonder at the flying scarab may suggest, students did not come to plays only in order to drink deep of classical learning. Occasionally Milton's courtiers, grooms and mademoiselles were present for the young men to gawp at, censure or impress. The plays themselves sometimes made fun of the townspeople, and the presentation of plays also gave scope to traditional college rivalries. On 6 February 1611 a production at Trinity was the flash-point for fighting with neighbouring St John's. Stagekeepers attacked, and were attacked by, Johnian undergraduates seeking entry to the play in spite of pointed warnings to stay away. Stones were thrown, clubs and torches wielded, and a few participants even had helmets or rapiers; other weapons listed by witnesses include a coal-rake and an iron bar. (No-one appears to have been badly injured.) The St John's warriors included the head porter and Maurice the cook. Either they were displaying college loyalty worthy of the staff of Tom Sharpe's Porterhouse 350 years later, or they were well rewarded by the students.

By 1611 a sizeable body of "Puritan" opinion held that this sort of conduct was only to be expected if activities as ungodly as play-acting were allowed to go on in the first place. Colleges (except those with Puritan leanings: Emmanuel, Christ's, Sidney Sussex) disagreed with this where their own shows were concerned. But since the 1560s, with what now seems extraordinary invidiousness, they had worked to prevent townspeople putting on their own entertainment—music, mercifully, excepted. Bear-baiting and puppet-shows were banned.

Visiting companies of players, once welcomed, were seen off or paid off. Once the Lord Chamberlain's men, the company of Burbage and Shakespeare, tried to tour to Cambridge and were turned away. Conceivably Shakespeare himself was one of the frustrated actors. The university wanted, as ever, to control and police the town, to make clear who was in charge, and to protect its allegedly tender charges from the corruption to be associated with performances at inns and fairs rather than in college halls. The sorts of horrors to be expected are graphically depicted in a painting by Pieter Bruegel the Younger in the Fitzwilliam Museum, "Village festival in Honour of St Hubert and St Anthony". Here on a simple booth stage a play about adultery is in progress, with the woman and her lover—a devil disguised as a monk—happily together on a settle. Spectators on a nearby roof obviously have not paid. Nearby, eating, quaffing and inebriated revels are in full swing. In the foreground a peasant vomits beside a large tub. A child is encouraged to down his pot with the others. Everywhere are signs of drunkenness, unruliness, irreligion, but crossbowmen, local agents of law and order, pass by oblivious to it all. St Anthony's Pigs wander about in a not too subtle comment on the peasants' idea of fun.

Banning non-college plays may have made life dull for the average citizen. It also increased the divide between the sort of plays seen in Cambridge and elsewhere. Nevertheless, there was some overlap, and students were often keenly aware of London theatre. Increasingly in the seventeenth century they were able to read published versions of at least some plays. In the St John's play *The Return from Parnassus* (c. 1601-2) the London actors Kemp and Burbage are brought on as characters; performers and audience are encouraged to laugh both at the professionals' ignorance and at their own pretentions when Kemp tells Burbage that university plays often "smell too much of that writer Ovid, and that writer Metamorphosis, and talk too much of Proserpina and Jupiter." Yet, he goes on, "here's our fellow Shakespeare puts them all down... and Ben Jonson too."

Gammer Gurton's Needle

Cambridge did not only produce plays smelling of Ovid. *Gammer Gurton's Needle*, one of the earliest surviving comedies in English—as opposed to medieval plays containing comic elements—was published in 1575 but probably first performed in about 1562. The author, "Mr. S. Mr of Art", was probably William Stevenson, a former fellow of Christ's.

Gammer Gurton's Needle is the tale of the eponymous elderly woman's loss of her trusty "nee'le". (The rustic-spoken and not notably intellectual "grandma" is no doubt named as a college joke at the expense of the village of Girton, about three miles from Cambridge.) Gib the cat started the whole farcical train of events, before the play began, by stealing the milk meant for Gammer's servant, Hodge. Gammer, who was busy mending Hodge's torn breeches, leapt up to chase off the cat and mislaid the needle. She has been looking for it, she declares in the weary but audience-aware tones of the pantomime dame (the whole cast, of course, was male), "a long hour before these folks"—the spectators—"came here." Woe is her; soon she will be reduced to crying "Alas, my nee'le, we shall never meet—adieu, adieu for aye!" Her maid Tib completes the couplet with what little consolation she can: "Not so, Gammer! We might it find if we know where it lay!" The plot thickens when the mischievous "bedlam" Diccon persuades Gammer that her neighbour Dame Chat has made off with the needle; he tells Chat, on the other hand, that Gammer thinks she has stolen and eaten her chicken. As a result, after much cross-purpose bandying of insults, the two women come to blows, with Hodge cheering his mistress on from the safety of the house: "Hoise [hoist] her! Souse her! Bounce her! Trounce her! Pull out her throat-boll!" Further farcical incidents follow. Hodge decides that Gib has in fact swallowed the needle and now wants to show his valour by somehow extracting it with a knife—Gib could be played by a college cat, but an undergraduate with preposterous costume and worried expression seems more likely. Theft, however, still looks to be the more probable explanation, as Hodge tells the local vicar, Doctor Rat, pointing his tale with frequent repetitions of "See now"—an early equivalent of "Right?" or "Know what I mean?" Rat is the next person to fall victim to Diccon's sense of humour: assured by him that he will catch Dame Chat with the needle, Rat crawls, at night, through a hole into her house. Here he is soundly drubbed by Chat and her maid, who have been warned to expect Hodge to come to steal chickens. The laugh now is on country parsons (what many of the audience and players would later become) rather than villagers. As the sensible Master Bailey points out to the incensed cleric, in the dark people cannot be expected to tell that he is not a thief: "I am sure your learning shines not out at your [pause for the expected "arse"] nose!" Gradually, at last, everything is sorted out; the needle is found still sticking in Hodge's breeches.

This "pithy, pleasaunt and merrie comedy" was, according to the title-page of 1575, "played on stage... in Christes Colledge in Cambridge." The puritanical leanings of Christ's, Milton's future college, did not yet extend to downright opposition to plays. But there was certainly a stronger tradition of performance at King's, Queens', St John's and Trinity. Alan H. Nelson, editor of the comprehensive *Records of Early English Drama* volume for Cambridge, argues that the hall in Trinity was purpose-built (1602-8) for the performance of plays. It was intended by the Master of the college, Thomas Nevile, as an answer to the great sixteenth-century hall at Christ Church in Oxford, where plays were also performed.

As in the professional playhouses, speech, costume, gesture and music, rather than developed scenery, were the main vehicles of communication. Sometimes, however, more realistic elements do seem to have been employed. At a daylight performance in St John's in 1578-9, for instance, nets covered the hall windows to give a partial illusion of darkness. (Lighting after dark was provided by torches, hand-held or in braziers.) And on two occasions the use of live hunting dogs on stage is recorded.

Royal Shows

College drama took on an especially high profile during royal visits, themselves often semi-scripted theatrical events. When Elizabeth I came in 1564 she attended performances of Plautus' *Aulularia*, Edward Halliwell's *Dido*, and Nicholas Udall's *Ezechias*. A large stage (forty by fifty feet) was erected in King's chapel—no hall was deemed big enough for the great occasion and extra spectators. The Queen's throne was on stage, side chapels were co-opted as the "houses" traditional from classical drama, the noblemen had priority seating, noblewomen occupied the roodloft, and dons, students and lesser courtiers crammed in wherever else there was space.

Elizabeth watched the long plays attentively, but long before she took her position as chief spectator she was involved in her own performance. Dressed, a contemporary noted, in "a gown of black velvet pinked: a caul [netted cap] upon her head, set with pearls and precious stones; a hat that was spangled with gold and a bush of feathers", she proceeded to King's along a lane "strewed with rushes, and flags hanging in divers places, with coverlets, and boughs; and many verses fixed upon the wall." As she passed by the scholars cried out "'Vivat Regina!', lowly kneeling." Everything was minutely organized, much of it on the instructions of "Mr Secretary Cecil", the future Lord Burghley, who was both Elizabeth's right-hand man and Chancellor of the university. At the west door of the chapel Cecil welcomed her, kneeling, and the university bedells, also kneeling, kissed their staffs of office and delivered them to Cecil, who passed them on to the Queen. Since she "could not well hold them all," she "gently and merrily re-delivered them, willing him and the other Magistrates of the University, to deliver justice uprightly, as she trusted they did." Cecil limped or "halted" as he came forward to take the rods, and so she quipped that "although the Chancellor did halt, yet she trusted that Justice did not halt."

Such comments, ponderous though they may seem now, enlivened formal proceedings, put people at their ease, and enhanced Elizabeth's reputation for ready wit. As the University Orator launched into his long Latin welcome, which might have been even longer had he not been kneeling on the first step at the west door, she sometimes "broke forth" into his litany of praise for her virtues with "Non est veritas, et utinam…" ("It isn't true, and would that…"). This may have been the first time most of the university audience had heard a woman speak Latin, let alone use it to interrupt the Orator. Later she thanked him in English, claiming gracefully that she would have answered him in kind "but for fear she should speak false Latin; and then they would laugh at her." A dire fate might have befallen anyone who did; besides, she was a good Latinist. It is difficult to know how far she was improvising or semi-improvising her part, but it often sounds, if witnesses remembered right, more like bravura acting than simple recitation of a script.

On went the opening ceremonies. The Queen met "four of the principal Doctors", attended evensong in the chapel and marvelled at its beauty and at last—until it was time to re-emerge for the first play—was allowed to move towards her accommodation in the Provost's Lodge. Before she finally reached it she was presented with "four pair of Cambridge double gloves, edged and trimmed with two laces of fine gold; and six boxes of fine comfits and other conceits".

As well as plays, Elizabeth listened keenly to scholars' public disputations during her visit. Having heard one such debate in Great St Mary's, she did vouchsafe, after an initial coy—but in this case probably premeditated—refusal, to make a Latin speech. Only "the intercession of my nobles, and my own good will towards the university" made her speak, but in a spirit of "foeminilis pudor" or "womanly shamefacedness". As usual, she managed to keep male audiences flattered by paying lip service to contemporary notions of the "weak and feeble woman", while at the same time demonstrating her "masculine" power and intelligence. Suitably amazed by the speech, the hearers cried "Vivat Regina!" once more and she replied "Taceat Regina"—"Let the Queen be silent"—and soon "cheerfully departed to her lodging."

Royal visits caused much excitement; some graceful and learned young scholar might attract royal notice, or at the least those present might see some fine and famous people and some good theatre. They also caused those in authority considerable anxiety lest the excitement got out of hand. So when James I came in 1615, strict prescriptions and prohibitions for fellows and students were issued. Not only must everyone wear correct academic dress—various caps and gowns, no "huge cuffs, shoe roses, tufts, locks and tops of hair"—but there was to be no resorting "to any inn, tavern, alehouse, or tobacco-shop at any time during the abode of his Majesty here." (No doubt the collegians' places were filled by lesser members of the royal entourage and other hangers-on.) "Nor"—perish the thought, particularly since the king was known personally to disapprove of the habit—must anyone disrupt the disputations or plays by presuming "to *take tobacco in St Mary's Church* or in Trinity College hall, upon pain of final expelling [from] the University."

The sort of conduct to be feared on such occasions is suggested by the prickly prohibition issued when the Chancellor and foreign ambassadors came in 1629. At the play there was to be no "hawking, whistling, hissing, or laughing", nor "any stamping, or knocking, nor any other such uncivil, or unscholarlike, and boyish demeanour upon any occasion." No one was even to clap until the end of the performance unless the distinguished visitors "do apparently begin the same." Yet these are just the sort of reactions which seem to be invited by one of the plays that King James and the teenage Prince Charles saw in 1615 at Trinity, George Ruggle's neo-Latin comedy *Ignoramus* (given by a cast mostly from Clare). Ruggle satirizes a lawyer, based partly on the town Recorder, Francis Brackyn, who, as the play's editor E. F. J. Tucker puts it, suffers from a "total inability to speak in any other tongue than legalese, with its quaint admixture of anglicized Latin and Law French." The king—fortunately, since it took about six hours to get through—"was much delighted by the play, and laughed exceedingly." James came back to Cambridge two months later to see *Ignoramus* again; "which," John Chamberlain told his friend Sir Dudley Carleton, "hath so nettled the lawyers, that they are almost out of all patience." In the longer term, Ruggle's play is thought to have given the word "ignoramus" to the English language.

Stourbridge Fair: The Festival Theatre

While the young men were savouring farce and learning in their halls, townspeople could enjoy themselves, if the university did not interfere too much, at such annual events as Stourbridge (originally Sturbridge) Fair. This large trade fair, stretching between the modern Newmarket Road and the river, was established by the early thirteenth century and was still flourishing in Daniel Defoe's day. "The shops are placed in rows like streets," he explains in *A Tour Through the Whole Island of Great Britain* (1724-6). In the streets were

> all sorts of trades, who sell by retail, and who come principally from London with their goods. Scarce any trades are omitted: goldsmiths, toyshops, brasiers, turners, milliners, haberdashers, hatters, mercers, drapers, pewterers, china-warehouses... with coffee-houses, taverns, brandy-shops, and eating-houses, innumerable, and all in tents, and booths, as above.

There were also many wholesale dealers, especially "in the woollen manufacture". These operated from vast tents or booths and attracted not only immediate buyers but—in more modern fashion—thousands of pounds' worth of orders. Cloth from all over the northern and western counties was on sale, and such was the reputation of the fair that a prodigious quantity of hops was brought here to be sold from as far off as Kent and Surrey; "there is scarce any price fixed for hops in England, till they know how they sell at Sturbridge Fair." Hops and other heavy goods were sent by river to Lynn "and shipped there for the Humber, to Hull, York etc. and for Newcastle upon Tyne, and by Newcastle, even to Scotland itself." And every morning in came "all sorts of wrought iron, and brassware from Birmingham; edged tools, knives, etc. from Sheffield; glasswares, and stockings, from Nottingham and Leicester and an infinite throng of other things of smaller value." Ned Ward, London tavern-keeper and satirist, provides, in *A Step to Stir-Bitch Fair* (1700), yet another long list, although with a slightly different emphasis: the "world in epitome" at the fair includes "a multitude of gentry, scholars, tradesmen, whores, hawkers, pedlars and pickpockets."

When Henry Gunning (1768-1854) first knew the fair in the 1780s, little had changed. If the trade in woollen goods had now begun to decline, eating and drinking went on in the old uninhibited way. This aspect was enjoyed to the full by senior university officials as much as anybody. Each 18 September the Vice-Chancellor and his colleagues would assemble at the Senate House, "where a plentiful supply of mulled wine and sherry, in black bottles, with a great variety of cakes, awaited their arrival." Suitably fortified, they proceeded in carriages to the fair. The University Registrary (or Registrar), from the carriage he shared with the Vice-Chancellor, proclaimed three times that the fair was open. The officials then alighted at "the Tiled Booth" for "the dispatch of business—and of oysters", ale, and "bottled porter in great profusion". (Oyster shells are still found on Stourbridge Common.) Soon they came back for dinner, elbowing their way to the dining-room through the mass of unsympathetic "peasantry". Here "before the Vice-Chancellor was placed a large dish of herrings; then followed in order a neck of pork roasted, an enormous plum-pudding, a leg of pork boiled, a pease-pudding, a goose, a huge apple-pie, and a round of beef in the centre." The other half of the table had the same arrangement, with the herrings set before the Senior Proctor. The wine was, according to Gunning, "execrable", but toasts were proposed and "mirth and good-humour prevailed, to such an extent as is seldom to be met with at more modern and refined entertainments." The town Corporation dined meanwhile at a private house where "they were served with an abundance of venison and game, which at that time (as they could not be purchased) were considered great luxuries."

Fair-goers more generally were able, in the eighteenth and early nineteenth centuries, to enjoy rope-dancing, fireworks, and dramatic "drolls". Attractions in 1751 included "the learned French dog from Paris" who "reads, writes and casts accounts by the means of typographical cards." Gunning explains one method of displaying such creatures' sagacity: some people "acquainted with the University" would

> *enter into a confederacy... with the owners of these learned animals, to give them a string of questions and answers, and to point out some mode by which they might discover the persons to whom the answers were particularly applicable... Persons guilty of indiscretions, which they flattered themselves were known only to their most intimate friends, were astonished at finding that the sapient pig was acquainted with their proceedings, and pointed them out with but little hesitation to the assembled crowd.*

Human prodigies were also presented. In the 1780s, among other equestrian events, you could watch displays of horsemanship from "the Wonderful Child of Promise"—the Infant Phenomenon of the day.

In the mid-eighteenth century more permanent playhouses began to replace the traditional makeshift playing spaces at the fair. A succession of buildings appeared off what is now Newmarket Road. William Wilkins, Senior, built a theatre here in 1808 ("spacious and lofty", according to the *New Cambridge Guide* of 1809). Wilkins' venture survived only until 1813, but its replacement was opened in 1814 by his better-known son William Wilkins, Junior, architect not only of Downing College and the new courts at Trinity and Corpus but of the National Gallery and University College, London, and of the Theatre Royal, Bury St Edmunds. This new Theatre Barnwell had a capacity of 700. At first it was allowed to function only during the fair (which survived officially until 1933), and for a much longer period only out of term time in the hope of minimizing the number of young men likely to be corrupted. After a period of some commercial success the venture foundered in the 1870s. Then, following half a century of use mainly as a mission hall, in 1926 the Barnwell was bought, refurbished and renamed the Festival Theatre by the wealthy director Terence Gray. Under his aegis productions were often adventurous: his lover Doria Paston designed Cubist sets, and a *Twelfth Night* with Sir Toby on roller skates was much remembered. Gray left in 1934 and, although for a time the Festival continued to flourish without him, attracting such leading actors of the day as Robert Donat and Jessica Tandy, it closed five years later. It was reopened for wartime musical entertainments before being acquired by the Arts Theatre for uses including costume storage. In 1995 the Arts put £876,000 of its National Lottery grant towards fully repairing the decaying building, and announced that when the work was completed the Festival would be used for experimental theatre work. In the event, however, the Arts Trust sold the Festival in 1998 to help settle its debts and save the Arts itself. The Georgian playhouse has now been restored for use as the Cambridge Buddhist Centre. (The entrance is beside 38 Newmarket Road, the house built for William Wilkins Senior in about 1800.)

The Greek Play

In 1882 William Beales Redfern converted a church hall, between Emmanuel College and the University Arms Hotel, into what was known from 1883 as the New Theatre Royal. It was built for large audiences and often described as "barn-like"; after its rebuilding in 1895-6 there was room for 1,400. (It later became a cinema and was demolished in the 1960s.) Redfern, who was mayor for four successive terms in 1883-7, was keen to impress on the university that this was to be a respectable establishment. (Control of licensing passed to the local Council only in 1894.) One way of doing this was to agree to host what would become a notable university institution, the Greek Play, in November 1882. The plays have always been given in their original language, and with one exception in 1885, used all-male casts until 1950. Since the late nineteenth century they have taken place every three years.

Some productions, inevitably, were worthy and academic. This is not really an option available to modern directors, who must respond to the challenge of engaging a mainly Greekless audience. Jane Montgomery, the director of Euripides' *The Trojan Women* in 1998 and Sophocles' *Electra* in 2001, adopted some interesting and fairly radical solutions. (In 2001 accessibility was also, more simply, increased by the provision of English surtitles at the Arts Theatre.) Some flavour of *The Trojan Women* is given by the *Varsity* description of Michael Spencer's set at the Arts, "a disused swimming pool [which] evokes a place of joy and physical grace gone silent and dangerous. Blood seeps through the cracked tiles." Ruth Hazel, in a review for the Open University, comments on the Electra of Marta Zlatic (a memorable Hecuba in the earlier production):

> *Her cropped hair and the signs of self-neglect and of abuse showed that her refusal to conform and accept the current status quo had exiled her to a no-man's land between life and death. [W]ith her angular, distorted movements and harsh, anguished vocal delivery, [she] seemed at times scarcely human, as if hovering between the underworld of the dead and the morally degraded world of those now living in the House of Atreus.*

The Greek Play has become a more dynamic event since the days when Rupert Brooke, as an undergraduate at King's, could cause a sensation in the non-speaking role of the Herald in Aeschylus' *Eumenides*. According to his friend and "patron" Eddie Marsh, the "radiant, youthful figure in gold and vivid red and blue, like a Page in the Riccardi Chapel, stood strangely out against the stuffy decorations and dresses." His tunic was short enough to delight many in the audience, although A. C. Benson felt that the "pretty figure" was "spoilt by a glassy stare."

The ADC

In 1854 it occurred to an Etonian undergraduate, Francis Burnand, in his first term at Trinity, that "private theatricals" would be much more amusing than the usual round of "cards, drinking, and supper". Supper, of course, could still follow. So, in their rooms opposite Trinity above a grocer's, he and his friends started acting. Soon they conceived the idea of putting on a more ambitious performance and decided to approach the Vice-Chancellor for his permission. In 1880, the year he became editor of *Punch*, Burnand gives his account of what followed in *The "A.D.C.": Being Personal Reminiscences of the University Amateur Dramatic Club.*

The encounter with the Vice-Chancellor, Dr Guest, is written up in Dickensian manner. He was, says Burnand, "a short, wizened, dried-up, elderly gentleman, with little legs and a big head, like a serious Punch doll, wearing his academical cap, and with his gown hitched up over his elbows, which gave him the appearance of having recently finished a hornpipe before I came in." After some delays and misunderstandings the eighteen-year-old Burnand stammered out the nature of his request. (As befitted the future prolific author of burlesque and farce, inappropriate puns and jokes raced through his mind but remained, thankfully, unuttered.) Dr Guest started at the words "theatrical performance". "'Um!'... and, giving his gown a good hitch up over his elbows, he put his head on one side, as though he were meditating the commencement of another hornpipe on the spot." But instead of dancing he put a series of questions to the young man. Was he "of Trinity?" A fellow? A scholar? A graduate? The tenor of his questions on the play was equally unpromising: it would not, he elicited from Burnand, be a Greek play, nor a Latin, nor even Shakespeare. Reluctant to reveal that it would be the popular *Box and Cox*, Burnand gave the author's name, "Mr Maddison Morton", but had to confess that Morton, too, was not a fellow of Trinity and so was forced to utter the title. "Even then," he claims, "I was afraid he would ask me if 'Box and Cox' were Fellows of Trinity" and "regretted not having introduced them as *Mr.* Box and *Mr.* Cox... If I could only have metamorphosed them into the Rev. Mr. Box, M.A., Fellow of Trinity, and Dr Cox, D.D., Fellow of Caius, it would have been perfect." The Vice-Chancellor nevertheless said that he would put the proposal before the college "Heads", whose meeting he was about to chair.

Three days later the expected refusal arrived. Plans for Messrs Box and Cox were shelved. Nevertheless Burnand and his friends decided to found a theatrical club, without advertising its precise nature to their elders. This became, in 1855, the Amateur Dramatic Club. The club leased two disused rooms over a stable at the back of the Hoop Inn in Jesus Lane, and "a capital carpenter, one Lovett" made a stage and proscenium arch. In 1859 the premises were much extended, and a new stage built, when the Union Debating Club gave up the Hoop billiard rooms.

The actors at first took precautions "in case of a raid by the Proctors." "We had a speaking tube," Burnand remembers, "run through from the Hoop bar to our green-room... and outside the windows of the stage we had a ladder placed," down which the performers would have descended, caps and gowns concealing their costumes. As it turned out, however, when a proctor came to investigate the club rooms he raised no objections. If some dons remained hostile to all kinds of theatrical activity, others began to take an active part in helping the club. But it was the attitude of the Prince of Wales, a man rarely averse to the pleasures, which effectively forced the university to recognize the ADC. As an undergraduate in 1861 he joined the club, went to several performances, went backstage, and even came again with his more evidently irreproachable wife, Princess Alexandra, in 1864.

The main early repertory of the club was burlesque, some of it, like *Villikins and his Dinah* (1855) by Burnand. (His later offerings for the London theatre included *The Frightful Hair, or, Who Shot the Dog?*, "an original travestie on Lord Lytton's *The Rightful Heir*".) *Box and Cox* was soon playing, Vice-Chancellor or no Vice-Chancellor. Eventually some restrictions were imposed, with students banned from putting on burlesques in 1871 and performances limited, until 1882, to the first term of the year only. Not all club members chafed under such restrictions; for them the advantages of belonging were more social than theatrical. Their subscriptions, however, helped to keep the ADC alive long after the Hoop Inn had gone. In 1973 financial survival was made easier when the building was leased to the university, which also employs several staff to run it.

Comedy always remained a staple of performances by the club, but in the twentieth century serious drama became at least equally important. Productions in the rebuilt playhouse which opened on the same site in 1935, following fire damage in 1933, included in 1937 the first modern airing of *The Revenger's Tragedy* and in 1943 the second ever version of T. S. Eliot's *The Family Reunion.* The ADC continues to present a very wide range of student and some other productions. With a capacity of only about 220, it remains one of the city's most intimate playing areas.

The Arts Theatre and Marlowe Society

The Arts was conceived and achieved by Maynard Keynes. King's, where he was bursar, intended to build new student accommodation at Peas Hill, and this was integrated with the playhouse. Yet the college did not provide much of the money for the scheme; Keynes used some of his own skilfully invested wealth to force the project through. He provided nearly £30,000 of the total £32,000—about £800,000 in modern money—and got back £17,000. The Arts opened in 1936. The opening season included Keynes' wife, the Russian ballerina Lydia Lopokova, as Nora in *A Doll's House* and Hilda Wangel in *The Master Builder.*

Recurrent financial problems notwithstanding, the theatre remained open until 1993, by which time, according to the new Chief Executive Stephen Walton, "the whole place was old and tired, the kitchen would have been condemned, there were cockroaches in the auditorium, the place was unventilated in summer, cold in winter... It was unfriendly, grubby, expensive to maintain." After much work, £3 million raised by the theatre trust, and a saving lottery grant of £6.64 million in 1995, the completely rebuilt Arts Theatre opened in 1997. By 1998 it had come perilously near to closing once again as a result of remaining debts and difficulties with various funding bodies. It managed to survive as a result of measures including selling the

Festival Theatre and shedding the Cambridge Arts Cinema. This small but very popular cinema (formerly the Cosmopolitan), in Market Passage, was famous for showing foreign language and other "art" films and for its annual film festival. A support group fought hard but unsuccessfully to save it. They were sceptical about the plan to open instead a three-screen cinema in St Andrew's Street, since this, unlike its predecessor, would be under commercial management. This enterprise, the Arts Picture House, has, however, shown a much wider range of work than some of its critics feared, and has continued the festival.

The Marlowe Society, founded to act work by Shakespeare and his less known contemporaries, was formed after a production of Marlowe's *Dr Faustus*, with a cast including Rupert Brooke as Mephistopheles and the mountaineer George Mallory as the Pope, at the ADC in 1907. The following year the society put on Milton's *Comus*, directed by Brooke, who also played the Attendant Spirit, at the New Theatre. (The classical scholar Francis Cornford was Comus, in shiny robe and panther-skin, and his future wife the poet Frances Darwin designed the production; her cousin Gwen Darwin, later Gwen Raverat, worked on the costumes.) From the 1930s, however, the society usually presented its annual offering at the Arts. The dominant figure in the society between then and the 1960s was George Rylands (1902-99), always known as "Dadie" because of his own childhood mispronunciation of "baby". Rylands, an English fellow at King's, was Keynes' associate and then successor as chairman of the Arts. He influenced several generations of undergraduate actors and directors towards simple staging and above all the clear speaking of verse.

"Dadie" became a Cambridge character. In his eighties and nineties he was spoken of usually with affection. Those who knew him when he was younger had more mixed feelings about him. The conductor Raymond Leppard remembers "moments of extreme exasperation at his bland, devastating demolition of our more pretentious views. Lovable and maddening at the same time..." Noel Annan, former Provost of King's, wrote after Rylands' death of his various neuroses, his drink problem, and the outrageous homosexuality which made him, in Annan's view, a travesty of himself. Stephen

Spender would perhaps have agreed with some of this, but revised his earlier opinions during a walk with Dadie in 1980, recorded in Spender's journal: "I thought how I had missed a life of friendship with him, because his clever mocking brittle manner made me think that affection—for someone as gauche as I have been all my life—was only an act, but I was wrong."

Rylands was one of a number of Cambridge influences on Sir Peter Hall. Hall lived in Cambridge from the age of eight and later at Shelford when his father became stationmaster there. He went to the Perse School where, as he relates in his autobiography *Making an Exhibition of Myself* (1993), teaching Shakespeare through drama had been pioneered in the 1930s by Caldwell Cook. This tradition was still thriving; Hall's first Shakespeare memory is of himself and other eleven-year-olds "armed with wooden shields and swords and cloaks, shouting *Macbeth* at each other" and his appetite was whetted for an author "thrilling and blood-soaked and full of witches". Equally important was his habit, a few years later, of standing at the back in the Arts Theatre for sixpence every Monday night. Here amongst much else he saw John Gielgud, whom he would later direct, play Hamlet.

Hall read English at St Catharine's College (1950-3), although he was more often to be found at the ADC or Arts. He performed in Marlowe Society productions under Rylands, whose voice he remembers as musical, emphatic, and with "a constant upward inflection", which "sustained the sense if not the emotion." Such, he recalls, was Rylands' interest in "our line endings and our iambics" that he was much less concerned with "whether we were bumping into each other." He went to lectures by F. R. Leavis, and later came to feel—ironically in view of Leavis' disapproval of the theatre—that he was responsible for "all the textual seriousness at the basis" of his own work and that of Trevor Nunn, who came to Downing in 1959, was supervised by Leavis, and like Hall went on to head both the RSC and the National.

It was probably John Barton, however, who had the strongest immediate effect on Hall and Nunn. Barton came to King's in 1948 and went on to become a research fellow and Lay Dean. Nunn remembers, in his foreword to Barton's *Playing Shakespeare* (1984) how, as an admittedly impressionable eighteen-year-old, he first saw on the stage of the Arts

> *The young man with the Renaissance face... noble beard, high forehead, an expression in the eyes both haught and hawk and rich brown crinkled hair... In 1959 John was a Cambridge legend; he had directed countless university productions to professionally high standards, he had become a young and romantic don... with the Elizabethan Touring Company he had pioneered small cast touring Shakespeare productions... None of that contributed much of course to the legend—no it was the fact that he chewed razor blades for fun, that he knew every line of the First Folio by heart, that he spoke Chaucer's English, that he was a brilliant and extremely dangerous sword fighter, that he was hilariously absent-minded, obsessed with cricket, a chain-smoker, an expert on Napoleon and some-body who enjoyed working sixteen hours a day without a break.*

The worrying habit with razor blades is confirmed by Peter Hall, who explains that at rehearsals he would gently flop them over on his tongue "to ease the enthusiasm which threatened to possess him"; "occasionally, a tell-tale trickle of blood would seep out of the corner of his mouth as John elucidated a particularly difficult textual point." Hall also experienced the swordsmanship, when he was Tybalt to Barton's Mercutio at the Arts and they duelled dangerously and at some length—too much, Hall thinks now—with rapier and dagger. Barton says that having sustained minor injuries in this and several other productions he "evolved a technique of making everything *look* as dangerous as possible, while at the same time ensuring the maximum of safety"—a form of fighting "more theatrical and exciting than the real thing". Barton's larger contribution was, as throughout his career, to show actors how, as Nunn puts it, to appear not to be "delivering a previously written text" but thinking and discovering the words out of character and situation; "The words became necessary. It wasn't verse speaking. It was acting."

Footlights
The Footlights Club, since its foundation in 1883, has channelled the comic or would-be comic energy of many undergraduates. Since the

mid-1950s it has often achieved the more difficult distinction of launching not only professional careers, but entire new trends in comedy.

Jonathan Miller, who read medicine at St John's before embarking on his career as doctor, director, psychologist and "intellectual", was one of the early stars of the more experimental period. With unequalled mastery of gesture and inflection he parodied the great tradition of Cambridge philosophy, speaking as Bertrand Russell:

> *One of the advantages of living in the Great Court, Trinity, I seem to recall, was the fact that one could pop across at any time of the day or night and trap the then young G. E. Moore into a logical falsehood... I recall one occasion with particular vividness. I had popped across and had knocked upon his door. "Come in," he said. I decided to wait a while in order to test the validity of his proposition. "Come in," he said once again, a trifle testily, I thought. "Very well," I replied, "if that is in fact truly what you wish."*

They go on to test the statement that Moore has apples in his basket, and become fast friends as a result. A rather more surreal Footlights act originated in the decision of Miller's future *Beyond the Fringe* collaborator, Peter Cook, to entertain his friends, one lunch-time at Pembroke College, "in the persona of a religious eccentric who claimed to be carrying the Holy Bee of Ephesus in a cardboard box, an insect which he said had once buzzed about the true cross."

Cook was Footlights President in 1960. Among subsequent Presidents were Tim Brooke-Taylor (1963), Graeme Garden (1964), Eric Idle (1965), Clive James (1967), Clive Anderson (1975) and Hugh Laurie (1981; the previous year, most unusually for a member of the Footlights inner circle, he rowed for Cambridge in the university Boat Race.) Laurie's friends Emma Thompson and Stephen Fry were committee-members. Other members who took up comedy professionally include Eleanor Bron, John Bird, John Fortune, Sandi Toksvig, Sasha Baron Cohen of Ali G fame, and David Baddiel. John Cleese, a law student at Downing, was yet another; in the programme for *Double Take*, at the Arts Theatre in 1962, he was billed as "an enthusiast for verbal humour" who "is nevertheless always prepared to stoop to slapstick, where he ranks the custard pie above the banana skin." In keeping with the shift away from the earlier Footlights song and dance tradition, "He says he cannot sing, and keeps a locked piano in his room to prove it."

May Week

May Week, the post-exam period in June—originally in May—is the culmination of the year's undergraduate drama. There are so many open-air productions (and rival attractions) that audiences can be very small. Clive James, in *May Week Was in June*, recreates the atmosphere of a production which was, however, well attended. At *As You Like It*, around the pool and the hedges in the Fellows' Garden at Clare, the young actors "deployed their hired costumes as they had been taught by some preposterously solemn young director." From the back of the audience "the theatrical dons ... threw decrepit fond looks at Orlando. They thought him charming. In that weather I thought them charming. They had their place in this enchanted forest. Absurdly I was sorry that I must soon lose mine."

The pool and hedges are still useful features in productions at Clare. During the long vacation some college grounds, including those at Girton and Emmanuel, are also used for the Cambridge Shakespeare Festival. Since audiences include many overseas visitors and students, a clear playing style is required—sometimes, but by no means always, unadventurous compared with what happens in May Week.

The colleges' May Balls are a more widely known May Week event. Michelle Spring's detective novel *Nights in White Satin* (1999) describes a ball at St John's. "May Balls evolved," her private investigator Laura Principal tells us, "so that students could let off steam after exams and, in spite of their differences, they all occupy a cusp between excitement and excess." On the way to St John's towards sunset

> *the men stood out sharp and clean against the soft grey stone of Cambridge; the women looked bright and exotic. They filled the narrow streets with their scent, the clatter of their heels, their laughter, their high spirits. Cocky and loud they came, or tight and restrained;... loosened up with drink already, or holding out for excesses to come.*

There are fireworks, dancing to "the insistent rhythms of Hot Chocolate", champagne, smoked salmon, melon—indeed, it seems to Laura Principal, who is in charge of security at the ball, that "there was a torrent of food... A landslide, an avalanche. Eats on the scale of a natural disaster." Suddenly, amid this hedonistic festival, a young woman "took her splendid young self—the elegant white curve of a dress, the silver armlets, the dainty sandals, the corona of curls—and disappeared" and the investigation is launched. But for most students, free from the conventions of crime fiction, enjoying May Week presents few problems and remains, as Clive James says, "a time for youth to celebrate itself".

Music

At a service in King's College Chapel in 1901 the Provost, Augustus Austen-Leigh, took the tenor part. According to A. C. Benson, who taught at Eton at the time and was visiting his old college, he screeched rather than sang, "leaning against his stall, all doubled up, holding up music-books... his mouth like the mouth of a roach."

Perhaps it was an off day for Austen-Leigh (or for Benson); he was musical enough, at least, to be President of the Cambridge University Music Society (CUMS), in which capacity he had been involved in one of the most famous of Cambridge musical events, the Jubilee celebration for the fiftieth anniversary of the society in June 1893. This was made possible mainly, however, by the organizing energy of Charles Villiers Stanford, conductor of CUMS and, since 1887, Professor of Music. At the Guildhall the composers Saint-Saëns, Tchaikovsky, Boito and Bruch, representing their nations, performed their own work with the musicians of the society. Saint-Saëns gave the first British performance of his piano fantasy *L'Afrique*, Bruch and Boito conducted extracts from their operas *Odysseus* and *Mefistofele*, and Stanford stood in for Grieg, who was ill and unable to attend, with the first *Peer Gynt* suite. The piece which seems most to have impressed the audience was Tchaikovsky's *Francesca da Rimini*, another British premiere. The composer's English biographer Ernest Markham Lee describes

a man with sorrow-lines upon his brow, and grey, almost white hair, step-
ping up to the conductor's desk, among the plaudits of the throng! I
remember his serious set expression as he faced round to his band, his
wildly energetic baton, and the awful fury and madness of his music...
[T]he rushing scale-passages, weird, frenzied, wild, were something in
music that to us was uncanny and new.

The next day the distinguished visitors received honorary degrees and dined among a hundred guests, under Austen-Leigh's auspices, at King's.

The occasion also marked Stanford's stepping down from CUMS. He had worked hard for the society and for musical studies in Cambridge, but would now—partly because of his financial and other disputes with the university—be based mainly in London. He remained professor until his death in 1924 but his appearances in Cambridge were usually brief; tradition has it that they were confined to the Railway Hotel by the station.

Music had, of course, functioned in Cambridge in earlier times. College chapels provided, and still provide, one of the main opportunities for university music making. Congregations have often been uplifted more successfully than Benson; the odd officer may screech from his roach's mouth, but the choirs are experts. (Two of the best known, King's and St John's, are made up of choristers from King's College School and St John's College School as well as undergraduate choral students.)

The town musicians or "waits" with their shawms, viols, sackbutts and cornetts, provided music for civic and university occasions and shows between the fifteenth and seventeenth centuries. William Gibbons led the waits for two periods in the 1560s and 1570s and conceivably his better-known son Orlando was also a wait at the beginning of the next century. The composers Robert Fayrfax and Christopher Tye had been awarded Cambridge degrees in the early sixteenth century. William Boyce wrote and performed his ode for the installation of the Duke of Newcastle as Chancellor in 1749.

In modern times there was something of a renaissance. Ralph Vaughan Williams (1872-1958), who had studied at Trinity, maintained contacts with Cambridge music; his best known piece with a Cambridge context is his music for a production of Aristophanes' *The Wasps* in 1909. Edward Dent, a fellow of King's from 1902-18 who returned as professor in 1926, stimulated interest in unjustly neglected work including Handel's operas. The Cambridge Handel Opera Group has given biennial productions since it was founded by its conductor Andrew Jones in 1985. Among more recent composers connected with the Cambridge music faculty are Professors Alexander Goehr and Robin Holloway; John Rutter, at one time Director of Music at Clare, leads the Cambridge Singers in performances of his own and other work. And well-known former students have included such pioneers of the early music movement as David Munrow, Christopher Hogwood and Sir John Eliot Gardiner, the conductor Sir Andrew Davies, the tenor Robert Tear and the pianist Joanna MacGregor. Musicians have benefited from the introduction of a Music tripos along the lines of other subjects in 1947 and—together with concert audiences—from the opening of the West Road faculty building and concert hall in the mid-1970s. The hall, designed by Leslie Martin, has famously good acoustics. It was refurbished recently at a cost of more than £2 million and is one of the main focuses of classical music making in Cambridge. The many groups performing here include the still flourishing CUMS.

Rock concerts (and visiting jazz, opera, ballet and comedy) often take place in the Corn Exchange. Cambridge Folk Festival takes place annually at Cherry Hinton Hall. The Boat Race, in East Road, and the Junction, in Clifton Road, are other active live music venues. Roger Waters, Syd Barrett and David Gilmour of Pink Floyd were born and grew up in Cambridge. There have also been many university bands, but, as Mark Weatherall says in *From Our Cambridge Correspondent*, "few... have made it big, and great university bands of the 1980s and 1990s such as The Exploding Hamsters, President Reagan is Clever, and Brother's Cup have left their listeners with nothing except good memories."

Art: the Fitzwilliam Museum

The museum was founded by Viscount Fitzwilliam's bequest to the university of £100,000 in 1816. Building commenced in 1837 and the doors opened to the public in 1848. The original architect was George Basevi; after he fell to his death from scaffolding at Ely Cathedral in

1845 the work was continued by Charles Robert Cockerell and later by Edward Barry.

The exterior of the Fitzwilliam shows, in the opinion of John Julius Norwich, neoclassicism losing its "former purity and coolness, becoming more dramatic, restless, almost Baroque" (*The Architecture of Southern England*, 1985). Barry's entrance hall is a spectacular polychrome ensemble of mosaic-patterned floors, pillars, niches, caryatids copied from the Erechtheum, a cupola with statues, polished stone, classicizing busts on plinths, richly gilded capitals. It reminds Norwich of the hall of "a very grand London club". Ellis Waterhouse, writing in *The Listener* in April 1961, saw the "heavy coloured marbles" as an "indestructible and sinister Propylaeum" in contrast to the delights of the galleries; possibly the careful cleaning and conservation programme of 2002 would have persuaded him otherwise.

Downstairs the museum displays a variety of ancient artefacts. The Greek exhibit with perhaps the most unusual history is what Edward Daniel Clarke, subsequently Professor of Mineralogy, travelling in Greece in 1801, believed to be the upper part of the cult statue of Demeter from Eleusis. (In fact it is a caryatid from her temple precinct.) Before reaching Cambridge it had to be prised away from local villagers who, since they believed it made their land fertile, were understandably reluctant to see it go. A bribe was paid to a Turkish official and the statue was cleared of the dung that—in accordance with the fertility belief—surrounded it. At this point a bull charged up and butted it, confirming the villagers' superstitious suspicions, but they were persuaded when a Greek priest was produced, in full vestments, to strike the first pickaxe blow. At last Clarke's one hundred and fifty workers were able to haul the weighty "Demeter", in a wooden frame on rollers, to the sea. Eventually—the statue was salvaged when the ship carrying it went down off Beachy Head—it reached England.

The Egyptian section includes samples of Amarna art, the "naturalistic", or at least differently and more dynamically stylized art of the heretic Pharaoh Akhenaten: the king celebrating a jubilee beneath the descending rays of his beloved sun-disk, the finely moulded limestone head of one of his daughters. More traditional Egypt is present in some superbly decorated mummy-cases and the massive seven-ton sarcophagus-lid of Rameses III. The rest of the sarcophagus is in the Louvre while the Cairo Museum is left with Rameses' despoiled mummy. Similar separations have delivered to the Fitzwilliam some detached sarcophagus masks. A gilded wood mask from the twentieth or twenty-first Dynasty has a degree of mystic serenity, the look of one whose heart has been weighed and accepted. Divorced, however, from the usual funerary context and the panoply of colourful gods, it seems on the whole human, our contemporary, with its steady, slightly melancholy gaze.

There are also exhibits from less familiar areas of the ancient world. A small gallery is dominated by the case containing a Romano-Syrian syncretistic deity in basalt, probably third-century AD. Zeus, Hermes, and the local warrior-god Hadad combine. The gallery lighting has been arranged for some years so as to create, in the glass as we look at this figure, clear reflections of the limestone grave-markers behind us. The figures, among them a reclining man who banquets while his wife and sons look on, are from Palmyra. Partly enhanced by the light effects, they partake of the usual somewhat enigmatic Palmyrene air. They are not quite Greek, Roman, or eastern, not quite of this world yet emanating from it.

The Fitzwilliam has notable collections of armour, ceramics, coins, drawings, manuscripts, and medieval and early Renaissance painting. Among somewhat later paintings one of the most interesting is Veronese's *Hermes, Herse and Aglauros* (1576-84), part of the founder's bequest of 1816. In a rarely used story from Ovid's *Metamorphoses*, the jealous Aglauros tries to prevent the god reaching her sister Herse, with whom he is in love. Hermes will turn Aglauros into a black stone; here he is in the act of touching her with his caduceus. Herse sits, one breast and one knee revealed, her lute and music laid aside, but fairly impassive. Aglauros, too, seems to put up only limited opposition. She is on the ground but her arm only curls up to, rather than clutches at, the god. Her hair remains in place and, besides, we cannot see her face to gauge her state of mind. Hermes himself shows no anger or aggression—a calm certainty, rather, of what must happen, and even a degree of tenderness for his victim, if a god can feel such an emotion. Herse's lapdog does look somewhat surprised but again the reaction is decorous: a stare, perhaps a growl, but no yapping. Myth unfolds with leisurely inevitability. Perhaps the picture is intended to illustrate some such truism as "Amor vincit omnia", perhaps the statue of a satyr implies some condemnation of lust, but Veronese's emphasis is, as often, more on colour than on morals.

Both colours and morality are stronger in the best-known Renaissance painting in the collection, Titian's *Tarquin and Lucretia* (c. 1570). Titian prefers this scene of horrifying, irresistible energy to the more traditional depiction of a more composed Lucretia, killing herself having told her father and husband that Tarquin has raped her. Titian said that he had put "greater labour and artifice" into this work than anything else he had produced for many years (he painted it probably when he was around eighty). Its effects are nicely calculated: the contrast between the rapist's russet hair and his victim's golden; his clothes and her nakedness (emphasised by her necklace and bracelets)—the finely woven doublet versus the brute fact of rape; pure white and fierce red; the thrusting forward motion of his dagger and knee, her falling back; his downward glare of desire or conquest and her upward look, partly imploring but aware of her helplessness; the violated domesticity of Lucretia's slipper and bed-linen. But the impact is one less of careful contrast than of immediate, shocking action, shocking in part because it evidently takes place in a house in contemporary Venice rather than safely mythical Rome. Two beautiful figures demonstrate the ugliness of rape.

Among many later works in the Fitzwilliam are Richard Parkes Bonington's *Bocadasse, Genoa, with Monte Fasce in the Background* (1824), where the buildings shine as if still wet with morning or with paint; Samuel Palmer's *On Chaldon Down, Dorset* (1835), in his distinctive amber-gold; and Ford Madox Brown's *The Last of England* (1860: a replica of the version of 1855-6 in Birmingham Museum and Art Gallery). International twentieth-century art is less well represented but there are a few good samples of Matisse, Picasso, Braque and Modigliani. From Britain there is an important group of Stanley Spencers, Gwen John's *The Convalescent* (one of a number of studies of the same figure, John's model Isabel Bowser), and Jacob Epstein's bronze bust *Oriel Ross* (1931). The room is dominated, however, by the sky-filled trees of Monet's *Poplars*, one of the series of fifteen canvases he painted in 1891. (In order to complete the job before the poplars were cut down he had, famously, to buy them at auction in conjunction with a local wood dealer.) Monet, a French reviewer said in 1899, "understood the poplar, which summarises all the grace, all the spirit, all the youth of our land."

The Museum of Classical Archaeology

The public gallery of this museum, on the first floor of the Classics Faculty building at the Sidgwick site since 1982, shows high-quality plaster casts of ancient sculpture, taken mostly during the nineteenth century. The original collection was kept in the Fitzwilliam. In 1884, much expanded, it moved to the so-called "Ark" in Little St Mary's Lane, where it played an important role in the teaching of classical art and archaeology. (The Ark, which was leased from Peterhouse, now houses the Ward Library and College Theatre.)

This single gallery brings together representatives of the National Museum in Athens, the Acropolis Museum, the Vatican, the Capitoline, the British Museum, the Louvre and many other collections. There are such well-known statues, blueprints for generations of sculptors and painters, as the winged Nike (Victory) of Samothrace, the massive Farnese Heracles with his appropriately massive club (from Naples), the Apollo Belvedere, two caryatids from the Erechtheum and at least five famous Aphrodites. Less generally familiar pieces include, from the west pediment of the temple of Artemis on Corfu, a large and menacing Medusa ready for conquest, snakes wreathed in her hair and tightly knotted round her waist, and a more elegant leopard. On a much smaller scale and cast from an original of 450 years later, there is a Hellenistic relief apotheosis of Homer, with muses, lyres and much drapery.

The room is top-lit, often bathing the exhibits in sunlight (aided by some artificial lighting); after a time it is surprising to look out of the windows and see English horse-chestnuts or the red brick of Ridley Hall. Here, as in many sculpture galleries, especially when there are few visitors, there is a sense of presence: everywhere strong, living figures gesture, ride, worship, fight, hurl a (now missing) trident or thunderbolt, hold up the heavens or just stand still with the simple dignity of youth or god. All this may, nevertheless, seem classically remote; one factor that helps to dispel the remoteness is the inclusion, near the beginning of the gallery, of two imaginative reconstructions of the way the figures were originally painted. Beside, and almost disconcertingly different from, traditional plain casts of the Auxerre goddess and the "peplos kore" (an Attic votive statue of a peplos-clad girl), are versions painted in garish red, blue and green. They develop red lips, black hair, clearly outlined eyebrows, eyes with pupils, clearly patterned clothing. Different again from the pure white tradition, and not needing imaginative reconstruction, are the casts of figures in bronze—rare survivors like the Delphi charioteer who, as Forster aptly puts it in *A Room With a View*, "drives undismayed towards infinity."

Niobe and her daughter are desperate where the charioteer is eternally controlled, caught on the cusp of disaster where he steers timeless. Originally this was part of a larger group with more Niobids, the whole brood punished by the gods for their mother's presumption. The remaining girl clings to Niobe, who tries hopelessly to protect her and looks up, less "all tears" as yet than shocked, agonized, imploring. (The original has had a complex history: it is a Roman copy of the Greek piece set up in Cilicia in the third century BC and transferred to the temple of Apollo in the Campus Martius in Rome in 38 BC; Niobe's most recent misfortune—a reminder of one justification for taking casts—was to be damaged by a bomb at the Uffizi in 1993.) Nearby is another well-known group of sufferers: Laocoön and his two sons, from the Vatican, struggling in the coils of the sea serpent.

Another notable copy of a copy—again a Roman version of a Hellenistic original—is the Dying Gaul from the Capitoline Museum. He was long supposed to be a Dying Gladiator who had been, as Byron says in *Childe Harold's Pilgrimage*, "Butcher'd to make a Roman holiday." Rome itself is represented by some interesting portrait heads and busts. The faintly smiling Pompey—the sort of knowing Roman politician who ought to be in *Spartacus* or *Gladiator*—is followed by a good range of emperors: a battery of heads of Augustus, suggesting the widespread distribution of his official image for propaganda purposes; Vespasian creased with experience from Copenhagen and a puffy, larger head of Nero from Munich; the big-eared provincial Claudius in bronze found in the River Alde in Suffolk in 1907 and now at Saxmundham Hall; some elaborately coiffured imperial women.

Kettle's Yard

In 1957 H. S. Ede, generally known as Jim Ede, took over four small, dilapidated cottages and converted them into a home for himself, his wife and his art collection. He showed visitors round in the afternoons and continued to live on site for some years after the university became involved in the project in 1966. Kettle's Yard is still more like a large house than most museums: there are not only paintings and sculptures but plants, stones, tables and chairs, rugs, books; there are, for better or worse, no labels. An overflowing personal enthusiasm for art, nothing more clinical or academic, is in evidence; Ede defined the place as less a gallery or museum than "a continuing way of life... in which stray objects... in light and space have been used to make manifest" an "underlying stability".

Visitors' reactions will also be personal. Some find the whole place rather "precious" and prefer to consume their art less comfortably than in a place called by its founder "a refuge of peace and order". Winifred Nicholson once pronounced that it "won't do" and that Ede was "as blind as a bat" where abstract art was concerned. (The works in the collection by Winifred and Ben Nicholson are mostly figurative. Ede credited both artists with opening "a door into the world of contemporary art" for him in the mid-1920s.) Kettle's Yard is particularly well endowed with non-abstract work, most prominently the maritime paintings of Alfred Wallis and sculptures and drawings of Henri Gaudier-Brzeska. Among the sculptures is Gaudier's *Dancer* (1913), where, Ede in his book about Kettle's Yard quotes Stanley Casson as saying, movement is "detected at a moment when it is neither static nor in motion: when it is potential and yet not stopped." David Jones provides some interesting and densely allusive work, including the branching, wreathing trees, hills, temples and creatures in the pencil and watercolour *Vexilla Regis* (1947). Jones told Ede's mother, who bought the picture, that one of its starting-points was the eponymous hymn, "Forth come the standards of the King":

> *in which are many allusions to the tree and the Cross, and to the Cross as a tree etc. The general idea of the picture was also associated, in my mind, with the collapse of the Roman world. The three trees as it were left standing on Calvary—the various bits and pieces of classical ruins*

dotting the landscape... [T]he rushing Ponies are, more or less, the horses of the Roman cavalry, turned to grass and gone wild and off to the hills... The tree on the left of the main tree is, as it were, the tree of the 'good thief', it grows firmly in the ground and the pelican has made her nest and feeds her young in its branches... The tree on the right is that of the other thief, it is partly tree and partly triumphal column and partly imperial standard... Nevertheless it is shadowed by the spreading central Tree and the dove, in fact, hovers over this tree of the truculent robber for somehow or other he is 'redeemed' too!

More recent art, not always susceptible to this sort of explication (and Jones insisted that "none of this symbolism is meant to be at all rigid"), is the main subject of exhibitions at Kettle's Yard Gallery, built next to the house in 1970 and several times expanded since then. It was designed by David Owers and the ubiquitous Sir Leslie Martin.

Appendix: Some other places of interest

Cambridge

Anglia Polytechnic University, East Road. This was once Cambridge College of Arts and Technology, where Tom Sharpe taught in the 1960s and 1970s, presumably without encountering the farcical misfortunes and embarrassments of Henry Wilt, lecturer in English at the Fenland College of Arts and Technology in his *Wilt* trilogy (1976-84). In 1989 CCAT merged with Essex Institute of Higher Education to become Anglia Higher Education College; it became a polytechnic in 1991 and Anglia Polytechnic University (APU) in 1992. Among Anglia's facilities is the tiered 250-seat Mumford Theatre, which is used for both student and some professional productions. The Cambridge Drama Festival takes place here each spring.

Ascension Cemetery, All Souls Lane. This peaceful, secluded burial ground opened in 1869. Here are the graves of A. C. Benson, Sir John Cockcroft, Frances Cornford and several other members of the Darwin family, the astrophysicist Sir Arthur Eddington, Sir J. G. Frazer (author of *The Golden Bough*), the classicist Sir Richard Jebb, the economist Alfred Marshall, the architect David Roberts, and Ludwig Wittgenstein.

Broughton House Art Gallery, King Street, is a small commercial gallery on the adapted ground floor of an attractive eighteenth-century house with walled garden. There are monthly exhibitions. The gallery manages the Gwen Raverat Archive, a changing selection from which is also shown.

Cambridge Drama Centre, Covent Garden. Many of the plays, workshops and other events here are put on either by or for children and young people. In 2000 CDC merged with the Junction, Clifton Road to form Junction CDC.

Fisher House, Guildhall Street, is the Roman Catholic chaplaincy. The Chaplain's House was formerly the Black Swan Inn.

Information Centre, Wheeler Street. This was the reading room of the Public Library between 1884 and 1975: airy, domed and pillared.

Little Trinity, 16 Jesus Lane. A house of 1725 whose façade is "representative of the translation of classical principles into a decorous brick architecture" (Nicholas Ray).

Lloyds Bank, St Andrew's Street. Originally Fosters' Bank, by Alfred and Paul Waterhouse (1891, extended 1935). It sports a clock-tower and has an extraordinary, rather Russian-looking interior with glazed tiles.

Orchard Street contains an attractive terrace of nineteenth-century cottages, built by Charles Humfrey and restored by the Cambridge Preservation Trust.

Railway Station. According to Kingsley Amis, "that curious railway station, with its endless single platform like something out of Kafka or Chirico, ought to tip off the sensitive" that Cambridge is a cold and inhospitable place. The station building was designed by Sancton Wood in 1845.

Trinity Street. Booksellers have operated on the site of the Cambridge University Press shop at 1 Trinity Street since the sixteenth century. The most famous was John Nicholson (1730-96), known as "Maps", who was, according to Henry Gunning, "indefatigable in the pursuit of business"; he went "from room to room in the different colleges, announcing himself by shouting 'MAPS' as he proceeded." There is a portrait of him in action, laden with heavy volumes but evidently undaunted, in the entrance hall of the University Library. No.14 is a timber-framed house of about 1600, once the Turk's Head Inn. No.30 (until recently Heffer's Children's Bookshop) has a late eighteenth-century timber shop-front. The main branch of Heffer's, the best known Cambridge bookshop (now owned by Blackwell's), is at No. 20. William Heffer opened a small stationer's shop in Fitzroy Street in 1876 and also sold hymn-books. Later the shop moved to Petty Cury and became established as the principal supplier of books in

Cambridge, transferring to the present large premises in the early 1970s.

Wolfson College, Barton Road. A mainly graduate college, founded in 1965 as University College and renamed in 1972 following a benefaction from the Wolfson Foundation.

Near Cambridge

American Military Cemetery, Madingley. Many American units were based in East Anglia during the Second World War. 3,812 of their dead are buried here, and the 5,125 missing in action are commemorated by a long Wall of the Missing in Portland stone.

Anglesey Abbey, Lode. In January 1946 James Lees-Milne noted in his diary "Wonderfully appointed house, soft-treading carpets; full of semi-works of art... I do not covet it or anything in it." Lord Fairhaven, with whom Lees-Milne was dining, left the property to the National

Trust in 1966. The Fairhaven collection includes, as well as a fair amount of semi-art, some Claudes and a luminous Bonington. The house, on the site of a medieval Augustinian priory, is seventeenth-century and later. There are fine and much visited gardens.

Barton. The church has remains of fourteenth-century wall paintings and a delicately carved wooden screen of 1388.

Chesterton. The village has now been largely absorbed by Cambridge, but retains more rural edges along the river. The mainly fourteenth-century church was restored in the 1840s but there are many interesting earlier gravestones in the churchyard. Chesterton Tower, the fourteenth-century residence of rectors sent from Vercelli Abbey (to whom Henry III had granted the rectory), now contains offices.

Cottenham. Kelly's Cambridge Directory for 1847 salutes Cottenham for the superiority of its cheese and describes the place as "a large respectable village and parish". The church, "which is situated at the extremity of a very long street, is a noble structure, with lofty tower and four ornamental pinnacles." Twentieth-century editions of the Directory explain that the cheese declined because pastures were converted into arable land, but the long street and "the bold Jacobean design" of the tower (Norman Scarfe) are still worth seeing.

Denny Abbey, near Waterbeach. Remains of a Benedictine and subsequently Franciscan religious house, founded in 1159 and altered many times. The Farmland Museum includes a seventeenth-century stone barn.

Duxford. The airfield here was an important military station during both World Wars. Spitfires and Hurricanes based at Duxford played a significant part in the Battle of Britain and between 1943 and 1945 it was the headquarters of the 78th Fighter Group of the United States 8th Air Force. In the 1970s the airfield was acquired by the Imperial War Museum. About 180 historic aircraft are on display, including a Concorde. A land warfare hall contains tanks and artillery.

Ely. Sacheverell Sitwell declares that "There is no more wonderful and imposing building in England" than Ely Cathedral, "varying, as it does, from the castellan turrets and modulations of its exterior towers to the fern-frost delicacies of its Lady Chapel, and to the miraculous Octagon, an engineering feat without parallel in its day—still less in ours when there is much work of engineering but little art" (*Sacheverell Sitwell's England*, 1986). The nave was built between 1083 and 1189. The Octagon, choir and Lady Chapel are mid-fourteenth-century.

Newmarket. Here, says Henry James, "the very breeze has an equine snort." This may be relished at the race-course or at the National Horseracing Museum in the High Street.

Shelford. The villages of Great and Little Shelford, south of Cambridge, figure as Great and Little Barley in Philippa Pearce's *The Minnow on the Say* (1955). As a child she lived at the Mill House—her father was the miller. She still lives in Great Shelford.

Wimpole Hall. Eight miles south-west of Cambridge is "the noble house, seat, or mansion of Wimple... formerly built at vast expense, by the late Earl of Radnor, adorned with all the natural beauties of situation; and to which was added all the most exquisite contrivances which the best heads could invent to make it artificially as well as naturally pleasant" (Daniel Defoe, *Tour Through the Whole Island of Great Britain*, 1724-6). Radnor had enlarged, at the end of the seventeenth century, the earlier house built by Sir Thomas Chicheley at mid-century, and further development came between 1713 and 1730 under Edward, Lord Harley (later second Earl of Oxford), best known as a bibliophile. The National Trust has owned Wimpole since 1976. The most notable room in this elegant house is the Library, the work mainly of Sir John Soane. Originally it housed the great collection of manuscripts of Harley and his father, the first Earl; these were bought by Parliament in 1753 and went to the British Museum Library—later the British Library. In accordance with Harley's literary interests, in the Gallery there is a portrait by Jonathan Richardson of the poet Matthew Prior (1664-1721), who died at Wimpole. (He was educated at St John's College, Cambridge and was a political ally of the first Earl.) A less expected example of Soane's work is the well-appointed Bath House of 1792. "Capability" Brown was involved in the design of the grounds. The church, next to the house, is dominated by memorials to the owners, principally the Yorke family—Earls of Hardwick—who succeeded Edward Harley.

Wysing Arts, Bourn. A centre for visual and applied arts with a gallery and studios in converted farm buildings. There are frequent exhibitions.

Further Reading

Peter Allen, *The Cambridge Apostles: the Early Years.* Cambridge: CUP, 1978.

John Binns and Peter Meadows, ed., *Great St Mary's: Cambridge's University Church.* Great St Mary's, 2000.

Michael H. Black, *A Short History of Cambridge University Press.* Revised edition. Cambridge: CUP, 2000.

Christopher Brooke, general editor, *History of the University of Cambridge.* 3 vols. so far. Cambridge, CUP, 1988-97: vol. 1, to 1546, by Damian Riehl Leader (1988); vol. 3, 1750-1870, by Peter Searby (1997); vol. 4, 1870-1990, by Christopher Brooke.

Graham Chainey, *A Literary History of Cambridge.* Revised edition. Cambridge: CUP, 1995.

Rupert Christiansen, ed., *Cambridge Arts Theatre: Celebrating Sixty Years.* Cambridge: Granta, 1997.

John Durack, George Gilbert and John Marks, *The Bumps: an Account of the Cambridge University Bumping Races.* Cambridge: George Gilbert, 2000.

Peter Fox, ed., *Cambridge University Library: the Great Collections.* Cambridge: CUP, 1998.

Peter Harman and Simon Mitton, ed., *Cambridge Scientific Minds.* Cambridge: CUP, 2002.

Ronald Hayman, ed., *My Cambridge.* London: Robson Books, 1977.

Robert Hewison, *Footlights!: A Hundred Years of Cambridge Comedy.* London: Methuen, 1984.

T. E. B. Howarth, *Cambridge Between Two Wars.* London: Collins, 1978.

Elisabeth Leedham-Green, *A Concise History of the University of Cambridge.* Cambridge: CUP, 1996.

David McKitterick, *The Making of the Wren Library, Trinity College, Cambridge.* Cambridge: CUP, 1995.

Rita McWilliams-Tullberg, *Women at Cambridge.* Revised edition. Cambridge: CUP, 1998.

Richard Mason, ed., *Cambridge Minds.* Cambridge: CUP, 1994.

Charles Moseley and Clive Wilmer, *Cambridge Observed: an Anthology.* Cambridge: Colt Books, 1998.

Alan H. Nelson, ed., *Records of Early English Drama: Cambridge.* Toronto: University of Toronto Press, 1989.

Sarah J. Ormrod, ed., *Cambridge Contributions.* Cambridge: CUP, 1998.

Nikolaus Pevsner, *The Buildings of England: Cambridgeshire.* 2nd edition. London: Penguin, 1970.

Ann Phillips, ed., *A Newnham Anthology.* Cambridge: CUP, 1979.

Tim Rawle, *Cambridge Architecture.* London: Trefoil Books, 1985.

Nicholas Ray, *Cambridge Architecture: a Concise Guide.* Cambridge: CUP, 1994.

Edward Shils and Carmen Blacker, ed., *Cambridge Women: Twelve Portraits.* Cambridge: CUP, 1996.

Frank Stubbings, *Bedders, Bulldogs and Bedells: a Cambridge Glossary.* Cambridge: CUP. Revised edition, 1995.

Alison Taylor, *Cambridge: a Hidden History.* Stroud: Tempus, 1999.

Mark Weatherall, *From Our Cambridge Correspondent: Cambridge Student Life 1945-95 As Seen in the Pages of 'Varsity'.* Cambridge: Varsity Publications, 1995.

Some Cambridge Novels

A. S. Byatt, *Still Life.* Chatto and Windus, 1985.

Penelope Fitzgerald, *The Gate of Angels.* Collins, 1990.

E. M. Forster, *The Longest Journey.* Blackwood, 1907.

E. M. Forster, *Maurice.* Edward Arnold, 1971.

P. D. James, *An Unsuitable Job for a Woman.* Faber and Faber, 1972.

Charles Kingsley, *Alton Locke.* Chapman and Hall, 1850.

Rosamond Lehmann, *Dusty Answer.* Chatto and Windus, 1927.

Tom Sharpe, *Porterhouse Blue.* Secker and Warburg, 1974.

W. M. Thackeray, *The History of Pendennis.* Bradbury and Evans, 1850.

Jill Paton Walsh, *The Wyndham Case.* Hodder and Stoughton, 1993.

Virginia Woolf, *Jacob's Room.* Hogarth Press, 1922.

Index of Literary and Historical Names

Index of Places